Also by Rick Moody

The Long Accomplishment

The Long
Accomplishment

A MEMOIR

of HOPE *and*

STRUGGLE *in*

MATRIMONY

Rick Moody

Henry Holt and Company   New York

Henry Holt and Company
Publishers since 1866
120 Broadway
New York, New York 10271
www.henryholt.com

Library of Congress Cataloging-in-Publication Data

Names: Moody, Rick, author.
Title: The long accomplishment : a memoir of hope and struggle in matrimony /
Rick Moody.
Description: First edition. | New York : Henry Holt and Company, 2019.
Identifiers: LCCN 2018044743 | ISBN 9781250214799
Subjects: LCSH: Moody, Rick—Marriage. | Authors, American—20th
    century—Biography.
Classification: LCC PS3563.O5537 Z46 2019 | DDC 813/.54 [B]—dc23
LC record available at https://lccn.loc.gov/2018044743

First Edition 2019

Designed by Kelly S. Too

For LKN, HJM, TFNM, eilífu

The Long Accomplishment

January–September 2013

In order to have a second marriage you can believe in you may have to fail at your first marriage.

I failed spectacularly at mine.

It is not my place, here at the outset, if ever, to evaluate for you the way that my wife behaved in my first marriage, though because marriages are intricate, dynamic, complex relationships, you would not unreasonably infer that she played her part. This is in the nature of things. Failure is often as collaborative as success. Instead my job here is to discuss briefly what role I played in that failure, before going on to tell you about redemption in difficult times, redemption undeserved, redemption so unforeseeable as to appear to require a belief in grace.

I am writing down these first lines because they are the beginning of the story, though I am still not inclined to cherish the particulars of my conduct where my first marriage is concerned. I did not rise to the occasion of matrimonial language, the beautiful, powerful vows that go with the enactment of marriage. I, who care about language, did not prize the language, but rather ignored it.

I remember reading an interview with John Cheever in my early years as a student, in which Cheever says (in *The Paris Review*, I believe) that there are certain lies that everyone understands to be lies but that are still useful to civilization as moral ideas, compasses with which we might navigate the storms of our being. Among these, according to him, are the vows of marriage. I found this remark, made by a married person himself, painful to contemplate, but also somehow compellingly frank. My own parents, it seemed to me when younger, should not perhaps have been married, and they were wise to get out of the business of marriage while they were still in their thirties, waiting to remarry until they were certain they had settled down some. Theirs was not a marriage that indisputably reassured about the sturdiness of the institution, and that was what I knew from earliest childhood, the sadness, anger, grief, and isolation of a marriage that had endured beyond what was practicable. I love both of my parents, and I have often marveled in my adulthood at what a good job they did in remarriage. But I saw them express affection toward each other, while married, infrequently enough for it to be both surprising and hard to remember in any detail. Though one can presume, on the basis of their three children (my brother, my sister, and myself) that some kind of love took place at some point in the late fifties and early sixties, I knew little about it.

This was one factor in the tremendous reluctance I had about marrying in my twenties and thirties—the ache of the history of my own parents and their separation. My parents divorced after thirteen years. Meanwhile, my mother's mother, whose acute alcoholism was the end of her in her sixties, after multiple hospitalizations, was effectively bedridden in a sort of nineteenth-century-novel way during the later period in which her husband, my well-known grandfather, F. M. Flynn, helmed the *New York Daily News*. No one outside of the family knew of her suffering or her demise or of the barrenness of the marriage between them, at least in the later years of their union. Of my grandmother Flynn, I remember only that she had a nurse, and that she did the crossword puzzle assiduously each Sunday. We went to visit her some. But she (and my uncle, my mother's brother) died in the mid-1960s. I never got to know either of them well.

After his wife's death, my grandfather Flynn never remarried.

My father's parents were similarly remote from each other (as I wrote some years back in a book called *The Black Veil*). They lived two floors apart, they kept to diurnal schedules that were very different (my grandfather went to bed at sunset, my grandmother stayed up till late), they had separate interests, they did not seem to communicate very much.

Was it because of all this suffering, however unintentional, that I understood nothing of monogamy? That I never even tried very hard to understand monogamy? Family history is perhaps part of it.

I can go back through my teens to romantic triangle after romantic triangle: the teenaged girl to whom I lost my virginity, at boarding school, who had also been involved with my roommate; a cherubic tenth grader I was seeing later in senior year who knew little about the sultry torch singer girl I was hooking up with; the long-term girlfriend in college who went on safari with her family to Kenya, whereupon I took up with a fellow intern at my summer job; my later girlfriend in college, who transferred to another school for a semester, which prompted an entire odyssey of extracurricular experiments with friends.

Under no circumstance did it seem that monogamy was an impulse that I wanted to explore, and it was not that I didn't love anyone with whom I was in a relationship at the time; more it seemed that I loved *everyone*, and could not bring myself to make a choice among them.

My first wife was someone I met in an improbable internet-ish sort of way after a rather traumatic breakup with a prior lover who had the temerity to refuse to be monogamous with *me* (she was bisexual, and wanted to keep it that way). My first wife seemed earnest and totally available, and she lived in Chicago, which was nowhere near where I lived in Brooklyn, and right from the start it was more of the same, for me, by which I mean both love and inconstancy, deceit and impulsiveness, failure at intimacy. I was often at the artists' colonies, like Yaddo and MacDowell, and as often seemed to happen in those days, I could not but find that certain painter utterly charismatic, and I was only too happy to counsel that fellow writer about her own unhappy marriage, and so on. I aspired to do better, but I did not do better, and in this attenuated string of short-term indulgences and experiments, it seems now, there was little but selfishness and manipulation.

And then something really awful happened.

In November of 1995 (on All Souls' Day, in fact, and almost exactly twenty years ago, as I write these lines, and from where I'm working in New England, I can only look on the riot of almost excessively beautiful autumnal color and think of this sequence of events, as if it's an old school film loop of hardships), my sister was putting her children to bed òne night when she had a seizure, and her heart stopped, and no one was able to revive her. Had I put down here the necessary pages of a biography of my sister (older than me by three years, and possessed of two children, ages four and six at the time of her death), the gregarious, funny, winning, beautiful, short-tempered, self-destructive, frequently drunken, incredibly loyal, heart-breakingly devoted mom who was my sister, you would have a better idea what a shock this was to me and my family (which, for the record, also included, at the time of my sister's death, my just-married brother, Dwight, eighteen months younger than I, who would, with his wife, Colleen, go on to have three children, two of whom are now in college, and the third in high school). But suffice to say that at thirty-four I had never known the scourging of sudden loss. Of time and its depredations, I knew the turn of the seasons, and the getting older of the very old, and in that it seemed there was an order to life and death.

My beautiful, outrageous sister, at age thirty-seven, should not have been subjected to this sudden turn of fate. And her kids, her wonderful funny kids (who are now my formidable and upstanding niece and nephew, fully grown), should not have had to suffer what they suffered through. The suffering should not have spooled out in front of them, piling up the complications and reverberations across the many years, in the way that it did.

I had gone through a lot myself, in my twenties, again as I have written in the earlier memoir called *The Black Veil*. For example, I struggled with alcoholism and depression, but I had come through most of those problems. Of my early thirties I remember that I was feeling provisionally good about things. I had an occasional spring in my step. I was publishing my first books, and though I had lost a really great, rewarding publishing job, I had figured out a way to make enough money to survive, if inexpensively, and I was living by my wits, and I believed that things, to one degree or another, were going to get better. I believed that life was constituted in such a way that it improved.

And then my sister died.

The wreckage associated with this loss was immense. There was the splintering of family certainties that comes from having the most social, most family-oriented person in your family suddenly disappear. There was the total philosophical depletion that comes with prolonged grief. (I couldn't *do anything* for a while. For example, I can recall spending several days, at one point, thinking about getting a new power strip for all the cords that led from my computer and printer, thinking that this might be one thing I could manage, and just doing *nothing about it*. For months. Just sort of sitting and idly thinking about the power strip, and then weeping about my sister, and thinking about the power strip some more. There seemed no meaningful thought I could have, there seemed no reason to do the next thing, so why not the power strip? I'm sure I ate and showered, but that was about the extent of things. Some months later I believe I finally purchased the power strip, as a kind of initial sign that minor improvement was possible. Perhaps at that time I also replaced a burned-out lightbulb. The simplest things, with sustained assault, were just barely possible. Sleep occurred sporadically, and was marred by gruesome thoughts. I managed to stay sober, which was imperative to getting through the loss, and I managed to check in with my family now and again, all of them wrecked, but by and large I did very little, for a long time.)

When I began to come out of the acute phase of this loss, I noticed that some of the spiritual certainties that had accrued to me after sobering up and getting out of the psychiatric hospital in the late eighties, evaporated before me, as if they were water vapor boiled off by the convectionary action of calamity. The sense of order and rightness to a lifetime's sequence of events collapsed. And as far as the moral certainty of the time, I no longer had any of it. On the contrary, I felt like the world was a Darwinist world, a consume-or-be-consumed world, a world of disappointment and searing loss and regret, and that there was no point in *not* pursuing some of the really overwhelming compulsions that my brain occasionally offered up.

Off the rails I went. Whereas in the years before my sister died there had been some very occasional ethical thinking about the needs of others, some ethical thinking about the implications of respect and compassion, now recklessness swept over me like a category five hurricane. In the middle of these reckless years my first wife, who was not yet quite that, asked me to marry her, and I turned her down. Because why bother? I refused to have children, too, so there was no good reason for her to wait for me, but wait she did, while I was off on a fever dream, in some kind of compartmentalized, isolated world of compulsive behavior that only people who suffer with addictive illness can really understand well. I lied to her, I lied to my family, I lied to myself, I lied to my multiple lovers. Partially or wholly invented stories about where I was or whom I was with were so regular that I wouldn't have even thought to use the word *deceit*. The stories never bore up under attention, on the rare occasions that I was worth attention. Every time I put down or trash-talked a certain kind of sexual behavior as damnably perverse, I found myself electing to pursue it, so that the field of activity got more and more profane, more and more dishonorable, so that all mornings had the features of a hangover, if without any of the actual alcohol. It is worth saying that I hated myself in many potent and baroque ways, and I told no one this, and in the milieu of literature and civic life, in more cases than not, people seemed to me to think I was a reasonably good guy.

The only thing that operated as a leavening agent in

all of this was the love of my sister's kids, whom I saw as often as I was able in those days. They loved my first wife, still do, and we took them to the movies, and got them gifts when we could, and saw them in the summers a lot. When my total resistance to the domestic first began to yield to something like adult thinking, in my late thirties, it was because I loved these kids.

In fact, I think I got married, therefore, because I came to see that children, through the prism of my sister's children, were an illumination in the crabbed and half-lit space of narcissistic young-adulthood. My sister had the two, and eventually my brother had the three, and my going along on my way with only *books* to show for myself seemed like a kind of recoiling from what is productive and lasting in life. I remember an older friend saying to me once: *Well, children are what you do with a life.* It took me years to understand her words, and I had to hurt myself and others a great deal to get there.

So I agreed to get married, which is not the same as enthusiastically embracing marriage, because in the end I wanted to have a child, but without any intention of not continuing on with all the compulsive activity on the side. One affair lasted for seven years, one lasted for five (they might have overlapped a bit), at one point there were at least three being conducted at the same time, maybe four if you count some occasional indiscretions with yet another party. I felt morally upright because I had never been to a prostitute or a massage parlor, but if that's morally upright then there are alcoholics who are not alcoholics because they never drank rum or scotch.

My wife and I quickly landed in couples therapy, maybe not more than a year or two after our wedding, and she, who had endured all of this, and had known about much of it, suggested that the only way to go on was if we were *both* allowed to pursue the arrangement that I pursued with such zeal and irresponsibility aforethought, and though this seemed like a tolling of the funeral bell to me, not an act of liberation, I said *yes*, simply because I didn't know how to stop. And then, while we were doing that, practicing what is called the open marriage, we were trying to get pregnant. Or she was trying to get pregnant. I was sort of trying to do what was expected of me.

Somehow, it seemed, I had reproduced many of the features of the bad writerly marriages that I knew about from reading all the biographies, the writer husband who has to go away for a year to write his book, and who takes up with a younger, more innocent writer of his acquaintance, and uses this casually imbalanced relationship to rail against his own misery. I rationalized my conduct in many of the usual ways: *It was good material*, and I needed to feel passionately in order to write passionately. And so: I tried to have sex in a crowded café once (without being noticed), I went to a bar with trans sex workers, I allowed myself to be beaten, I had sex on the pay phone at a writers' colony while around me novelists worked away on their opuses, I stashed willing partners in a vast portfolio of distant cities, I had electrifying correspondences, both through the mail and online, I waited patiently, I exploited the internet, I gathered in the willing slowly and quickly and sometimes indifferently. The motto, in a certain precinct of my divided self, was *anything that moves.*

I should say, in this supercharged historical moment, that there was never a time, ever, in my life, when this behavior extended to anyone who didn't explicitly want it. While I leave open the possibility that people may have *thought* they wanted to be the other half of my self-destructiveness and then didn't feel so terribly good about it later (as I often did not myself), all of what I'm describing here was with people who had similar preoccupations. Indeed, the moment when compulsive sexual behavior is thrilling, the moment that you chase, forever falling away from it, like the waterfall from the ridgeline, is the moment when the other person says *yes.* I never wanted anyone who felt otherwise, and never wanted anyone who wasn't of age, and never wanted anyone who didn't think it was all a grand adventure of passion, taboo, secretiveness, and desperate longing, or a sudden powerful remediation of loneliness. Indeed, loneliness was an uppermost feeling for me in those days. Lonely in my marriage, lonely in my affairs, lonely in my person, lonely in a crowd, lonely with myself. The desire to be touched (even when, in the end, it often made me feel worse) was the thing that seemed like it was going to help, even if my intimacies were rarely intimate at all. To be perfectly explicit, that is, I never wanted to hurt anyone. And the way I conceptualize this now, from *after* the years I'm describing, is that often the relationships were ritualized in such a way as to cause **me** physical pain, or humiliation. That is, at least then, I inclined toward my own physical pain, and liked to have people inflict some of it upon me, and the same was true to some degree with humiliation. The person I wanted to hurt, therefore, occupied the same physical space as the narrator of these lines, was identical to him. While certain contemporary thinkers of human psychology may say that these particular paraphilias are healthy and just another lifestyle choice, in my case they are not and were not, they were a direct result of despair, grief, contempt for self, loneliness, and desperation. Hurting anyone else was a horrifying byproduct, something I tried to avoid, though in the context in which a lot of this conduct was taking place, there were ramifications after the fact, sometimes, very painful breakups, and people were miserable then. I understand this, and I have a long list of regrets.

At last, in the midst of all this, I remember attempting with my wife to fertilize the relevant egg in Rome, in an almost fraternal way, and then my wife was pregnant. When I told all of this to a despoiled young lover from the Southwest, who deserved a lot better than me, that my wife was pregnant, she told me that there was no one on earth as evil as I was, that I would in fact be the *death* of her (these were her very words), and that I would then have that on my conscience.

My experience of the bliss of domestic life, the time of fatherhood, at first, was that there was no real place for a father in it. I suppose the traditional thinking holds that I should have felt duty toward my newborn daughter, but I didn't feel duty, not at the outset. I felt like my work time was being taken away. But gradually I began to get some time with my daughter alone, and in having some time alone with her, with going through the process of changing diapers and taking her to church every Sunday, alone, which is something I did from her earliest years, it began to emerge that maybe what had been accomplished in my marriage was the making of this wonderful girl, this weird, funny, loving, perfect little kid, with an easy smile and lots of curiosity about the world, and maybe the marriage would not survive its having made it to the goal line of its purpose, but at least I had helped to bring about *this*.

Of course, I had poisoned the marriage, long before, no matter what my wife had done or wanted to do with her own choices. I had adulterated the meaning of the vows, and had not much bothered about what they all meant.

And: not terribly long after my daughter's birth, I gave a reading at an ashram. Why give a reading at an ashram? One of the monks who ran the ashram was a poet, and he contacted me out of the blue and asked if I would read at his ashram. Because I always felt it was important to say *yes* to any question asked of me that had a spiritual cast to it, I said *yes* on this occasion (and you would reasonably inquire why I was so given to spiritual investigation when I was behaving so erratically and myopically, and my only response would be: it is the problem individuals who *most* need the spiritual life), though I expected the worst. The worst, at a literary event, means: a very small audience that doesn't quite get what you are doing at all, an audience that looks at you with an expression (each and every one of them) of mild confusion, a feeling that is next-door over to boredom. Put it this way: I never walk through the door of a reading venue without that sinking feeling of the time in Washington, DC, when my own mother was one of only three people in the audience. And the ashram, on the day in question, and its audience, delivered as expected. They had just finished up meditating, I think, when I arrived, and there were only ten or so, two of whom I had known from my *home birth class!* (The home birth class that preceded my daughter's birth in the bedroom of our one-bedroom Brooklyn apartment.) They were there, and I liked them, and so I did my reading, despite the expressions of confusion that were next-door over to boredom, and then I talked to a few people afterward, and one of these was a young woman who insisted she had met me before, though I had little recollection of this, and who was telling me a little bit about her work, she was a visual artist, and I couldn't quite make out all of what she was telling me, because there was chatter around me, and because there were others who wanted to talk with me after the reading, like the couple from *home birth class*, and I was distracted. The young woman gave me an invitation to her show, her exhibition of photographs, at a gallery in Chelsea, and then she left.

And then I turned over the card, and realized I knew a fair amount about her work. I had read about her work, read interviews, seen reproductions. What the hell was Laurel Nakadate doing at the ashram? On Lower Broadway?

This was the beginning of a path through and out of the shame spiral of the previous years, and it would be great, for the narrative that follows, if I could tell you that it was a love-at-first-sight moment, or that I knew instantly that the visual artist who had been at the reading would somehow have a lifeline available for me, and would be ready and able to use it. But obviously it was more complicated than that. The exchange between us was no more than five minutes (and apparently we *had* met once four years before, though I can't really remember it, and we were friends on Facebook) and it was hard to concentrate, but she was indisputably Laurel, she of the challenging and incendiary video art, and the most I can say is that one of the great rewards of being a little bit known in the writing and arts communities is that if you really want to know more about someone whose work you admire, you can find a way to make that happen. And I did want to know more about Nakadate's work, about the emotional risk of it, about the intensity of it, and I really wanted to know how the smiling, wry, straightforward woman could also be the person who made that work. She was the Laurel Nakadate of the video work, that is, but also Laurel the person, and that was the part that became interesting before long.

It wasn't obvious, therefore, that the reading at the ashram was momentous, that there are mysterious principles involved in the daily rotation of our hunk of rock in the heavens, because life sort of went on in the way that it went on. I had thought, in those days, after the woman from the Southwest had told me how evil I was, that maybe the love of the greatest songs, or of the greatest love poems, was a thing that was mostly behind me now. With the advent of my daughter, I felt, in the first year of her life, like adulthood was more frequently about responsibility, and I had been exceedingly lucky in many ways, was able to write about whatever I wanted to write about, and had a country house, and a family who mostly cared about me, and what did it matter if marriage was not what I had wanted. At least there was a little child.

I did, in fact, because it was permitted under the rules of my *open marriage,* get to know Laurel, the person, better, but in the platonic way. I went to see her show in Chelsea, we went for a walk, we talked quite a bit about her relationship, I watched the movie she was making and offered opinions about the use of music in it. She came to see my band play (I was in a sort of a postmodern folk band for eight or nine years, called the Wingdale Community Singers, wherein I wrote some lyrics, and sometimes some music, and sang and played a bit of guitar, along with a couple of like-minded friends) and she really liked my bandmate Hannah. At some point, nine or ten months after the ashram, we went to see *Avatar* together. What an innocent and strange thing to do, to see a movie neither of us was going to like. Maybe we went to ridicule it. Some three or four months after that, when it seemed like her boyfriend or partner really never *was* going to move back to New York City, it seemed as though it might be appropriate, not totally unwarranted, to admit that we had some feelings for each other. The growth of these feelings was along the platonic axis, but it also came to exceed the platonic axis. It was a feeling that exceeded its container.

From a thematic standpoint, it is worth pointing out that my intense respect for Laurel was such that I tried to keep the out-of-control and somewhat mentally ill Rick Moody clear of her address and, contrary to my normal operating procedure, I tried to be useful and helpful to her and her life, which I was very interested in getting to know. I tried to be in love, instead of needing anything other than that. It was occasionally an uncomfortable fit, but one that always seem to have growth associated with it.

The months went by and my daughter got a little bit older, and in this highly orderly, if melancholy, domesticity, this marriage giving out beneath its weight, my daughter thrived. There was no big fight with my wife, no long sequence of hard, long talks about how things were going at home. Instead, my wife and I went to visit her family for Thanksgiving, and one night we went out to dinner, left the toddler with her grandparents, and had a decent meal, despite the fact that we just didn't seem to have that much to talk about anymore, probably mostly because of me. At one point my wife repaired to the bathroom for a moment, while we were awaiting the dessert course (it was pie, this restaurant had really good pie), and then came back out to the table and said: *Do you think it's possible that it's just time for us to separate?* I will say, to her credit, she smiled as she said it, and was just calling the end what was already evidently the end, and it was more about accepting what was than trying to get the facts to be otherwise, and she was very adult about it. It was I who had hitherto felt like he had to try to hang on, who thought that was my job, when there was nothing much to hang onto, except that habit of growing away from someone you thought you once knew well.

I had been sleeping on the couch for more than a year, and I had been staying alone in my country house several nights a week, partly to write, and partly because I like being alone better anyhow. And because, after about a year or so, I found that I did harbor feelings of love about the visual artist who'd been at the ashram. There was not necessarily a reason to believe this, really, because as I say I sort of thought I'd loved *everyone*, but by the same token I didn't know if I could do better unless I worked hard and treated her with respect, and I didn't have a chance to do so if I were still married.

My wife and I needed to be separated six months, the lawyers said, to get a divorce, and so we needed to separate completely, after hiring the lawyers, which we did in the spring of 2012, and that was when the civilized, reasonable, adult, and progressive tone in our separation was replaced by force, manipulation, self-preservation at any cost, and endless bickering about money. When I engaged my lawyer, who was a specialist in *collaborative divorce*, she said that the average divorce in her practice took somewhere in the area of twenty-two weeks. By the end of 2012, we'd been at it over twenty-two weeks, and we had no end in sight.

Laurel and I decided to get an apartment together, in Park Slope, and I sold my writing studio on the coast, and bought a house in Dutchess County, and Laurel and I began traveling back and forth between the two, Park Slope and eastern Dutchess County, trying to get a life together off the ground, while every couple of weeks I would go and meet with my first wife and the lawyers, and be so filled with disgust and hatred for mankind and his works that I sort of could not do anything else. The money part was monstrous and cruel and brought both of us nearer to ruin, and it did not favor the father of the child. I understood I would have to give up some stuff to leave. A lot of stuff, apparently. It was the hardest interpersonal negotiation I had ever had in my life. I had seen lawsuits, I had been fired from a job, I had broken up with some people before, in lasting and painful ways, but nothing was as hard as the legal process called divorce. Divorce was like agreeing to have all your skin peeled off electively, after which you walk around like that, like a guy with *no skin*, for all your neighbors and friends to see.

Meanwhile, how does a spree of self-centeredness, moral fuzziness, and destructive sexual abandon come to an end? It can happen all at once, with an arrest for going to the prostitutes one too many times, or for trying to carry cocaine onto an airplane with a college student, or in a drunken car accident, and while I didn't do any of these things during my first marriage, I did wear it down with studied casualness. Not because I had some systematic program of resistance in mind, but because I felt like I didn't care, and couldn't be bothered. Bit by bit, marriage became a position I thought I could no longer comfortably inhabit. The little humiliations, like running into people with whom I had behaved inappropriately, or waking up feeling ashamed, or simply thinking about being indisputably middle-aged and still behaving like I was in my early twenties, these all acted against the set of assumptions, the nihilism, that appeared to make possible my behavior. I assumed that marriage, and love, were tragic affairs, in which the essential indecency of humans would inevitably be revealed, and in which the animal instincts always outflanked the civilizing impulse. But over time, beginning with my daughter's birth, and then through the long months of divorce, and into the sixth decade of my life, I started to feel like I wanted the things that I had never wanted before, like a sense of family. A family of my own design, in which I got to make decisions for myself. Another way of putting it is this: there's an intense loneliness to addictive behavior, not only because the performance of addictive behavior requires so much deceit that you are required by it to be largely unknown by the people closest to you in your life, but also because the major part of your decision making is given over to the pursuit of *supply* (as some people in the recovery community put it), and there simply is not enough time for the small, rewarding interactions with the near and dear that allow one to feel witnessed, appreciated, loved. With the repetition, compulsion, and dishonor of infidelity, this loneliness is made worse. One's actions entail loneliness, and then it's the very loneliness that one attempts to repair with further repetitions of the compulsive activity. It can feel like some constant boomeranging of disaffection. At some point, I, the narrator of these pages, could take no more. Scoured clean of that time of my life, and beginning, perhaps at last, to accept the loss of my sister, and the loss of my marriage, I decided I wanted to do better. I wanted it for Laurel, and I wanted it for my child, and I wanted it even for myself, and in this way I began treatment for my sexual compulsion. I have to say it was a tremendous relief to admit complete defeat. As with my alcoholism, and my depression, awakening to a problem, and feeling the help rush in to fill the spot where secretiveness once lay, is to experience anew the joy of living. Sunlight really *is* a good disinfectant.

The year 2013, then, began twelve months into my recovery, and in the last months of my divorce negotiation, and during the planning of our wedding, Laurel's wedding with myself, and it is the first year of our marriage that this book intends to document. It intends to document October 2013 to November 2014, or roughly the length of a calendar year, in the way that Henry David Thoreau documented his year camped out next to a mud puddle on Emerson's property, except that instead of documenting the natural world, what I want to document is a year in a second marriage, an extremely hard-won year in a marriage, and to try to show that in a year of incredible difficulty you can still nonetheless pursue the elusive goal of love, that shared purpose, no matter how old or in what state of mitigated attractiveness, if you are bent upon that lofty end.

LET ME SAY, however, that in spite of the aforementioned "joy of living," if I were to pick an emblem, an objective correlative for the year 2013, it was a Charles Manson autograph.

The story comes from the writing world, at least initially, and it starts like this. I knew this literary fellow who was doing some hard time. I think a number of writers knew him. Another writer told me that this guy, doing the hard time, wanted to write to me, and would I write back? I had no objection to writing back, because my own behavior had always made me sympathize with people given to the occasional horrible decision. I felt sympathy for the victims of crimes, of course, but I also felt great waves of compassion for the men and women who somehow seemed to do a poor job of living their own lives, and who then wound up in the penal system. I wrote back to the guy doing the hard time, and we wrote back and forth throughout the rest of his interval inside, and later when he was living as an ex-con in Ohio. I helped him name his dog. We talked about contemporary literature, of which he knew a lot. I think he knew Allen Ginsberg personally, and maybe William S. Burroughs. Often the guys living on the edge of the law know and admire the Beats, have you noticed?

Some time later, when this guy, who insisted that he had not committed the crime for which he was interned (I have no reason to disbelieve him), was just another person on the margins of the literary world, I had occasion to review a certain book that I much esteemed. The book was *Building Stories*, by the graphic novelist Chris Ware. I ordered the book, and then I also got a free copy from the organ for which I was reviewing, and then suddenly I had two copies. This is not the strangest thing in my life, but it happened to coincide with my partner, Laurel, telling me about a certain conceptual art project named One Red Paperclip. I think the blogger who undertook this work is called Kyle MacDonald. And MacDonald, through a series of fourteen trades, managed to turn a single red paperclip into a farmhouse in Saskatchewan. I think probably MacDonald was an unusually shrewd negotiator, and he had some very excellent allies in his project, or (and this part is undeniable) he got a lot of very good publicity for his project, and this enabled trades that anyone would admire or find exceedingly creative.

I had been looking around to try something similar, because it sounded like so much fun, and I decided that I would trade my second copy of *Building Stories* to whomever offered me something really incredible for it, after which I would try to trade that item to someone else, and so on.

This proposition, the bartering of the extra copy of Ware's book, generated a fair amount of discussion on Facebook at one point, and I believe one guy did invite me to stay for a week in Italy, or maybe Greece, but because I am shy and can't really stand being anyone's guest for very long, I did not take the week in Greece. How foolish! I think there were some other interesting offers too. But I decided that the best offer, for no reason that I can re-create now, was the postcard signed by Charles Manson.

Of course, it came from the guy I knew who was staying in the federal penitentiary. Apparently, he had not only been corresponding with literary writers in those years, but also with some more hard-core criminal types. I don't know the extent of it. But somehow he had found himself attempting to correspond with Charles Manson. If you are my age, you perhaps, like I do, associate Charles Manson with a certain kind of California—with LSD, and the out-of-control period of the Beach Boys, with deranged interpretations of Beatles songs, with the Summer of Love and its philosophies converted all at once into the obverse, malevolent and incoherent evil. You associate Charles Manson with that book *Helter Skelter*, by Vincent Bugliosi and Curt Gentry, and with the photos of Lynette "Squeaky" Fromme in the police cruiser relieved of her firearm, after her attempt to assassinate President Gerald Ford. Maybe the younger persons turning these pages don't know as much about Manson and his band of followers, or associate him primarily with any list of dangerous and legendary serial killers that includes Richard Ramirez, John Wayne Gacy, et al., all available on the internet. But the psychedelic California, the bad acid California of that lost time, that's how I think of him.

I can't say exactly why my friend thought procuring and storing up the Manson postcard was a good idea, and perhaps it was simply that he was killing time in prison and wanted some memorabilia associated with his residence. I can't say exactly why I thought it was a good trade either, except that perhaps it would be easy to trade to someone else. I think I still felt bad about my friend's incarceration (he was soon released, and is on firm footing these days), and so I wanted to help him out. Apparently, I couldn't see the obvious menace of the object.

My friend's cover letter, which followed with the post-card, said:

New Year's Day, 2013

Hi Rick,

*Here's Charlie, hope he arrived intact. The poem on the back
is not by Manson, but by his "prison secretary." Signature
on front is Charlie's (signed MacManson). Note the swastika
through his last name. What a guy, that Manson.*

Then my friend wrote a few pleasantries, and concluded with: "Ah the curse is lifted (just kidding) (maybe)."

The Manson signature is on the front of an old-fashioned
picture postcard. Laterally across a photograph of a squir-
rel standing in a posture that I suppose I would describe
as fully erect, sort of waving at the camera with one hand,
from his perch atop a stump. The inscription, in blue ball-
point, does, in fact, say "Charles MacManson." And there
is a sort of a swastika.

The poem, on the reverse, goes as follows:

Friends, countrymen,
Lend me your ears,
All knowledge is moonshine
We are here and it is now
                    The Little Zen
                    For Charlie

Let's review the lamentable facts. I wrote a book review
of a book I really loved (the first sentence of the review was
"This book is a masterpiece"), and then I decided to trade
my extra copy of that book, hoping that I could, through

some conceptual art smarts, convert that book, ultimately, into a house in Nova Scotia, or maybe Newfoundland. And somehow I determined that the first thing I should trade for was a postcard signed by a guy with a swastika carved into his head, who was responsible for the murder of seven people. It is true that when I was an undergraduate at Brown University, there was a professor in the film department who had once made it his business to publish a chapbook of Manson's remarks from his sentencing hearing in 1971, and in the giddy, sometimes repellant political environment of Brown, circa 1983, this publication was considered genuinely revolutionary. However, I have also read comments by Sharon Tate's sister, that is, the sister of one of Manson's victims, and I found them heartrending and persuasive; I can only say that I felt that the Manson signature, which I imagine is one of many circulating out in the world (items signed by Manson start at $100 and go up from there on various true crime collectible sites), would be valuable for my bartering project.

You would have thought that the appended note at the bottom of the covering letter, "Ah the curse is lifted," would have been the sign, or that I would have felt a slight chill at reading the poem by Manson's "prison secretary," with its ominous and Eastern, "All wisdom is moonshine / We are here and it is now." Sort of reminds you of that koan that suggests that if you meet the Buddha in the road you should kill him. And yet: much of the contemporary outsider language orbiting around Charles Manson tends to overlook the horror done by him, and so I can only say that I did what many others have done, which is to say I neglected the facts for a moment. I averted my gaze, and allowed the Charles Manson signature into my apartment in Brooklyn, where it sat in my drawer.

The trouble began almost immediately.

It would be too obvious, and the mechanism too transparent, if I were to tell you that the death and destruction that visited themselves upon my life, and the lives of my wife, Laurel (who was only my fiancée at the time of the acquisition of the postcard), and my daughter, were *caused* by Manson. And so let me reassure you that it is not that obvious. The Manson curse is simply a slow-acting metaphor. Not immediately identifiable. Mostly at the beginning of 2013, I was trying to finish a novel that I had told my publishers I was writing for almost four years, and of which I had written 250 pages without conviction of any kind.

And I was trying to finish my divorce. Regularly, as I have said, I was going to a lawyer's office.

Collaborative divorce, as I have said, involved the two separating parties hiring lawyers familiar with the collaborative divorce process and then sitting down for regular meetings in which people discuss the various issues until they come to some joint decision about what should happen to the property being divided. It sounds great in theory. I am sure it works well for some couples.

In practice, the meetings took place in a mostly undecorated windowless room at my lawyer's office, and involved four people saying awful things to one another. First my wife and I said awful things to each other, and then we waited while the lawyers said awful things to us. Then one of the lawyers would say: "Okay, let's pick it up there in ten days." Though I understood that the legal professionals were decent and hardworking, I felt great overpowering waves of contempt for nearly everyone involved in negotiating my divorce.

My wife looked at me, across the table, with an expression that was pitying, irritated, and smug, and her lawyer always was most melodious when asking if I was hiding more money. And was I willing to surrender half of my copyrights for the work produced during the period of our marriage? I had never had anyone talk to me in this way before. Not even my parents, when I was at my most unpleasant, in my early twenties, when they were exasperated and didn't know what to do with me. Even they didn't talk to me like this. And apparently I was paying tens of thousands of dollars in order to be talked to like this.

I knew several other people getting divorced at the same time, including a visual artist friend, whose wife had considerable familial resources and had therefore hired very expensive lawyers with the avowed intention of destroying him financially. She *told* him she was going to destroy him. She would probably argue that he deserved to be destroyed, and of course my insight into the internal dynamics of their marriage is limited. But who really deserves to be destroyed? Why is dominance a legitimate goal in the process? Doesn't that make you into the thing you hate? What I know is that I saw my friend during his divorce, and I saw another friend, a writer and artist, whose husband was threatening to bring out in court the facts of her flirtation with heroin now decades in the past, just in

order to try to secure an economically favorable outcome—
I saw that friend during her divorce, her drawn features,
her intense agitation and anxiety. It was a confraternity,
my close friends in the throes of divorce, class of 2013,
all of them somnambulists, as they watched, apparently
powerless to intervene, as decades of ambition and security were obliterated.

Every other activity in life was contaminated by it, this
process of divorce, and by *contamination*, I mean the literal
thing, as if divorce were a particularly nasty virus for
which there was no vaccine yet, and it went about engendering hemorrhagic fountaining in your daily affairs. If
I took my daughter to a birthday party at her friend's house,
a friend who knew my ex-wife, I could feel the mixture of
curiosity and disdain for me at the party, a sort of nause-
ated fascination; I could feel the tendency of certain friends
to pick a side that was not my side; I could feel people
making up their minds without inquiring into the facts
of my life; and then there was the going to pick up my
daughter at her mother's apartment, which had been my
apartment not long before, whose boxes I had moved into
that space, myself, whose dishes I had washed, and seeing
the doormen there, only some of whom had elected to be
nonpartisan initially as regarded the divorce. They no
longer would call me by name. Or the uncomfortable rides
up in the elevator, to pick up my daughter, where, for example, that ambitious academic on one of the lower floors
had apparently decided that it was simply politically sound
to have nothing to do with me on the elevator, and who
therefore waited with me for the elevator in silence. There

was not a moment that was uncontaminated, there was not a moment in which I was not a homunculus, a protruding of additional tissue that my ex-wife needed to have cut out.

I am certain that many of the people who participated in this divorce-related contamination are not bad people, and probably did not know they were doing it, or certainly did not experience the moment at the elevator in exactly the way that I experienced it, but that is just what it means, in life, to choose the ready path, the superficial path, in evaluating a social situation. Stopping yourself, in the midst of your haste, and really thinking about what other people might be feeling is the hardest thing to do, and I am bad at it myself often enough, but I *want* to stop and think about what the other person is thinking because I believe the ability to do that is what indicates growth in our time here. The goal is never to deny the subjectivity, the personhood of the other person, but rather to affirm that subjectivity, to affirm it in all its stupendous and contradictory humanness. And yet this denial happens every day.

I threw in with the other sufferers of divorce. I knew their look of dejection, their pounds shed, their incipient alcoholism, their profound cynicism, their inability to finish any creative work, I knew that feeling, I know it now, and I don't care what they did in their marriage, or who is to blame (because in almost all cases it's not a person who causes the marriage to fail, anyhow, it's the internal dynamics of the marriage, it's the *folie à deux*), I only know that to wade into the divorce part of marriage is to root around in the cesspools of humanity, in the lowest circles of hell, and no one who has not gone through a difficult divorce knows exactly how exquisite the horror is. Divorce *is* like wartime surgery, it's like surgery in the field, it's like amputation in the field, without opiation, or divorce is like watching pieces of your body fly away in front of you and trying to gather them back in before wobbling over to the battlefield surgeon, and what is lost are the very ideas of love and faith and belief. In divorce, it's the person to whom you once expressed the marital vows avowing something diametrically opposed: *I want your future to be insecure, I hope it's worse for you from here on out.*

Every week or two, I went to go see the lawyers. And then when I was lucky enough, when I wasn't being penalized for reasons I couldn't understand, I got to see my daughter.

She was about four at the time.

Now, it is worth saying that my daughter is among the very best things that have ever happened to me. If not the very best, then tied for the very best. Throughout my thirties, when I wanted to be one of those men who disdain reproduction, because my writing was *so important*, and kids were going to get in the way of my vaunted creativity, I didn't yet know that my daughter was going to be tied for the very best thing that ever happened to me. I have a friend whose partner said to her once: "There's an *unfreedom* associated with children." I think now of the tremendous vanity of the childless Rick Moody, and of the many mistakes in my life's journey that I associate with that time, the selfishness of my earlier self, the selfishness,

I would go so far as to say, of a certain masculine idea of literature or art-making that I practiced unapologetically when younger.

My daughter, who finally appeared when I was age forty-seven, mitigated the better portion of my vanities, and she did it in an inadvertent way, with her fervent and unstoppable enthusiasms, her love of all the stuff I would have said I didn't want in my life, her monochromatic obsession with pink, her Disney princesses, her five books a day, her verbiage, her mild stuttering (which started not long after the divorce), her elegiac love for her cousin, Tyler, and so on. I was, and am, a father who has trouble getting out of his head and into the world of children, but who is incredibly happy once I do so, and who can tolerate the repetitions of children's games as though they are musical compositions, but my difficulties with the mechanics of parenting are no indicator of the amount of love that I feel for my daughter. I am often overcome by it. In moments when I am doing other things (it happened, in fact, last week in the checkout line at the supermarket), I will powerfully feel the need to weep because of how much I love my daughter. When the Judeo-Christian tradition uses the metaphor for God that he or she is a father or mother, a parent, I understand God that much better, the helpless love of a parent for a child, and I think this is an ingenious metaphor, because if it accords with the surfeit of helplessness that I sometimes feel for this child who I didn't even know I wanted until I was in my mid-forties—maybe God does, in fact, care in ways that are interesting.

I am sure that my daughter's mother feels the same way, and I am glad for my daughter that she has two parents who feel this way about her, but the fact that this became, for a moment, a contested item in my divorce, the amount of time that I would spend with my daughter, was among the darkest and most annihilating stretches of human discussion I've ever had to live through. I had already dealt with the idea that I wasn't going to see her every day, and now it was a matter of debate whether she was ready to stay with me 50 percent of the time. Having to defend your right to see your child kind of makes you want to stay in bed all day. And abandon the novel you're supposedly working on.

To be clear, four years earlier, in 2009, I had taken a contract from my longtime publishers to write a novel, and I had this idea that I would try to write a conventional novel, in which there was a hero (a radio producer at some kind of fictional public radio network) who faced hard times (he was in Baghdad at the "end" of the Iraq War, and was badly injured by a roadside bombing near the Palestine Hotel) and attempted to recover from them. It sounds so reasonable. But it quickly became apparent that there was nothing left in me that could write this conventional novel. The conventional novel, when I heard people talking about it, or arguing in its behalf, brought out in me something like those episodes in the illness of Virginia Woolf, in which she could hear birds talking in Greek. The partisans for this or that issue-oriented contemporary novel sounded to me like birds talking, or more accurately like birds complaining.

So, in the beginning of 2013, I was supposed to be work-ing on that.

But it happens that at that time I was also working on a photo exhibition that would include the first-ever exhi-bition of photographs by my late sister, Meredith Moody.

My sister, during the last fifteen years of her life, took a lot of photographs, always intending to try to do some-thing with them, but never quite getting there. As with many women artists of the seventies and eighties, making a living and having children somehow got in the way of her artistic work. Moreover, photography was, at that time, still locked in a struggle with the art establishment in which it was sort of a bastard art form (or, at least, this is how I see the timeline of the form), and it was not included in the collections of the major New York museums. My sister loved Ansel Adams, loved that sort of painterly nature photography, and was always trying to reproduce that style with a 35-millimeter camera, shooting, espe-cially, sunsets in the Northeast.

When Meredith died, one of the things my family did to remember her was to start an endowed residency at an artists' colony in upstate New York, the colony known as Yaddo. Under the terms of this endowed residency, a woman photographer has free travel and up to two months of time to make work—shoot photos, edit photos, or print photos—after which, every year, my family purchases one of her photos. In this way, beginning in 1997, we began to amass a collection of photographs by these photographers, those upon whom was bestowed the Meredith S. Moody Residency at Yaddo, and when we hit the fifteen-year mark, we began to try to find a way to exhibit this work. I have to say, every year, when my father goes to visit the studio of whoever has won the residency, and brings back some images from her, and we all sit around a table and mull over the various images, it's like some blessing has been meted out upon our family, a blessing with which to paper over a scar. With each photograph we begin to feel, a little more clearly, how to recover from grief, and from the caverns of loss that one travels into.

The museum that agreed to show the work is, like Yaddo itself, in Saratoga Springs, New York, namely the Tang Museum at Skidmore College, and once they agreed to hang the images from the Meredith S. Moody Residency, we very tentatively asked if they might consider showing some of my sister's photos as well. In fact, initially, we thought about asking if they'd show exactly *one*. But what happened was that Laurel and I went to my mother's condo in Bucks County, Pennsylvania, and went poring through the several thousand prints and slides that remained of my sister's photographic work after her death.

It was a sunny day in Pennsylvania, and my stepfather was not yet as ill as he later became, and there was a stillness to the way they lived, in a slowing down of events, an arrest of the contemporary. My mother's house preserved, for example, a lot of my grandfather's things. It was sort of a mausoleum of antique furniture, with especial attention to my grandfather's professional stint in Japan in the twenties, and as such was both reverent about a time before I was born and painfully reflective. The moments that day were full of joy: Laurel and I sat on the porch and went through all the images, with a loupe, which is that little magnifying ring that photographers use to look at negatives and contact sheets. Laurel, because she's a photographer herself, has a really tremendous eye for what's interesting in a photograph, and she spent her whole youth looking through a loupe, and I have been looking over her shoulder a lot in this time of our being together, and I am now not totally uninformed. And we sat there for three or four hours, going through all the images. Certain ideas going back and forth between us, *Hey, look at this!* And, *This one is really great too!*

What came out of all this was not only a sense of my sister living again, such that I could feel *her eye* behind the lens, feel the implication of her, her choosing this moment to shoot this image, and then this moment, and this moment, but there was also a sense of a hidden body of work. A body of work that my sister had hidden from her family in plain sight. Though we looked at a great number of landscape images that my sister had attempted almost ceaselessly over the years, always with the recognition of the sunset exceeding its ability to be captured in two dimensions, there was a completely different tendency in my sister's work, and it nearly leapt up off the contact sheets. My sister was really good at capturing social occasions, informal social occasions, among her friends and her family and off the cuff at weddings she photographed, and these social images brought out the best of her as a photographer. These images captured what she saw in people, hidden moments of complexity and comedy, unassuming moments, moments in which people exhibited the least artifice, the most character. We collected a hundred or more of these images and then cut them down to twenty, and sent the twenty to the Tang Museum.

The best of these images are striking and animated photographs: for one example, some kind of party functionary paused on a lane in the suburbs, on some kind of ATV, carrying a gigantic multicolored passel of helium balloons to an unknown party. The driver's expression—he who resembles to some degree the novelist Richard Brautigan, which is to say, white-haired, droopy, with a mustache, and wearing the fashion item most contraindicated for middle-aged men: short pants—is beleaguered, full of ennui, as if the riot of color bobbing above him is somehow being extracted from his very being, such that the party's joy is his loss.

And there was a whole sequence of images from a summer party in which a young boy, with his fossil of a grandmother just behind him, seems to be lamenting some kind of bloody nose, though the exact cause of his pained gesture (grabbing at his sinuses with both hands) has been hotly debated inside my family; there was a photograph of a streetwalker in Jersey that my sister was apparently very thrilled to get, but which is noteworthy for the benignity of the expression of the woman in question.

The further I got into this project, of trying to preserve my sister's photographs, and thus the instant in which she took each photograph, the instant in which I could feel an implication of her behind the lens, the more I liked it, and I did this, gazed upon my sister's photos, often to the exclusion of the aforementioned novel I was supposed to be writing. That the Tang Museum agreed to exhibit some of my sister's images with the collection she had helped to inspire—of women photographers who had been to Yaddo—*was* some kind of bandage in the big structural wound of her passing away. And there wasn't that much else that seemed so important. Writing a novel about a conventional hero in a conventional way seemed unimportant, not to mention impossible.

Meanwhile, in the intellectual or literary part of my life, which was part of my life I was desperately trying to fit in, in the period I'm describing, I did happen to be reading Dante's *Paradiso*.

Was reading Dante somehow engendering the feeling I had at the time of a Manson-related curse? Because Dante is about the moral and ethical architecture of the world, in which all things are balanced? Was I (according to Dante) somehow *due* some bad luck, because I had had it so good, had so much, and had done so much that was reprehensible during the period when I had it so good? I had read *Inferno* several times, and I had read *Purgatorio* several times; *Purgatorio* opines that even if you only say "I'm sorry" with your last breath, you can still make it out of eternal persecution, by will and transformation, into heaven. But *Paradiso* is more blissful than this. *Paradiso* is all about light and geometry and love. I had been defeated by *Paradiso* throughout my adult life, and therefore I never got to see the beautiful last cantos, where Beatrice guides Dante up to the very highest circles of heaven, where God is perceived as pure light, and in a way it is an indication of how hard it was for me to understand love, and to see it as a motivation, that I had always quit reading before *Paradiso.* I identified, especially when young, with *Inferno,* and its depersonalized suffering, and then later I came to feel the beating heart of redemption in *Purgatorio,* but it was in the beginning of 2013 that I struggled up through the oscillations of light in *Paradiso,* scaled its impossible latitudes, where Dante falls again and again into the inexpressibility of what he's seeing, namely the emanations of love.

That this—my blissful paging through Dante with friends—was happening at the same time as I was acquiring a postcard signed by Charles Manson and grinding through a divorce, is perhaps a fine example, or so it seems with a retrospective gaze, of the peaks and troughs that were about to come.

October

It was always a problem, for me, that in *Walden* Thoreau gave short shrift to autumn. All the preparation for growing, knowing beans, it's all there in the spring section, and then there's a lot about summer, too, the lengthening of shadows, the twittering sounds of the forest. Even the desolation of winter comes in for significant attention, but what about autumn? It's the harvest season, after all, and for me there's always a great surge of feeling in the idea of the harvest, the preparation, the celebration of fertility, the time after the labor of harvest. The harvest still has great symbolic value. Halloween is less about the costumes, and more about the idea that pumpkins are harvested at that time of year, and I personally find gourds meaningfully tragicomic and resonant as objects and images. The threat of frost makes all things sweeter. As a child, as a younger person, I would wait through August in a kind of aesthetic suspension, awaiting that first night that was a little bit cold, when the air was crisp and new, and the harvest moon crested over the horizon line like an indictment of frivolities. The autumn light was more cinematic, more perfect, when the haze of the summer blew off. The stars, the shooting stars, the jets on their way to Europe. All in the autumn night sky. You could have *clarity* in autumn; summer was for chumps and guzzlers and people on motor bikes wearing inadvisable sandals and cargo pants. Autumn was when things started to happen.

We were getting married in autumn.

That Laurel and I were getting married at all, that we were having a ceremony at all, was surprising in some ways. Because Laurel is fond of noting that as a child she used to have nightmares about marriage ceremonies. She didn't want everyone *looking* at her. And in my late twenties and thirties, it seemed like I was never with anyone romantically for five minutes when there wasn't a discussion of marriage, after which, whether in mind or body, I began to flee the scene. Yet Laurel and I didn't have any kind of prolonged thinking about when or where or how we were going to get married, except that it would take place after my divorce settlement was final. The inevitability of the marriage was a fact of the relationship, it was just a thing we were going to do. And this was genuinely new for me.

My first marriage ceremony was immense, in terms of specifics and logistical issues. It included multiple trips to evaluate possible venues, it included a meeting with a cake specialist, it included not one but two bands, it included a very expensive photographer, it included an abundance of visits to outfitters, for both the bride and groom, and so many fights about outfits to be worn that at least one friendship was ended over the selection of outfits, and it included arguments about who was coming and who wasn't coming, and it included friends scheming to be invited, even though we were trying to *keep it small.* I needed a honeymoon to recover from the planning of the honeymoon. At one point, an executive decision about what kind of underwear I was going to wear was made for me, without my input. I disliked all of this. It was perhaps a measure of my insecurity about getting married in the first place that I was significantly unpleasant about the details of the marriage ceremony and didn't like talking about it, and repeatedly tried to duck out of big-ticket issues, like where we were going to stay on the honeymoon, and who was paying for what. When all those wedding planners try to help you figure out your wedding (and I would have died before using a wedding planner, but it's hard not to be pulled into their public dialogue about wedding planning when talking about these things), they never tell you that, in the end, it's *all* about who pays for it, not about how you feel about ceremony. This is, in fact, how in a capitalist economy, people rate the success of their weddings, by how much is spent. It's sort of like the Kwakiutl potlatches, where the combatants destroy their own property: that wedding is best in which the principals, or their families, are most fiscally ruined on the way to the union.

So for the second marriage ceremony I desired the

opposite. I wanted everything to be organic and simple. And this was an approach to the problem that I shared with my wife-to-be.

The first decision we made was to have the ceremony at our house upstate. This was a fine decision for a number of reasons. For example, the space was free, it was outside of the city, it was relatively accessible, it was a beautiful spot. But more than all of these things, our house was a good idea, because we were getting married in autumn. In the Northeast.

From our house, the one at which we were about to marry, we could see the ridgeline of the Connecticut Berkshires (the Appalachian trail up there somewhere), and their craggy, postglacial granite outcroppings, and the density of oaks and maples as far as the eye could see; and in autumn, the ridgeline was a conflagration, and this valedictory with its heavy poignancy was just the place to marry. There are a couple of outdoor features to the house, including a patio off to one side, and we figured we would have the wedding on this patio.

The next decision was about keeping the wedding party to the absolute minimum. By inviting our families, especially because my family is not that small, we got up into the twenties, and then we invited just a few very close friends besides. In October, we got through these decisions intuitively, and very quickly. We had sort of tarried on a date, and decided, therefore, to do the actual service on November 9, and that gave us a little room to find a rug to put on the patio, and to scale up some music for the event. (We wanted my friend the singer and songwriter Jolie Holland to sing one song, and we had to find a way to get her east, and we had Tanya Donelly, another good friend, come down from Boston, and we had to square dates with her.) And we had to figure out a cake. In the end, we got my bandmate and friend Hannah Marcus to come up with a cake. She had been a confectionary expert as a young person.

I was teaching two courses at NYU that fall, an undergraduate workshop in creative writing and a writing-for-artists class in the MFA program in studio art. And Laurel was teaching at the School of Visual Arts. And my daughter was doing her pre-K year at a day care facility in Lower Manhattan. So we had our hands full, and didn't want regular life and the marriage ceremony to crowd each other out.

That's how we decided to have a little preliminary wedding at the City Clerk's office in downtown Manhattan. And, I must say, I *really* wanted to get married there. I love that joint. I love the long lines of dizzy-in-love people who want to get it done *now*, however inadvisable the haste. I love that the City Clerk's office is about all races and ethnicities, and, in 2013, all sexualities and gender expressions. Gay marriage in New York State had only been legal two years or so when we visited there, and it was a subject I had always felt very passionate about, owing to the fact that my cousin Jack Moody and his partner, David Smith, had not been able to marry legally during the thirty-six years they were together. When David died (in a bicycle accident in 2007), Jack had all kinds of difficulty simply inheriting from his husband's estate. That the City Clerk's office would be much taken up with establishing the marital rights of my gay and lesbian brothers and sisters in the period of our own nuptials felt like a powerful emblem for the civic approach to tying the knot.

As our witnesses, we chose two of our nearest and dearest friends, Amy Hempel (she's the author of *Reasons to Live*, and *Tumble Home*, and other excellent books, and my colleague in many settings going back twenty years or so, also a close friend of Laurel's) and Randy Polumbo (sculptor, installation artist, and, when I first met him in Providence, Rhode Island, during my student years, a wild man from the east side of town—we'd been friends more than thirty years), and they came with us downtown. It was a sunny, warm day in October, and the office was right near where my daughter was in day care (her mom worked in Federal Plaza), so we were on our way there anyhow. No matter how often one successfully transacts business with the federal, state, or local government, there is still that feeling that the business is about to be thwarted, that you don't have the proper forms, that the proper forms do not exist, and even if they did, *you* could not have them. I was a little bit nervous. I always wear the same thing when I'm nervous: polka dots. Somewhere I saw a photo of Bob Dylan wearing polka dots, from the mid-sixties, and, upon purchasing my first polka-dotted shirt, from a western-wear store in Arizona, I made the polka dots my thing, in a frank effort to seize them from the-no-longer-freewheelin' Bob Dylan. Well, the polka dots and also the porkpie hat, which I have been wearing for fifteen years or so. I think my porkpie is sort of a variation on the "stingy brim," or that is what I have been told by certain incredibly well-informed gentlemen in their sixties who have approached me on the street to talk to me about my hat. Okay, so really it's a three-part outfit, for the moments of high anxiety, black jeans, polka-dotted shirt (white dots on a navy blue or black field), and porkpie hat. It's not, really, that I aspire to being fashionable in any way, or that I imagine my outfit is somehow stylish, although when I was young I wanted to be stylish. No, it's just that I like an outfit the semiotics of which I can rely on, and which I don't have to think about very much. And which favors my rapidly aging physical appearance.

I wore this outfit. And Laurel wore a red-and-white striped vintage 1950s sailor outfit. She was, in those days, doing a lot of online dress shopping for the outdoor, upstate wedding of November 9, but for City Hall, she was just wearing the sailor outfit. I think Laurel used to show up at her crits in the photo department at Yale, when she was a grad student there, wearing vintage Girl Scout uniforms. A certain amount of vintage style is not at all out of the realm of possibility for her. Laurel wears metafictional outfits, but she never laughs about them for your benefit. You have to work the meanings out for yourself.

My recollection is that we didn't have to wait long because we went early in the day. Amy Hempel forgot her forms of identification, but this was no great crime, because we only needed one witness and Randy was able to sign on that line. He lives right near City Hall, and therefore he apparently rolled out of bed and brought his driver's license, and was ready to serve. In the line to see the judge who would pronounce us wedded, there were, as I had supposed, a great number of gay couples, and it is perhaps no stereotype, but just the facts, that these guys were almost without exception exceedingly well turned out. To a degree that shamed us. We looked like the couple who had slept together after open studios in the Gowanus Canal area, and decided, still somewhat deranged by the events, that we should head to City Hall. None of these things were true, of course—our gear was more about constitutional, and (in my case) unrepentant, informality, a hatred of formality that borders on the obsessive, but there we were. Surrounded by gay couples and interracial couples like us (Laurel being Japanese American on her father's side) and poorer couples, and younger couples, all of New York City, as a matter of fact. The demographic was not dissimilar to the demographic that uses New York City mass transit, but *happier!* Everyone there was bending the narrative of their life's journey in this direction of love, of affirmation, on that morning, and we were with them, and it was hard not to feel some incredible group purpose, as if we were all in the baseball stadium with the Reverend Sun Myung Moon, and he was going to, in some explosion of nuptial simultaneity, pronounce us *all* married before God. I think the close quarters of multiple nuptial celebrants increases the volume of love, the kilos per cubic foot of air of love, in a room, geometrically rather than arithmetically, and the sense of purpose is therefore precisely infectious.

At last, we were ushered into an inner sanctum, an ultimate waiting room, with one other couple, two men, one of whom, in my memory, was wearing a gold vest under his tux, made even of gold lamé, and he was all shimmery, and I remember telling these guys that they looked particularly spectacular, and their response was a little shy, and I wondered if, in that moment, in New York City, there were not self-evidently a lot of fellow travelers who rabidly, wholeheartedly supported the mission of gay persons who wanted to sign off on monogamy with the support of the legal apparatus (even as I also understand, as the writer Wayne Koestenbaum said to me once, that there is a legitimate argument against gay marriage that goes: *Why should gay men want that?*), or whether, simply, those guys were scarred from all the cruelties cast upon them by straight unexamined-privilege types over the years, though I personally never felt like those kind of straight people.

But perhaps as I was thinking this there was a hush in the inner sanctum, as another happy couple emerged from the judge's interior space, which I thought of as the inmost section of the temple in Jerusalem, or the innermost part of the castle in Kafka's novel of the same name, to which one is *never* granted access, or to which access is granted, after which you must die. Nevertheless, it was now our turn.

What must go through the minds of the justices of the peace who effect this great turn of events for couples every day? Do they come to think of it as *just another job?* Would they rather have some kind of televised judgeship in which they resolve the disputes of small-time claimants? Our justice, a woman in her late forties, with long dark hair, perhaps from Queens or Long Island, if I were to attempt to guess, had not, I do not think, completely managed to forestall that tendency with respect to repetitious tasks, the tendency in which we exercise the minimum of consciousness required for the performance thereof. Which is to say: she was *almost* in a good upbeat mood, but not quite. This did not matter! Laurel and I had to say some stuff, despite the excision of all the *God* language, that was quite familiar to anyone who has ever seen a romantic comedy. Laurel does not like to read in public, at all, and yet all she had to do was repeat some stuff that was read to her first, and this she managed to carry off. The witnesses witnessed. It was all over in a matter of two minutes (in fact, they boast online that it takes only two minutes! Two minutes to change your life!), and then we were ushered out, and the couple behind us was ushered in.

I am always interested in the way that liminal moments in life can be so brief. Things can progress in the slowest of slow motion, for decades sometimes, and then change happens instantaneously, in just a minute or two. A friendship can fall apart, after hanging on in some asymmetric disarray for years, until you have a discussion about something really minor, your profound dislike of your friend's driving habits, and then the smoke clears and the friendship is over (I remember in college losing a friend because we disagreed on the relevance of philosophy to the work of Samuel Beckett). Change is happening all around us, all the time, and the fashionable idea that people never really change, that they grind along in the same way, making the same mistakes, fails to take into account how mutable, how constantly is the landscape around us changing, the ponds drying up, the marshes spreading themselves out across the roads, the oceans swelling, the ice shelves shearing off. Nothing is what it is for very long, especially when you consider how abbreviated is our time. In one moment, Laurel and I were affianced, in the most offhanded way, just having agreed that it was an inevitable direction of the years we had already been together, and then, in the two minutes of the workflow of a New York City justice of the peace, who probably married thirty or forty couples that morning, we were in law united, unto our deaths.

The other really odd feature of the City Clerk's office, where all this takes place, is that there's a photo backdrop room, right near where the ceremonies proceed. There the happy couple can have its photos taken before this backdrop, which many of you probably know. What is this cheeseball backdrop? I guess it's City Hall, which you can't otherwise stand in front of anymore, not since 9/11/2001, but as the City Clerk's office is no longer in City Hall, but on Worth Street, the whole idea of the backdrop is strange, highly simulated. City Hall, in the backdrop, looks a little bit like a French municipal building of the Napoleonic period. You could imagine some kind of international trade being negotiated there involving large batches of cinnamon, sardines, and maybe some Kalamata olives.

And thus why do people want their photo taken in front of this backdrop? Perhaps because it's *there*.

Laurel is a photographer of an exceedingly gifted kind, and she doesn't mess around when it comes to photographs. On the contrary. She will take a photograph forty times, even if it's a snapshot, to make sure it's what she thinks it should be. I have often stood next to her and photographed the exact same material she is photographing, and have found that I do not see what she sees. And that's a nice way of putting what I do by comparison. In fact, it's all about seeing, and while I pride myself on being able to observe, as a novelist ought to be able to do, I do not, it turns out, see things as through a lens, which Laurel definitely can and does. Some things, in Laurel's world, exist solely to be photographed, and have no other value. She is an especially aggressive collector of the image repertoire who is forever running out of room on her phone because of the tens of thousands of photographs, and she is forever therefore adding new hard drives to her collection of five or six of them that are measured in terabytes not gigabytes. The Napoleonic backdrop at the City Clerk's office, therefore, was an opportunity to see if we could find something in this image-making exercise that other people wouldn't be able to find. And so we spent some time there.

Randy Polumbo, my close friend of multiple decades, is also no slouch as a photographer, and often carries around a banged-up Leica that is unprepossessing and astoundingly great at the same time. He took the photos of us in front of the backdrop, in which we tried to jump and hold hands while doing so, which is a photo we have delighted in taking in many, many places over the years, we were happy and we were performing happiness, and Amy Hempel was laughing in an unrestrained way, and when that jumping photo was eventually accomplished there was not much reason to hang around. Anyway, it was starting to fill up in the City Clerk's office, and no one wants to be in a civic office building, even one as handsome as some of the New York City buildings are, for longer than necessary, because of the presence of concentrated institutional power.

What we agreed on, therefore, was that we would go get cupcakes. I am not sure how Billy's Bakery on Franklin Street landed on our radar, but it did. I think I had taken my daughter there. And therefore I already knew that in the morning Billy's is great. There are tables, and you can kind of hang around for a while. There's a red velvet cupcake available there, which I associate with the middle of the country, though Laurel says it's not really red and it's not really velvet. There's cheesecake at Billy's too. If, like me, you have a tendency to be addictive in any setting, and sugar is the least bad thing you are addicted to, you definitely know about Billy's.

We started west toward Franklin from Worth Street, and crossed Centre Street, and then right in front of what I believe is the New York City Department of Sanitation, we happened into the marauding path of a woman, possibly a citizen of Tribeca, pushing a perambulator with twins. Because we were living in Park Slope at the time, we were not unaccustomed to excess perambulator traffic, even traffic jams of the sidewalk engendered by perambulators. We were not unaccustomed to going into one of those toy stores on Seventh Avenue in Park Slope where there is scarcely room for two pedestrians of the adult variety to pass without frottage, but in which you find regularly that two perambulators, and their owner-operators, intent on occupying the narrow corridor of Barbies or Shopkins, are inevitably falling into dispute. We were not unaccustomed to perambulators blocking up the front doors of restaurants, and creating fire hazards and ideological conflict. Twins, and their double-wides, were slightly less common, but still part of life in our Brooklyn. What was this woman doing down by Sanitation and the New York City Marriage Bureau, as it's officially called, with her double-wide? She seemed as though she probably lived in one of the condos over in Battery Park City, or maybe in some loft of Tribeca that had been converted into something occupiable according to the dictates of a top-flight decorator, or perhaps she was a model who was smart enough to get out of the business. In any event, the woman, whose twins I did not get a good look at, and her double-wide bore down on my newly minted *wife* with a relentlessness that almost seemed to be malicious, until, like a Corvette threading through a crowded intersection in the last instant before the red light, she gave Laurel a significant brush with the double-wide, one that would definitely leave a mark; the heedless mom ran over Laurel's newly married foot, and then *continued on*. It was the perambulator equivalent of a rich person's hit-and-run. Laurel winced, crumpled up, and leaned down to assess the damage, which involved a bruise, and bleeding and later a scab, and we watched the proud downtown mother and her pair of twins head farther north to do more damage. One of our number, I won't say who, though it was someone who could use the epithet without risking being held in contempt in the court of women's rights, yelled *fucking bitch!* And you could see that while the woman thus addressed *heard* the epithet, twitched briefly, she did not linger over it, did not turn around, and just went on with her careening toward Pilates-with-child-care.

It would be wrong, of course, to impute extra helpings of meaning to the kind of inconsequential rudeness that happens every day in New York City, sometimes several times a day (and I am mindful of that proverb that says: *If you meet three assholes in a day, the asshole is you*), but, you know, we had been trying to get pregnant for many months by that point, without success, and on occasion, seeing the happy, fertile couples pirouetting around us, in Park Slope even more than anywhere else, was a bit like getting a boil lanced. Having the more successfully fertile mom try to mow down Laurel right after our marriage ceremony, was, it seemed, one brazen incident too many.

We went for cupcakes, however, and we tried to shake it off. They were good cupcakes. If the heavy labor of the day, bureaucratic labor, was already done, the trip for high-calorie snacks seemed like some intermediate space between the giddy excitement of ceremony and the beginning of the accomplishment that is marriage. We lingered in Billy's Bakery, I mean, until Randy had to go to work, and then until Amy Hempel had stuff to do. We lingered, as if trying to forestall the moment in which the marriage would really consist of the two of us.

But then the moment came.

In fact, Laurel was already pregnant that day, though we didn't know it yet. It had been my birthday a few days before, and the thermometer that we had taken to using to try to hasten things along had indicated that there was a certain fertility-enhancing conjugal activity that we needed to undertake on my natal anniversary, and that activity should have been good and just on one's birthday, but I had taken to hating the thermometer and its inhibition of spontaneity. It wasn't *cool*, the thermometer, nor was it *hot*. It was like the intrusion of a medical professional into the bedroom. I believe this is a common feeling when the first stirrings of fertility planning result in fertility not going as planned.

We did as we were told, and probably, in fact, that was the night that we became pregnant. Though we didn't know it yet.

And: Did I mention that we lived in a building right on Prospect Park West that was sort of the last *middle-class* building on Prospect Park West, whose board was heavily staffed up with schoolteachers and pro bono lawyers and nonprofit types, and which still had laundry in the basement and a single slow elevator and a doorman from Yemen who was only there in the evenings (the building wanted to save money)? We had landed there to be closer to my daughter, and Laurel, who was more an East Village or Williamsburg resident (or, as it turned out, right before we moved in together, the resident of a rent-controlled studio just above Gray's Papaya on Eighth Street), had found the place, and we were all three—when my daughter was with us—crammed into an artificial two-bedroom that didn't have enough sunlight.

For a long while, in our building, we lived next door to a couple who had wisely, back in the day, purchased *two* apartments on the floor, and conjoined them, and who, besides playing jazz piano at length, seemed totally harmless, excepting for the massive amount of weed they consumed. This we knew because each of the very few closets we had in our apartment seemed to abut the nearer of their two apartments, seemed to *vent* from their nearer apartment, so that, on certain days, it was only necessary to try to find a different sweater to wear to get a stiff contact buzz from the jazz-playing couple.

This, it seemed to me, was the moment of change in the Park Slope neighborhood of Brooklyn. I remembered well a good friend of mine who moved in on Fifth Avenue in Park Slope (when I was living over on the edge of Brooklyn Heights) when it still had street prostitutes. He had quite a stretch there of giving in to his sex addiction with the desperate recent immigrants of Fifth Avenue, until he got himself some help. By the time we got to Park Slope, Fifth Avenue was where you could get Brooklyn Industries T-shirts, and four subtly different iterations of Thai cuisine, and extremely expensive frames for your Metropolitan Museum of Art posters. What that was going to give way to, finally, was real estate speculation by the

Upper East Side and Tribeca crowds. The hedge fund managers and arbitrageurs were coming.

The pot-smoking, jazz-playing couple saw the proverbial writing on the wall, and were moving out to Flatbush, where the two million dollars or so they were going to get for their apartment was going to go a long way. So, one day, if not the actual day of our marriage, then somewhere in the weeks near unto it, we got on the elevator in our building and shared the cab with a rather short, extremely trim southern lady in her later thirties or early forties, and her very tall Flemish or Belgian husband, who before they revealed that in fact they were the couple who had bought the apartment that vented into ours, who had paid the very significant asking price for an apartment made out of two apartments that overlooked Prospect Park in the most desirable elementary school district in Brooklyn, asked us what we thought of our neighbors. Laurel said, *They're great, but they smoke a lot of pot.* To which I added, *So if you're moving in, keep the pot smoking down to a dull roar.* Everyone had a good laugh! Ha! Keep the pot smoking down!

To which the rather trim lady added, *Oh, we won't be smoking any pot at all. No worries.*

November

We decided to order pizza from Four Brothers Pizzeria (*Traditional Pizza with a Greek Twist!*) for the wedding upstate. We decided on Four Brothers not because it is the only restaurant in the area that does not have golden arches, but because we really liked George, the guy who operates Four Brothers of Dover Plains, New York. It seems that upstate there are so many Four Brothers franchises that there are *definitely* more than four brothers. Does the next generation not have a full sixteen or seventeen brothers? Because that's how many Four Brothers Pizzerias there seem to be. The Four Brothers franchise in Hillsdale, where my cousin Jack lives, has a lot of Richard Nixon paraphernalia in it. I believe Richard Nixon ate at this Four Brothers establishment, and earned the lasting respect and admiration of at least one of the four brothers. But what restaurant besides Four Brothers Pizzeria of Dover Plains could possibly suggest the local colors and local flavor of the greater Amenia area for our nuptial event? As regards our main course, George would hook us up.

We hit up my cousin Jack Moody, retired Episcopal minister, to officiate, and we managed to get our musician friends, Jolie Holland and Tanya Donelly, to sing. Amy Hempel was going to read a poem by Jack Gilbert (from which the title of this memoir is taken).

We had to fly in Laurel's relatives from distant corners of the United States of America. Laurel's mom, who was very frail in those days (and who would get even more frail), was going to stay with us, and her brother Nick and his new wife, Jen, were going to stay in a small studio on the property, away from the main house. Laurel's other brother, Nate, and his girlfriend and her son stayed down in the guest room in our basement, where my books are. My sister-in-law Colleen helped us prep for the party by doing our first-ever trip to Costco. We used one of those flatbed carts there, as though provisioning for an army, instead of the more conventionally enormous Costco shopping cart. It was like prepping for nuclear winter. And we loaded our flatbed with our doomsday amounts of finger food (*hand snacks*, as Laurel calls them), inoffensive varieties of crackers, and soft drinks. A few friends arrived early to help unpack all the goods, the crudités in sixty-serving flats. And there was no alcohol at all at our wedding— because one of the trothed had the ALDH2 heterozygote flushing reaction, and one of the trothed had GABA or one of the related alcoholism genes.

Laurel's high school friend Heather works in children's literature now, but she used to be a high-end hair stylist. She was very good at it, and she volunteered to do Laurel's hair, and her mother's hair, as well. This was sort of a beautiful thing, as Laurel's mother, in her illness, was not terribly talkative, though occasionally something wry, funny, and warm would outlast her silence. When I went up to the master bedroom of our house to get my shoes and jacket for the wedding, Heather and Laurel and Laurel's mom were all in there, pursuing hairstyle perfection in low tones. I could see how much Mary Ivie was enjoying herself.

When I think about Laurel's mother now, I often think of this moment, her sitting on our bed, awaiting her turn with the stylist. Three of her five children got married in a span of about a year (the second marriages for both of Laurel's brothers), and she went to all three weddings, and that was very nearly the last time she was able to travel. I think she wore the same reasonably fancy dress to all three ceremonies, a really nice dress of rose gold and dusty pink, dressy with a hint of the cloister. Laurel's mother was in significant distress, it's fair to say, but was also trying to live life and show up for her beloved children, despite her agony. Few people of my acquaintance have been as resolute and forthright about *love* as a life goal, especially not when facing the suffering she was facing. Mary Ivie wanted everyone to be loved, and to feel loved, and she would do her utmost, even in great psychic turmoil, to make sure this love was actualized, put into practice, among those around her. Therefore her participation in the wedding, her getting herself up in her wedding ceremony outfit, and having her hair styled just so, caused some kind of glow of love and honor to hover around Mary, no matter how much else was going on inside her at the same time. The glow was passed on to us.

I hadn't spent that much time with Mary before the wedding, maybe three or four visits to Iowa, where she was living in an apartment on the main drag in downtown Ames, above a shoe store, just down the block from the Tibetan and fair-trade garment store. Her apartment was bigger than two or three New York City apartments end to end, and she lived alone and with a bare minimum of furniture, perfectly curated, antique items, just a very few things, and without much in the way of other stimulation. There were some New Age appurtenances around, photos of various gurus, some books about theosophy, to which Mary gave much of her adulthood. But that was it. Mary's distress was such that her gaze was eerily penetrating. She kept herself up like someone who came of age as an adult in the sixties and seventies, with a sort of Stevie Nicks wiccan luminosity. She still hennaed her hair regularly, and Laurel helped her do it while we were visiting on a few occasions. But for all her countercultural religious longing, her penetrating gaze could make a conversation hard to sustain. She would drift off in conversations, as though she were strenuously listening, and then come back to look you deeply in the eyes, like she could see all the way down in there, over the lip of self and into the deeper heartache. The first night we were with her in Iowa we went out to the Thai restaurant in Ames, not far from her apartment, and we had the kind of strained conversation that you have with Mary, did she need anything, could we buy her food at the supermarket, did she need any clothes, no, no, no, not really, no, and then at one point she looked at me and said: "Well, I'm so glad she's not keeping you under wraps anymore! I'm very glad to meet you!" With a mad cackle that I'm told was her stock in trade when she was younger.

Her circumstances were reduced at the wedding, but that did not mean that she was not content, or that she did not feel great joy at seeing her youngest child getting married. She did feel these things, and if pressed she would even say so, but in saying so you could tell that mere words didn't describe everything else she faced.

My other recollection of Mary at the wedding had to do with my daughter, Hazel. She was four at the time, and it was hard to get her attention for anything. She had occupations on which she wanted to spend her time—many of them having to do with watching animated cartoons on the iPad or on the television. But Mary had brought Hazel a couple of presents at the time of the wedding, and wanted to present them to her. I had to work very hard to get Hazel to pay attention to this, but getting her to understand the solemn duty of having a step-grandmother was, it seemed, beyond my paternal capabilities, as indeed it has probably been beyond the capabilities of fathers before me. The morning before the wedding (in a living room that would have several dozen people in it in a few hours), Mary sat down with Hazel and offered her these presents she had brought (and with what money? Mary spent what little she had on her apartment and food, and the fixed income of Social Security afforded her nothing else), and Hazel very methodically unwrapped the first of these, which was a small molded plastic sandwich holder for Hazel's lunchbox, styled up with the Wonder Bread logo.

There was this immense gulf between the two of them, Mary Ivie, who had struggled so much, and Hazel Moody, contemporary daughter of privilege, at that moment, even though Mary's gift was given with great love and forethought, and purchased with entirely nonexistent disposable income, and even though Hazel was nothing if not a loving and easygoing child. I could feel the desire for a meeting of the minds, but could not somehow bring it to the proper conclusion, despite wanting to. Hazel quickly set aside the sandwich container, which I believe went into a drawer in her room, from which it has very occasionally been removed and examined since. She didn't know how to receive the gift, and Mary sort of hovered there, as if her quietness could be transubstantiated into a blessing, and then everyone looked away, and we all went on with the particulars of getting a wedding organized, because we had to.

Do I sentimentalize when I say that there was a painful surfeit of feeling for me in that moment, the lost attempts of the generations to speak across their differences to what is really important, the longing for family no matter what? When I think back about my own grandparents now, and my treatment of them, I feel some of my most crippling moments of shame, and I would spare Hazel that. Nevertheless, despite Hazel's inability to express the sufficient gratitude for the molded plastic sandwich holder, we took a photograph of her from that period and sent it to Mary, and Mary had it framed on her bedside ever after: Hazel in a princess nightgown she wore at our house every night, until it was in shreds.

The other ache of the wedding day was the condition of my own stepfather, whose difficulties, of a not entirely different cast from Mary Ivie's, were growing ever more manifest. He was still capable of having a reasonably good conversation, as long as it was focused on a reliable set of generalities, these having mainly to do with the weather, or his golden retriever, on whom he lavished his last bits of meaningful affection, but otherwise he had been stripped clean of the majority of his past, or, at least, all the recent episodes. There were a few memories of the Germans bombing England during World War II, when he, who is English, had, frequently, waited out the air raids in one shelter or another. But those were really the only potent memories, as if there were some kind of muscle memory involved in recollecting the war, as if bits of muscular tissue, the lower back, perhaps, or the sinews and ligaments that connect the head to the rest of the body, were involved in the recounting of the war, the old memories bodily stored where the amyloid plaques couldn't yet get to them.

I had so passionately resisted my stepfather as a younger person. There had seemed to be many reasons to do so! I could write a whole book about resisting my stepfather, and in that book I would attempt to make myself look good in vain. It's more honest to say that I treated him shabbily, and whether it had to do with being the oldest male child, and the guy who was (psychoanalytically speaking) the man of the house after my parents split for five years or so until my mother married my stepfather, I cannot say. The shabby treatment of one's stepparents is not a project that one thinks out. One treats the stepparents shabbily in a blind grief, an infantile grief. You follow the emotion to its logical conclusion, the emotion being something along the lines of *resist*! My stepfather could not have had it easy with my brother, my sister, and me, as we were well provided for by my biological dad in every way. My stepfather must have felt how difficult it was to be dropped in the middle of the drama of individuation that was three children in boarding school, all of them struggling with drug and alcohol problems of various kinds. Now it can be revealed: I understand it must have been difficult. And I regret those times.

But finding him in extremis as he now appeared to be at our wedding, a man with only episodic memory, a man of minimal emotional or psychological animation, excepting perhaps anxiety—when it was apparent that he didn't really know what was going on—with only a dim idea of who all these people were, was exceedingly difficult to watch. Both Mary Ivie and Ken Davis, my stepfather, would get dramatically worse in the coming years, so any snapshot of the wedding found them, actually, at a reasonably *good* point, though occupying a space in the room, here alone on a chair, there gazing out a window, that somehow troubled the surface of the party, or, contrarily, forced us all to go a little further, in terms of extending ourselves with people who couldn't really make themselves comfortable in the space of our celebration.

At some point, after a lot of running around and having fragmentary conversations, we understood that it was time for the ceremony itself, and even though we'd already been married at City Hall, there was a way in which this felt more like the ritual that *wedding* refers to, which perhaps means that getting married only achieves its full force when it is being witnessed by a full complement of friends and relations. This squares with Laurel's nightmares about getting married, from her childhood. It was about people *looking* at her.

We had curated the guest list very carefully with the nearest and dearest, and we had arrayed the house in the most informal way possible, and I was not wearing a suit, and Laurel had made sure to solve the problem of a dress with a minimum of expense and fuss (well, she had two, actually, one for *during* and one for *after*), and so it really was a wedding of two people who cared about each other in front of their immediate family and friends, not some kind of society-page wedding, which, at this point in life, would have appalled me. I thought, perhaps irrationally, that I would rather be torn apart by grizzlies than appear, for example, on the *New York Times* wedding page. Although in my capacity as a Universal Life Church minister (more on this below), I would be happy to *conduct* a *New York Times* wedding ceremony, if you need one.

And so it came to pass that my cousin, the Reverend Jack Moody, arrived, and I encountered him in the hallway snapping on his clerical collar and gathering up that scarf that they wrap around your hands, and fiddling with the pages of the script I had given him, a boilerplate thing with no church service surrounding it, adjusting his hearing aid so that he could hear properly, and then we were all filing out. There was no "who gives away the bride" stuff, which is how it should be, because the bride is not property. Laurel came out with her dad and me, as the Moodys (my mom and her husband on one side of the patio, and my dad and his wife, my stepmother, Sarah, on the other) were getting themselves settled in some chairs outdoors. The extended family and friends filled in around them.

It was brisk shading into outright cold. If we had just managed to arrange for the outdoor ceremony two weeks earlier it would have been so perfect! How did it get this way? Forbidding, solemn, but also powerfully evocative of the indomitable, with faint traces of loss coexisting with the poignancy of the autumnal scene. It is often Laurel's tendency to look back and to see how a thing could have been done better. She is a great artist in this way, because many truly great creative people of my acquaintance change their minds with lightning precision and ferocity. They *always* see all the sides of a problem, and though their revisions are inconvenient they are often right. So Laurel does not often rest in a decision the way I do. I make a decision, and even if it's wrong I hang onto it with a some-times sanctimonious contentment. I did it! I made another decision! The ramifications of this for the precise dating of our family wedding ceremony was that we vacillated about the day, and then, once we decided on the day, we regretted our decision, Laurel did especially, because it was possible that it was too late in the season to be practicable. The leaves were already beginning to fall. We had watched them go.

I had been following the daily forecasts, and, later, the *hourly* forecasts, for three or four weeks, and no matter what it said online (on AccuWeather, or any of the multiple weather apps I had on my phone), I told Laurel that it was going to be partly sunny and mild, when in fact mostly what was forecast during those three or four weeks was *drizzle.* I'm not sure we had ever come up with a secondary plan on what to do if *drizzle* turned out to be the mood of the day. However, because we were making informality our rule, we would have been able to adapt, which is less easy to do if you have spent, say, $100,000 on your wedding, and have a tent in the yard with caterers. If we'd had to do it inside, we could have done it inside.

But a strange thing happened when we got out onto the brick patio beside the house (which had upon it a round wool carpet with a slightly homemade artisinal vibe that we had recently purchased for this very purpose), and that is that the hitherto gray and ominous day, with its umber and sienna views of the low, exhausted Connecticut Berkshires (now the redoubts of the deer-slaughtering locals), suddenly gave way, however briefly, to the sort of shafts of narrowly defined *afternoon sunlight* that you associate with rainbows and sentimental renderings of the divine that are favored by the greeting card industry. I mean, yes, that the sun came breaking through the clouds. It couldn't have been too soon for Laurel, who had

bare shoulders, nor for some of the older people in attendance.

I did not take this for an omen, because if I believed in
omens, I would have to start believing in *bad* omens, the
sort that come with ownership of a Charles Manson autograph, and on that day I did not want to go that far. But if
it wasn't an omen, it was at least a nicely dramatic moment.
Jack Moody, with his vestments and ritual scarf, and his
Bible, whipped through the service. We had chosen two
songs we wanted to have, and one of them was by Tanya
Donelly, "This Hungry Life," and she sang first, at the
beginning of the service:

> This hungry life won't let you out whole
> But you can change a thing or two
> Before you go
> This hungry life
> Might not leave you with much
> But you can change your story
> And throw a hand up from the mud

My particular floodgate of wedding service–related
decompensation started during this song, which Tanya sang
with her husband, Dean Fisher (a couple, it should be
said, with one of those sturdy and incredibly supportive
and admirable marriages that their friends cling to as a
sign that it can be done, and done with grace and warmth),
accompanying on guitar. It's a devastating song on a good
day, but even more so at your wedding, and it was in this
little moment of devastation that I saw some flickering of

hope for the marriage coming down through the clouds, like the brief Hollywoodish shafts of sunlight, this despite the fact that it had already been a year with a lot of hardship, and I had to engage in marriage with the healthy part of my personality, at the same time overcoming the big roiling part of me that wanted to say *It'll never work*. That was the kind of thing I delighted to intone when younger, that only the simpering, the weak, the unrealistic believed that matrimony was rewarding, but I wept at the Tanya Donelly song for the hope of it, for the hope of wanting to try a little more, a little harder, with the matrimonial habit. And having Laurel there, Laurel who had nightmares about the public nature of getting married, and hearing this beautiful song sung by a good friend, was enough to make the hope for the thing, the hope that one might be known and cherished in matrimony, and know and cherish in return, feel legitimate.

After Tanya sang, Amy Hempel read a portion of that poem by Jack Gilbert, entitled "The Abnormal Is Not Courage":

I say courage is not the abnormal.
Not the marvelous act. Not Macbeth with fine speeches.
Not the marvelous act, but the evident conclusion of
    being.
Not strangeness, but a leap forward of the same quality.
Accomplishment. The even loyalty. But fresh.
Not the Prodigal Son, nor Faustus. But Penelope.
The thing steady and clear. Then the crescendo.
The real form. The culmination. And the exceeding.

> Not the surprise. The amazed understanding. The
>   marriage,
> Not the month's rapture. Not the exception. The beauty
> That is of many days. Steady and clear.
> It is the normal excellence, of long accomplishment.

Hempel edited down the poem, which begins, if you read the whole, with the Poles riding out on horses to face the German tanks, and she rightly felt that the Poles were not exactly in the spirit of a wedding, and I have quoted above only from her edit. Let's say the thing described here is simply constancy, so misunderstood and disregarded in the present, and when compared to the Poles riding out to face the German tanks, it seems likewise heroic, but even in the Hempel edit, constancy and the love of the domestic possibility, these are not less heroic (though not *abnormal*, as Gilbert would have it, either).

Out on the deck on a round rug, it did not seem hard to be there saying those vows, hearing those songs, hearing Amy Hempel read from Jack Gilbert's poem. I had no ambivalence, and this *was* an accomplishment. It was, the lack of ambivalence, something like Gilbert's "evident conclusion of being," an ultimate concern. So much language in Hempel's edit of the Gilbert poem is arresting language: "the thing steady and clear," in which we imagine we hear Gilbert speaking to his own considerable density of loving relationships, the "amazed understanding" that begins a relationship, a marriage, let's say, but is changed to something much deeper and more powerful in the later stages of being together, and intimate, with another person. It is "the normal excellence, of long accomplish-ment," which does not mean, I don't think, that Gilbert is extolling the endurance tests of long marriage, but rather that he is rewarding the regular and thorough attention of marriage, the ability to be there, to show up, and to accom-plish daily in scale what some people cannot accomplish ever. I wanted to be there, because I could see the isolation-within-relationships that I had so well practiced before wearing out, and wearing me out. I could see the long accomplishment as an emerging from isolation, a self-imposed isolation, an isolation of self-protective vanity, an enclosed and wounded isolation.

Hazel, my daughter, also wept during the ceremony, because she was hoping that her cousin, Tyler, my brother's youngest, was going to give *her* a ring, too, as he was the ring bearer for the day. She had to have it explained to her why this was not to be the case, but in the meantime she wept, in her very lovely pink silk dress (with a purple flower), picked out by Amy Hempel. Meanwhile, I could see almost every face, because it was a small wedding, and in brief moments I saw into them all. A strange bunch of people, really, including Gregory Crewdson, the photog-rapher, and Marilyn Minter, the artist, and her husband, Bill Miller, and writers Amy Hempel and Susan Minot and Helen Schulman, musicians Jolie Holland and Tanya Donelly and David Grubbs and Hannah Marcus, but also a brace of Moody cousins, and not a few divorced couples who brought their respective new spouses. Not a group that would immediately talk well to one another, per-haps, because when do the disparate entanglements of life prove easy and smooth in one room. But they were the true society that would launch us on our long accomplishment, and in doing so would make that accomplishment manifest, and accessible.

There were a lot of photographers, and at some point during the ceremony, Gregory Crewdson snapped on his iPhone an extraordinary image of the light from between the clouds as it shone down, before it vanished altogether. It was not your average iPhone photo. He entrapped the brief enlightenment of the sun shining down between clouds.

Tim Davis, Laurel's classmate from the Yale photo department, had us all stand on the lawn, and took a photo from up on the deck, but then later broke the bad news to us that the shutter on his camera wasn't functioning properly. Indeed, for all the photographers present, we had a hard time getting the perfect photo, if such a perfect photo exists. There was no professional wedding photographer, that is, a photographer whose specific job it was to photograph us, and that was fine with me. But we presumed because there were so many photographers present that we would somehow have perfect wedding photographs, by which I suppose we meant photographs that looked exactly how we imagined they'd look. As a practical matter, they saw us differently from our preconceptions. While Laurel prizes photographic excellence, my novelistic reply to the problem of the poorly executed memento photograph is simply to want to consign the whole thing to memory, and to be okay with the possibility that memory will be full of holes, and will itself fictionalize and streamline, and make shapely what is not shapely at all.

George from Four Brothers (a touch of Greek!) came with the pizzas, and from there on out, it's all a blur, excepting that I remember hearing my stepfather say that he was *not Rick* at one point, and I remember seeing my mother talking to Laurel's dad, Neil Nakadate, the just-retired American literature professor from Iowa State University, and I remember seeing a whole brace of children in Laurel's office crammed in around an iPad watching *Ice Age*, or one of those animated features from the same period, each of them craning to try to see around some body part of another.

We were married.

As I said, the mostly concealed fact was that Laurel was pregnant. It was an excellent secret to be undertaking the long accomplishment with an aura of fertility, thinking about what the future might bring, and thinking that the process finally seemed to have been bent in our direction. It was in this glow that we ate a lot of a leftover pizza in the evening (I remember Laurel's brother Nick doing an amazing job of foiling up an astounding number of pieces of leftover pizza, and some leftover apple pie, too, which we ate for months), setting aside what little ceremony we had bothered to observe.

The next day people scattered out of the Northeast on their four winds. And we embarked on our future. We had no honeymoon planned, because we had sort of had one on the Aran Islands of Ireland at the end of summer (on assignment for an in-flight magazine), and because we had work we had to do. This seems a mistake to me now. I think the tradition of making a sort of carnival of those first weeks after your marriage is a great tradition. I like tradition, in fact, which to me just means that you can look at things that happen only rarely but in a ritualized way and see the outline of broader implications, narratives of significance. We didn't have time for tradition, however, and I had to do an event in San Francisco that week. A friend had invited me to travel all the way there, and paid for my plane ticket, in order for me to give a lecture about the time, a few years before, when I was a judge for the National Book Award (the five finalists for fiction were all women, and the status quo of that era didn't *like* that, and an uproar ensued). Without fear of contradiction, I can observe that I have said all I need to say on that subject, and certainly did not need to say it in public to a cohort of MFA candidates.

But there are rules of literary ethics that are tailored for cases like this, and my understanding is that statute number one of literary ethics says: *Shut the fuck up and do your job.* Whenever I have one of those little glandular convulsions in which such and such a writer doesn't sufficiently appreciate my work, or such and such a department chair doesn't value my contribution to the department where I'm teaching, or the review of my novel was only 1,100 words in the relevant newspaper, or that former student of mine can fill a room at a reading, and is doing much better than I am doing, whenever I think these things, whether because of meager caloric intake that morning, or because of lack of sleep, I simply utter to myself this statute number one of literary ethics, which says: *Shut the fuck up and do your job.* In fact, this is almost certainly a handy little rule for people from all walks of life.

We did not want to appear ungrateful, in the immediate aftermath of our wedding, for free tickets to San Francisco, and if that meant that I was supposed to talk about the National Book Award, then that was exactly what I was going to do. Laurel was expressing some trepidation about flying while pregnant, but because my first wife had very quickly become pregnant, I was constructed of a blissful and ignorant notion that it would all definitely work out, and don't panic, that awful stuff happens to other people, unfortunates, and so we got on the plane, and flew to San Francisco, a town I once briefly lived in (1984), and we took a taxi (that beautiful taxi ride alongside the bay) to our hotel in Nob Hill. I do not remember the name of the hotel, but rather I remember that the elevators were blue inside, and reflective, and that it was a boutique hotel, with a lobby the size of an office cubicle, and employees who doubled as model/actresses.

We did some rather routine San Francisco stuff, like we ate at our friend Owen Ashworth's favorite Mexican restaurant in the Mission, and we had tea with Abe Burickson, of Odyssey Works (there's more to say about him later), and we had dinner with Laurel's friend John, who edited that strange and very satisfying periodical entitled *The Thing*, a periodical that was also an object. John lived way out in some portion of San Francisco that I think was uninhabited at the time I lived there, and he was so far from our hotel that he had to get an Uber vehicle to come for us, and indeed this was the first and last time I ever rode in an Uber car. It seemed so easy, and I had not taken the time to consider the implications of a taxi-driving livelihood, the socioeconomics of driving a cab, that were being slain by our decision to climb with abandon into the gig economy.

It would have been a perfectly acceptable business trip, of the kind I used to undertake regularly, to a city I still love, but then there would be no point in including this scene in this book. Actually, the trip was an indication that something awful was about to happen.

The something awful, specifically, was that Laurel felt, with increasing urgency while we were in San Francisco, that her pregnancy had changed. She could feel that something was wrong, and that sent us immediately, upon return, into the jungle of medical options for expectant mothers. As you may know, getting an OB-GYN to supervise your pregnancy is in New York City a blood sport. There must be women who call the OB-GYN the second they have a positive test. They must have the clinics on speed dial, hanging up only if the test is inconclusive. They call and get put on hold, and stay on hold for a month if necessary, awaiting the positive outcome. As a result of this fierce competition, and our own resistance to making a fuss, Laurel and I ended up (during this pre- and postnuptial pregnancy) with a practice on the Upper West Side, about an hour from Park Slope by subway, in the care of a doctor who seemed willing to take just about anyone. We had an intake meeting with this MD and she congratulated us, and her congratulations seemed genuine enough that day. But she then attempted to locate the baby's heartbeat and failed to do so, and told us to come back in two weeks.

Come back in two weeks? How do doctors expect people to live through weeks of this kind? Maybe if she had agreed to *freeze* Laurel for two weeks, cryogenically freeze Laurel, in a lozenge-shaped tube, we could have gotten through that period without incident, but considering that Laurel had already felt, in San Francisco, like there was something wrong, this fortnight was bound to be interminable and marked by paroxysms of worry. This gear marked anxiety is not unknown in the interior workings of Laurel, the gear that indicates that there is the potential for something going wrong, and you had best prepare. At the same time it's possible that she is often *right* about things being *wrong*, and at least there is consolation in rightness, and preparation correctly undertaken. In the same way that Laurel's mother had the penetrating gaze, the deeply soulful gaze, there is in Laurel conviction about disaster preparation. Betting against her was a good way to make life more difficult, and: she is sometimes exactly right. So when Laurel said there was something wrong, despite the affable MD telling us that *no heartbeat* was nothing to be concerned about yet, you knew that Laurel was genuinely suffering. Not a lot of sleep was had that week. After the appointment, which took place as soon as we arrived back from San Francisco, we had a listless walk through a nearby Whole Foods, where we spotted the mentally ill actress featured in the video work of a student whom both Laurel and I had taught at the Yale School of Art. She was sitting at a table talking to herself. It looked bad. And somehow the grimness of the moment seemed emblematic.

We went back to the OB to have another ultrasound the following week, during which appointment we were fobbed off on a younger medical professional, a midwife, someone who might have lived in our neighborhood and maybe taken shifts at the Park Slope Food Coop, by which I mean that she seemed good-natured, approachable, and weirdly nonengaged in a way that people seemed to be in Park Slope sometimes, as if they can only become animated in order to tell you about the dangers of additives in your shampoo.

The young midwife, sandy-haired and fit in a wholesome, Vermont sort of way, applied the gel to Laurel's stomach, and whipped out the ultrasound wand, and there was a long meditative silence, during which Laurel, fearing for the worst, went all the way into that worst possible place, as I held her hand, vibrating with worry that she would not, in her dignity and self-respect, display for strangers, and our negative projection became a spiritual presence in the room. What can I say about this turn of events, but that I wanted it badly to be otherwise, and I had given up preparing for the worst, though it was second nature to me, because someone on the team had to be positive, and I was determined, at least, to play the role if only because no one else could right then. The silence was like one of those appalling intervals of *dead air* on the radio, in which you can tell that thousands of dollars of revenue are failing to be generated, or the silence on a telephone call after a calamity has been announced, and the recipients of the news are scrolling through the other possible outcomes, hoping that any one of them will be the outcome they can select.

In this case, the Park Slope midwife ceased from rolling around the wand for a second and said the words that I wish I could forget, but have so far not been able to: "Sorry, guys, I'm just not seeing what I need to see."

Let's give her the benefit of the doubt and suggest that heartbreaking reproductive loss was her daily fare, and she just needed a quick way to get the news across, before she, like the would-be parents in the room, could dissolve into a puddle. Let's credit her in this way. Because the only other interpretation, which I have certainly entertained at various points, is that it's really possible on occasion for medical professionals to lose all semblance of human compassion. After uttering these words, she sent us upstairs for another ultrasound with an enhanced device, and we waited around for a long time with a lot of other expectant mothers, and then at last were seen by an ultrasound tech with a brusque Eastern European style. She definitely, as a mere technician, was going to protect herself from the rollout of bad news, and told us that she was simply going to send the results back downstairs, where our doctor would interpret the results for us. More silence, more wanding, and then I watched as she typed, laboriously, the words "No fetal heartbeat" onto her screen, ultimately shortened to NFH, without at any point telling us what she was doing, as though I were incapable of deciphering the medical jargon.

Many times, now, I have watched Laurel go through

moments of horrendous loss, and sort of seal off into a place where she can protect herself. It manifests as great impatience and irritation at first. She does not wish to display her vulnerability in these assaults. Who can blame her? I attempt to love her through the irritation, because I know the vulnerability that is just under the surface there. When we arrived back at our MD's office, where the results were going to be "interpreted" for us—the interpretation of the words "no fetal heartbeat"—we were, for some reason, told we would have to get on the back of the line of people who all had legitimate appointments for the afternoon, and an hour went past, and then most of a second hour went past, and the both of us, in that down-at-the-heels and threadbare office, began to get really irate. It is true, in my case, that I become visibly, irrationally angry in a prolonged way no more often than once every eight or ten years, and rarely raise my voice, but finally it became too much even for me, and I said very loudly to the women at the console in the office: "You are not going to make this woman with the dead fetus in her wait another hour so that you can tell us what we already know. So you had better let us see the doctor *right now.*"

This sort of approach doesn't work often, and I tend to be horrified by the people who regularly employ it, but it did work this time, and we were very quickly in the doctor's office, who was giving us the choice of a D&C or a prescription. That is, we went from the possibility of having a baby, and all the symptoms of pregnancy, to going through the horror of remediating a "missed miscarriage," removing the baby, in the space of a week or less. We couldn't decide which approach was less appalling, but accepted the chemical prescription simply because the prescription and its effects could start immediately. I think they wanted us to wait a couple of days for the D&C. Laurel had the facts about misoprostol at hand, namely that it was (and is) a nasty bit of business, and all I could think about were all the women who took it first for stomach ulcers, and then found themselves spontaneously experiencing pregnancy loss.

We filled the prescription, and then stopped at the heartbreaking Columbus Circle Whole Foods again, before we decided what to do next, the bleeding and stomach cramping, and all-around pain and suffering, which required not one but two applications of the fiendish misoprostol, these replacing the easy first weeks of love and desire in our matrimonial state and of thinking the same thoughts and finishing each other's sentences.

How could it get so hard so fast?

December

There are any number of reasons why a person with my history would go to church. Here are some. I went to an Episcopal boarding school during my high school years, for example, and we had mandatory chapel four days a week there. After four days of chapel a week for four years you just get used to going. Or: my mother is a fervent churchgoer and believer in church, who cycled through a number of denominations as a younger person, and who thus came to Episcopalianism through a laborious intellectual journey of the sort I admire, and who therefore gave to me what she got from her experiences. She believed, and she dragged me along, metaphorically, until I believed. Or: I had a drug and alcohol problem when I was younger, and in many recovery communities, going to church is considered an important part of overcoming an addiction, and I wanted to do everything that was recommended to me as regards overcoming addiction. As with everything about my drug and alcohol problem and its treatment, I took very seriously the idea that my answer lay in *still more spiritual development.* Or: my cousin, Jack Moody, is, as I have said, a retired minister, and spending time with him at church has been an important part of my adulthood. I like spending time with him, with family, on Sundays.

These would all have been good reasons to go, I suppose, and are all part of the reasoning that resulted in my going to church. They are practical reasons. And even more practical is the fact of my daughter, and part of going to church was wanting to find a place for her, a community for her, in a church environment. Maybe I wanted this because I don't feel like an especially acute ethicist. But also simply because I *like* community and belonging. I have wanted my daughter to have the opportunity for belonging too.

My regular attendance, as opposed to occasional attendance, at Trinity Church on Wall Street, New York, New York, began because during my first marriage I appreciated taking my daughter for the morning on Sundays and going to church without my wife. It was a way to create a tradition with my daughter, and an activity that was unique to us, apart from her mother, who wasn't terribly interested. Church was a space where I could feel that I was definitively doing some good, and spending real time with my daughter on a worthy project.

We went to a number of different services at Trinity Wall Street, some at Trinity itself, which is a big, imposing space right at the intersection of Wall Street and Broadway. At Trinity, I often felt like Hazel was insufficiently reverent, or that the other parishioners at Trinity were less interested in the vocalizations of my daughter. Later, we went to a 10:00 a.m. service at St. Paul's Chapel, which is a Trinity satellite space, directly across the street from the World Trade Center site. The 10:00 a.m. service had a progressive edge to it. There was actual dancing during the service, for example, which was not easy for me, and lots of singing in which we were often schooled at the beginning of the service by a cantor. There were silences of such duration that we were encouraged to meditate during them. And almost all the priests who served at the 10:00 a.m. regularly were gay. (This was a great thing, for me, in a period in which I wanted the church to be doing more, progressively speaking, on social issues and social justice, in part because I was disappointed by Trinity's ineffective response to the Occupy Wall Street movement, which was camped out at its very front door, and which might have been removed en masse to a Trinity-owned space on Canal Street after their ejection from Zuccotti Park, but was not. In fact, one day I was at church, with Jack Moody, and there was a guy from Occupy at coffee hour, perhaps for the free coffee and cookies, and he sat and talked to us for a bit, before the rector of Trinity Church came over and buttonholed him, this Occupy foot soldier. What began as sort of casual agree-to-disagree conversation became extremely heated, with the rector accusing Occupy of posting his private information online (doxxing him, as the lingo goes), to which the Occupy guy noted there was no general agreement to do any such thing, and that, in any event, he had not done it himself personally, and thought it was a bad idea. It was distressing to watch persons of two generations unable to agree on much at all, though at least to this observer, they were both right, up to a point, and both effective deployers of their respective messages. This encounter, and the bad blood of it, made me feel even more passionately that the church had an obligation to help the Occupy movement, and when Trinity seemed to tire of any such obligations, I felt greatly disappointed about it, as if the oligarchs had won again.)

At first, I resisted the singing and dancing and meditating 10:00 a.m. service, but like many church-related episodes of my life, *contempt prior to investigation* was followed by a significant warming to the service, especially to the drumming they often had at the end. Hazel really liked the drumming too. (And now she takes drum lessons.)

Hazel went from attending the services to occupying the day care space at Trinity during the church services, and then she went to both the service and the Sunday school classes, and during all of this, she was thriving in a way that was especially rewarding to me, her father. She made friends, and her exceptional enthusiasm for group activities, even the lesson-oriented Sunday school classes, made her much beloved of her teachers at Trinity. I feel that the decision to take my child to church is one of the best decisions I made as a father, and this despite the fact that I have many friends who look down on church. I remember once being at an event wherein a particularly serious priest (a woman priest) debated a physicist, and I remember the priest saying: "I have this feeling that you [the physicist] believe that if I were just a little less dumb, I wouldn't believe these things I believe." So often my feeling among my writing friends is exactly this thought, that if only I were less weak or a little less ignorant I wouldn't believe in this nonsense.

Our story, however, proves the opposite, and concerns a period in which Hazel was still spending an hour or so in the day care part of Trinity, before going to Sunday school, after which I would pick her up in day care, and we would walk across the Brooklyn Bridge toward home. She had a bunch of friends in day care, all of them the children of families who effectively spent most of the day at Trinity on Sunday and went back and forth between activities. I was very happy over a sequence of Sundays to find Hazel playing with a very diverse bunch of girls, with no burden of history, not yet, or not in any way that was immediately visible at all.

Among these pals in day care was a slightly older girl called Stella Gates. Stella was a really funny kid, with a mordant wit, an accepts-no-bunk sense of humor. Stella was capable of thinking things were very funny, but she was also skeptical, perhaps because as an African American girl she already knew a bit about race (more than Hazel, no doubt), had felt some of the sting, and was willing to put some of it aside in a church community, but not all. Hazel considered Stella her Sunday school best friend. I don't know, in truth, if Stella would have said the same thing, as she was almost two years older than Hazel, and she was a popular kid around Trinity, but Hazel surely worshipped Stella, and looked for her each week. We ran into her most every Sunday, usually in the company of her grandmother, who was Caribbean and warm and lively. Stella and her grandmother were part of a large and vital black community that frequented our church and made it better by doing so, by participating vigorously in the politics of the parish, by reminding parishioners, those who didn't think enough about race, how omnipresent it was for them.

So Hazel loved Stella, and loved spending time with Stella, playing on the little indoor playground in the day care wing of the Trinity parish house, while she waited for me to turn up after services or coffee hour. The church had a small indoor slide in its little indoor playground and some big soft tubes that the kids could crawl through, and there was always some new fanciful self-generated imaginative context in which the kids danced around these various furnishings.

A lot of stuff could go wrong in the hour or so of a church service, and on one occasion, for example, Hazel was off her game, or had otherwise expressed some low energy that was out of phase with her upbeat enthusiasm for life almost all of the time, and had subsequently thrown up on the carpet at church day care, while I was listening to the sermon and failing to pay attention to my phone, and I had managed to find my way back at the usual time to a church staff that was polite to a fault, considering my lateness. It was deeply mortifying.

But in the period I'm describing, in the fall of 2013,

Hazel had started going to Sunday school itself, as opposed to just child care, after which she killed a little time in the day care playroom in the Trinity parish house with Stella and a few other kids, for a half hour or so, while I went to coffee hour after the service. It was a fine development, that she was actually going to Sunday school and meeting kids there, and still getting to play a bit afterward too.

On a particular Sunday in late November, I came back to find Hazel and Stella playing on the indoor slide in the playroom. It was some kind of fairy tale fantasy game, some bubbly froth of imaginative playacting, featuring princesses and princes, or the like. I surprised the two of them at this, and they screamed, and bolted. They made me try it a second time, surprising them. They screamed again, and so it went until, accidentally, because I surprised them rather too efficiently, Stella whacked herself on the edge of the slide, and was really mad at me for a second. It hurt, and she sort of brushed me off as I laid a hand on her shoulder in an attempt to comfort her. She looked at me in a frankly suspicious way for a second, and my heart was broken, in that way that children can sometimes do, so purely and unintentionally. Stella was fine, of course, and just sort of needed to rub her shoulder for a moment, and all was forgotten, but I felt like I had really let her down, when she was so kind to Hazel, and I sort of couldn't let go of it. Maybe my apologies went on longer than they needed to.

I remember, that day, taking Hazel down the main staircase from the day care room, down past the reception hall of 74 Trinity Place (it has since been demolished, to give way to a completely new building—under construction right now), where, as was not infrequently the case, there was a spread that day for some reception or other, a few tables covered with cellophaned and catered items, or perhaps some brought from home. They held coffee hour in that space, too, where I had often, in Jack Moody's company, had some of those thoroughly awkward church conversations with relative strangers in which I realized how all the niceties of church simply covered up the naked discomfort of churchgoers, and how the longing for spiritual attainment, or grace, was an effect of the relative isolation of some of the most fervent parishioners. They *really needed* God's help. As I did, too.

Hazel and I left, in due course, as we always did by noontime, and I got on the subway for Brooklyn, and it was only later that we heard what happened.

What we heard was that after we left—about a half hour later—Stella went into the reception hall, and ate some of the capacious buffet that was arrayed there, and then became violently ill, and went to the hospital.

The first rumble of these stories trickled out over the Trinity web presence, a group thread, with a request for prayers for Stella.

Because, as I've said already, I often assume that the worst outcome is impossible, for its infrequence, I didn't believe any more about this prayer request than what it appeared to ask for: prayers. Maybe she'd gotten hurt at school, maybe her family was having some difficulty.

And: it's true that I don't believe in intercessory prayer, in the sense that while it appears that God, whatever God is, could conceivably remit the suffering of humans, God is more often, in my experience, a co-sufferer, a presence of sympathetic care while the worst and most unimaginable travails take place. (In my life, the suffering of my niece and nephew after my sister's death, for example, was not remitted by God. My sister's death was not forestalled by God. The incredible suffering of my parents after her death was not remitted, or commuted, or reduced in any way.) Experientially, that is, there are limits to what interventions God is willing to undertake. But as I have heard it said: God *allows* suffering to take place, and God is a participant in suffering, as indicated, if you believe in these things, in the sacrifice of his own son. So while I don't believe that intercessory prayer can bring about a mitigation of suffering in all cases, I believe that intercessory prayer alters the perception of the observer, and creates conduits of relatedness among the community of the like-minded. Intercessory prayer creates community, and a sense of calm in the midst of urgency, at least some of the time. Which means that I prayed for Stella, just as they asked us to do.

Very quickly the news got worse. Within a day or two it circulated on- and offline that Stella was not just violently ill and in the hospital, but that Stella was in a coma. As the news got became more grave and more alarming, my own illusions of all the possibly miraculous outcomes became more effusive and baroque. She's young! She's strong! She'll wake, and there won't be any impairment or cognitive trouble, because she's young and strong! Implicit in these fantasies of the unlikely was the sense, a very indelible sense, that I had *just seen* Stella. That we had played with her not a half an hour before she ate whatever fateful thing she ate in the reception hall. Hazel had just spent the morning with Stella, her very best friend at church, and there had been some real sense of warmth and connection, notwithstanding Stella's being irritated with me however briefly.

And as the news got worse, and the apparent cause of the problems—nut allergies—grew clearer, and the lack of preparation in the community for the problems at hand became more unmistakable, there came the time when I was going to have to talk to Hazel about it. There are some kinds of bad news that are childproof, in the sense that they cannot and will not permeate a child's protective membrane—the elderly are going to vanish eventually, pets are going to die at some point. Children can have a protective layer with these losses that are a feature of time and its scourge; they can weep over the loss of a grandparent, and move through that grief in a healthy way. But losing a valued friend, a coeval, a classmate, is not one of these childproof tragedies. As Hazel is very good at making friends but tends to keep the very close ones in a special and reserved place in her life, it could only seem a particularly difficult topic. I talked about it with her mother, my ex-wife, and we agreed to take it on, each of us, and to try to be judicious and nondramatic to the best of our abilities.

I was putting Hazel to bed in the little narrow bedroom she had when we lived in Park Slope, the one we had laboriously persuaded her to sleep in *by herself*, and sitting beside her bed while I said, "You know that Stella is very sick, right?"

To which she replied, "Mom said she is asleep but is having trouble waking up."

And I told her that that was part of it, yes, but that it should not affect her own sleep, and I asked if she needed to talk about it more. And Hazel, in a sign of what I imagined was the very self-protective capability of the small child, simply changed the subject.

I changed it back long enough to say:

"If you're worried, we can talk about it any time now. Just let me know. And I'll check in."

She didn't want to belabor the subject, as she still doesn't, four years later, with the heaviest conversations. She will bear down on things for a brief time, only to move on and come back later.

The story came to be at Trinity, yes, that Stella had an undiagnosed allergy, perhaps a peanut allergy not entirely understood, and she had eaten some nuts and had an episode of anaphylactic shock. It was just one of those horrible, unplanned-for calamities. But this was a house of worship, and people brought food, it was a thing they did, and it was not clear whether there was a policy in place as regards nuts. What was clear was that it was impossible to linger over the questions of blame or responsibility, among these legions of people who were praying for Stella, visiting her at the hospital, bringing meals to her family, and performing ministrations of a round-the-clock type. People were signing up online to help pray for her and all of the parents of other kids at Sunday school were feeling varieties of what I was feeling: shock, deep worry, and horror.

Stella lingered on for about two weeks, as I remember it, from late November into December, and though I was newly wed, and newly initiated into grief in our own household, with pregnancy loss, somehow Stella's descent into coma became a very centermost concern for myself and my family. I can remember sitting around the kitchen table with Laurel, outside of earshot of Hazel, utterly stricken, even shattered. With other parents, in the community of family and parenting, it is not hard to know the hope and joy that parents feel, and likewise the anxieties and worry and grieving that parents must undertake. And so it was not unusual in that time to see people from church, church professionals, with red eyes, broken up in trying to talk to us, the congregation, about what was happening. It was not unusual for parishioners to break down while talking to other parishioners, because we had rituals for death, fine and moving rituals, but the loss of a six-year-old is far, far worse.

It's different when a six-year-old dies. And that was what happened next. Stella died. I wasn't there, at the hospital, and I understood only what the community understood at large, that there came a point where the situation was not going to get better, and there wasn't going to be a recovery of brain function, and so it became time for her to go over to the other side, to the eternal grief of her vital and loving extended family, and to the very deep pain of her church community.

And so I had to tell my daughter that her best church friend had died.

Death has been a frequent enough guest in my family that I have had some sense of it even during the intervals when it is not immediately present. There have been low-key deaths, and then there have been these violent, sudden, unsuspectable deaths (my uncle, in a plane crash, my sister to a heart defect), and the latter is like when the ocean unexpectedly washes in, when the floodwaters pour across the levy, and then recede, leaving some great effluxion of disorder that you have to sort through, item by painful item. Many things happen when the floodwaters recede. For example, as I have said, your certainties and preconceptions give out, and your ability to resist sieges of emotion fails, and every small thing—a pigeon dragging one of its legs, or a song that you long considered excessive and sentimental, a neon sign missing a letter— is perceptible as an aspect of some total poignancy of the world that you couldn't have noticed before, didn't notice before, and suddenly you have no defense.

This was exactly how I experienced the period of telling Hazel about Stella's death, and then going to Stella's memorial service. That all my adult systems for preventing the leakage of the world's emotional complexity into my own person failed, and I was adrift in unalloyed loss.

At the memorial service, for example, which was at Trinity, and which was conducted by the Reverend Mark Bozzuti-Jones, an extremely inspired preacher and pastoral counselor, who with my cousin Jack had baptized

Hazel, the expression of the loss of Stella was so utterly painful that even in the awaiting of the service people were weeping and hugging one another in the aisles, and trying to put into words what could not (even in this account) be properly expressed, the sudden overpowering undoing of this kind of passing. The Reverend Bozzuti-Jones, a large, kind, and loving presence of a man whose affability, serenity, and good humor is not routinely stoppered by the horrors of the day, was himself silenced, during his sermon, by the poignancy of the mass for the dead. If the goal of such a memorial service is to prepare the way for the congregation, so that in moving into and through the recognition of loss, and experiencing it, experiencing the details of grief, they can come back out again and go on with life, then Father Bozzuti-Jones somehow managed the purpose, the trajectory of the service; he briefly incarnated the loss, and hung it up on a scaffolding of Christian life, so that it wasn't just a pointless thing that didn't need to have happened. He managed a service that gave us a way to go on, to appreciate Stella in memory. Such is the reason for a faith community.

Thereafter, there were grief counseling sessions for the Sunday school families, and discussions. And Stella's grandmother, even as we neared Christmas, came and gave out some toys to the kids who had played with Stella at Sunday school, or who knew her. I remember thinking the gesture was at once incredibly generous and so exquisitely painful as to be impossible to reckon with, her decision to come among us. Hazel accepted a toy, but all I could think of as I looked into the eyes of Stella's grandmother was her unfathomable pain.

Hazel, in the aftermath of Stella's death, began a spell of not sleeping very well. In fact, Hazel had a number of mild psychosomatic complaints that may have had a physical cause, but which were certainly exacerbated by her sensitivity, and these were all more florid in the immediate aftermath. She said she missed Stella. It kept coming up, as you can well imagine. And there was nothing entirely helpful to say about this, it seemed, but that we knew exactly what she felt, and that it was a way of trying to keep Stella here, to summon her up through longing, the shimmering of her. Hazel *still* says she misses Stella, and if I had known then that Stella was going to become a permanent and unforgettable fact of Hazel's early childhood, I might have pursued further grief counseling for her then. And yet this is what life is, right? It's composed of these momentous separations.

At the same time that Stella's death scarred the Sunday school community, the parents of Trinity, it also catalyzed them. In the aftermath of Stella's death, it became clear that there were something like a hundred adults using the Sunday day care system at Trinity, and only a small portion of them were going to services regularly. A very enterprising priest who was coming up through the ranks then, Emily Wachner, seized on this, and not long after Stella's death, a family service was established at St. Paul's Chapel, which almost instantly gathered together the community of parents and kids who had been through this experience, and made a home for them. That service has persisted, successfully, ever since. It is probably among the more crowded, lively, uproarious, chaotic, and loving family services in Manhattan.

There is one related question about Stella, and that period of grief: Was the intensity of it just about Stella's death? Or was it also about the struggle, for Laurel and myself, to bear a child? I think it would be hard to argue with the idea that the two things, the two varieties of grief, were genuine events in our lives, and that there was an accumulation of loss, a loss that like some kind of remainder in chemistry or mathematics was to be carried over into any setting in which we found ourselves. It was about feeling for a child, and feeling an absence of a child. It was about parenting, and thinking about parenting. Laurel was a real advocate for Hazel in this time of grief, even when Hazel insisted that she was okay. All of that was happening, rippling out around us, and then soon it was the first Christmas of our marriage, with all the jockeying for a Christmas tradition, in our new, uncharted, and also divided family. We were trying to keep going forward. And yet: Stella Gates continued to visit us. She was a person and she was also a tumultuous memory. If Stella Gates had a legacy, though, in our household, as with all the households who had known her through her faith community, it was that she created opportunities for getting people together, and to rally as a community. She's still doing it for Laurel and myself, and for Hazel, and for many others too.

January 2014

If it's the winter of 2014, as the above chapter title indicates, this narrative must move inside for a couple of months. The winters in the Northeast are not like the ones I remember from childhood. Winter in the Northeast has its inevitable seasonal affective disorder, a kind of deep blue despond that sets in around February and doesn't really budge until the average daily temperature gets above fifty degrees Fahrenheit, but winter doesn't often feel like it could endanger lives the way, for example, a day in Concord, New Hampshire, did, when I was in high school, and with wind chill we approached fifty below. New York City is cold and damp, and often windy, but it's not Minneapolis. In New York City, there is light deprivation, a winter of the mind, of bare trees and dog-befouled snow drifts, and deep, dispiriting lakes of slush. And these are the landscapes of the next couple of months. Trying to teach my daughter to sled, on the occasional snow day, and then, when sledding didn't quite take, going inside for sprees of *Dora the Explorer* and handicrafts.

The moving inside of the story implies that there are episodes that are internal some of the time, and the danger for me is that an internal trajectory implies that Laurel and I weren't outwardly engaged with events unfolding beyond home, and that would be misleading. We were outwardly engaged throughout the year that I'm describing, and here are a couple of examples.

The calendar year 2013 had its Boston Marathon bombing, to which we were glued on the television, not only because of the epochal, raw facts of the case, the bending of history toward extremism, but because Laurel had lived in a house directly across the street from the spot in Watertown, Massachusetts, where Dzokhar Tsarnaev hid in David Henneberry's parked boat. Indeed, Laurel's former boyfriend, who still lived in the house they had shared, was sheltering in place during the lockdown of Watertown, and was multiply interviewed on CNN and other news outlets in the aftermath of Tsarnaev's surrender. Laurel's old life in Boston (which began when she went to Tufts, and continued during her time at the MFA program at the Yale School of Art) was brought back into relief, into our living room, likewise the way city life had come to change, perhaps for good, because of what happened in Boston. The coverage was sensational in contrasts, for us, of the bleakest sort.

And, later, in 2014, I was also completely preoccupied with MH370, the Malaysian airliner that vanished over the Indian Ocean (if indeed that is the correct location), thus far never to be found again. And, in a way, even now, I can't fully express the extremity of my reaction to this particular story. I too worried about Crimea, I too lived in dread that the upcoming midterm elections were going to doom the legacy of a president I deeply admired, I too worried about the Syrian Civil War, and the use of chemical agents there, I too worried about income inequality and the future of health care in this country, so why did the missing Malaysian airliner have such a lasting impact on me? There was a merciless isolation about MH370. To such a degree did I follow the story that I wrote about it at one point, a sort of a prose poem, about what it must have been like to be on the flight at the moment it *turned* from its foreordained course.

Throughout my middle school and teen years I was preoccupied with places like the Roaring Forties, with their violent winds, the Southern Ocean adjacent to Antarctica, undisciplined landscapes where things were especially wild, and where humankind was unwelcome or at risk; I liked all trips to the poles, ships lost at sea or frozen into permafrost, lone mariners drifting out toward the desolation of Oceania, and especially deep portions of the watery underworld that one finds in the Pacific. That the lives of those aboard MH370 were entwined with these dramatic and infrequently traveled parts of the earthly landscape made it impossible for me to look away.

All of this to say that the world is not in this book to

the degree that it might be, but that the backdrop of domesticity is always of the world. The two things interpenetrate, the domestic and the cultural. The world imposes itself on domesticity, on the philosophy of domesticity, on the need for it, and the way we talk about it, and that is not lost on me now, in retrospect, nor was it at the time, in winter, when we were indoors, sometimes watching the news (sometimes reading it in the glare of a smart phone), sometimes watching with my daughter, sometimes fretting.

In 2014, let it also be said, we procured our health insurance through the Freelancers Union, and in particular we got our health care from Freelancers Medical. Freelancers Medical, may it rest in peace, was one of those great experiments in health care delivery that involved a really nice office (ours was in downtown Brooklyn), really attentive and caring staff, and free tea, free yoga, and acupuncture. The first time I visited the office (which had a $0 co-pay for primary care), I became teary about the whole thing, for the simple reason that I couldn't remember a time when health care had felt unconflicted, civilized, pleasant, and *human*. With doctors, you sort of expected to be treated like a cheap cut of meat, brisket, let's say, and somehow the profession seems to take kind, caring, aspiring doctors and turn them into people who ponder statistical likelihoods instead of listening to human beings. Freelancers Medical was just the opposite. When you went in and met with your "wellness coach," and ours was exceedingly kind, she had your file at hand, and treated you like an individual, instead of a small interruptive set of symptoms. Frankly, I loved going there.

Of course, some fissures in the delivery of services began to emerge: for example, the Freelancers people really didn't want to send you along to a specialist, as the whole point of Freelancers Medical was to manage your primary care so as to expose your insurer (the Freelancers Union itself) to a minimum of high-cost specialists. They were treatment averse, really, or they were interested in extremely low-cost and practical treatment, after which they were uncomfortable. They liked to suggest more acupuncture. They were extremely nice about it.

At a certain point, despite a number of interactions with Freelancers Medical about our inability to get pregnant that were close to the traditional advice ("Why don't you *relax!*") we finally asked to be referred to a reproductive endocrinologist. A list was produced, mostly untested, as the whole of the Freelancers Medical practice apparently didn't number that many people getting treatment for infertility. From the list we selected a no-nonsense older lady on the Upper East Side, though I can't remember why. Was she at the top of the list? She took our insurance (for a while, anyway), and she had a hard-boiled exterior that Laurel and I both liked, from the first, at our consultation. Her initial observation was that we should never have had a *chemical abortion* to clear out our *missed miscarriage*, because chemical abortion involved awful drugs that no woman should subject herself to, and her second observation was that Laurel needed surgery to get rid of residual "products of conception," as these are brutally termed, and that in turn led to the discovery of some cysts and polyps inside that were possibly occluding our ability to get the

job of pregnancy done, and thus January 2014 began a year
when Laurel had surgery something like five times. There
was always some other surgical intervention you could do
if things weren't going your way, and always there was a
surgeon who understood the knife to be the safest and
most effective way to get quickly where you were supposed to be going. After pronouncing Laurel free of "the
products of conception," having shaved off some bits of her
insides, and after Laurel had recovered from that surgery,
we were encouraged by the Upper East Side doctor to try
the first layer of assisted reproduction, which is IUI,
intrauterine insemination. A more grandiose turkey baster
approach.

Laurel had to get pumped up with a drug called Clomid, the gateway drug of fertility treatment. As with all
the various drugs associated with assisted reproduction
technology, Clomid has plenty of side effects, some of them
serious, like ovarian hyperstimulation. Clomid makes the
people taking the drug miserable and uncomfortable. Having watched several friends take it, in addition to Laurel, I
can give you my anecdotal nonspecialist observation about
the medication: it makes people unable to process human
emotions in productive ways. And, while no husband or
other partner is permitted or encouraged to say this aloud
while a loved one is taking Clomid, or indeed afterward
(I am violating an understood vow of silence), I am repeat-
ing things that women I know have said themselves, and
am not characterizing Laurel particularly. It is of course
possible that repeated losses and the inability to get pregnant causes these emotional convulsions too. Or maybe

repeated loss *and* Clomid cause these things. Maybe Clomid exacerbates a feeling that is already present. But no matter the cause, one had best prepare.

And: if you're the father or donor in a particular IUI cycle, you eventually will come to have your first encounter with the little closet at the practice in which you are meant to *produce your sample.* At the Upper East Side lady's practice, it was my first time *producing my sample,* and I had done nothing to prepare for this new part of my life. I had not taken a single vitamin, nor had I considered, in any rigorous way, exactly *when* the sample was to be given, with respect to recent episodes of sexual activity, and so on. I believed in my heart that I was plenty fertile (I did have a daughter, and had occasioned unplanned pregnancies in the past), and I believed therefore that I needed no special effort. But as someone who had needed to foreswear the American entertainment pastime known as pornography only two years before, it caused me mild anxiety, the little closet, especially once I was led down the stairs to the closet by a Slavic brunette, slightly truculent, who had seen it all before. I didn't really *want* to have anything to do with the American pornographic product line secreted away within, I considered it (in the period of my sexual sobriety) morally unsound, unfair to women, a contaminant bad for the psychic lives of men, but I also didn't know how to *produce the sample* otherwise. Apparently, there were couples who did this sample production business at home, and they tried to corral the *sample* into a handy Tupperware of some kind, after which, bearing the container (by taxi, or subway, or bus, or on foot), they rushed into the office of the reproductive endocrinologist with the sample in their bra or breast pocket, in order to keep the sample warm. But that approach seemed a little uptight, and, besides, you never knew, under the circumstances I've just described, how *safe* the sample would be. What if you got stuck in very bad traffic? What if your breast pocket had a hole in it? How long until the little swimmers began to run out of vital reproductive élan? What if they perished before you got to the office?

Yes, I was once a consumer of pornography, as many American men are, especially the ones who claim otherwise, and I should have been able to use it without incident, even in this time in my life in which I was no longer interested, at least if the goal was to produce this genetic material, which was then going to be centrifuged, so that the not terribly good sperm were weeded out, and the really good ones were prepared for the inseminator. (It wasn't really a turkey baster, but not as different as you might imagine either.) And so there I was in the little closet, and you could hear the HVAC, the sound of footfalls on linoleum outside, but otherwise it was pretty quiet. There was a chair to sit on, and, by the sink (there's always a sink, of course) a big stack of sexually explicit magazines.

Though it's out of sequence to mention this, I can tell you that, in the course of the next two years, I think I went into the little closet eight times or thereabouts, and I became incredibly jaded about it, finding the little nuances of *providing the sample* incredibly funny, when reflected upon. You had better laugh at such a thing, because the only other approach would be convulsive sobbing.

I flipped through the stack of pornography thinking, of course, of all the guys before me, each of them trying to get it done as quickly as possible. Interestingly, the Upper East Side lady had a wealth of images, some gay pornography, some photo spreads of the cheerleaders of the Big Ten schools (a vintage copy!), enormous breasts, tiny breasts, amateur porn, and a little trans porn, just in case some guy attempting to produce his sample needed that. In fact, *whatever he needed* would be acceptable, of course, furries, bigfoot, whatever, because all that was important was that the guy *provide the sample* quickly, so it could be carried to the centrifuge and bumped up with whatever medium they introduce into the sample. If depilated barely-legal cheerleaders of the Big Ten schools were your thing and that was the only image that could guarantee your sample, then hats off to whoever bought the stuff in the first place. Didn't those magazines get sticky? Maybe the Slavic nurse had to go to the newsstand every couple of weeks, and grab a whole bunch of whatever was most up to date.

I know that some guys just absolutely cannot *produce the sample* in a semipublic setting. I saw the before and after of this problem. They go into the little closet and they sit there, trying to get and stay aroused, thinking about their wife down the hall on one of those examining tables that has stirrups affixed. They try to think past the wife and the stirrups and the examining table, and they use, if they must, the amateur photos at the back of the book, or whichever florid depiction is vital to the cause. There are men, even then, who cannot seem to get past the awkwardness, the implicit surveillance (the nurses at the nurse's station, the techs, the people shepherding them into and out of the various closets involved), and they sit there in the waiting room, while some other guy goes in, and then they look away when he comes out. The shame and intensity of the closet is immense. Imagine, as is not infrequently the case, that you are the infertile one, that you have male factor infertility, and you don't have enough sperm, or enough motility, or your sperm all have two heads (this is a real problem, especially with older fathers, of whom I am one, and it was sort of my problem), or are too degraded to do their job correctly. The weight upon the guy, the mitigation of his masculinity, if he has an unfortunate conception of his masculinity *as potency*, is significant. Some guys just can't do it.

I can tell you that when a friend of mine referred to the experience of the closet as "grim and joyless," he was hitting the nail cleanly on the head. One manages to *produce the sample*, but without any feeling but an acuteness of shame. I did it under doctor's orders. I looked at the stack of pornography under doctor's orders. And then I wandered out of the closet, leaving behind *the sample* for someone else to pick up and carry to the centrifuge. A little later on, the first time, the Upper East Side reproductive expert lady said, of my sample, "We can work with this!" Though what she meant was that my seventeen million sperm were at the low end of acceptable, but enough that she should have been able to find a few genuine live ones in there—without two heads.

When I was a teenager reading *Portnoy's Complaint*, a

copy of which I took out from the library at St. Paul's School, I thought my adventure in self-abuse was important, a defining narrative of self-discovery, an adventure of self, whose every new iteration, whose every fantasy, and especially the revelation of various less-routine preoccupations, was somehow thrilling. When I was a teenager doing this, it seemed important, if messy and desperate. But in my fifties, doing it contrary to my wishes, by reason of doctor's orders, I felt disgusted, and hoped, of course, that I wouldn't have to do it again.

But I did. I did eight times, I believe, and at four different medical addresses, and I came to enumerate for myself the differences among the various facilities. For example, the Upper West Side university-affiliated reproductive clinic had a lot of *video* in their closet, which must have helped to bring off the most hard-to-crack cases. I worried, of course, that the video would be audible from the hall, and that the nurses (and other patients!) had to spend the whole day walking by the XXX video room on the hall listening to the video imprecations of the paid sex workers, like they were going by one of the peep-show booths of the old Times Square, and I therefore managed to confine myself to the magazines. They also, at the university-affiliated clinic, had some kind of sterile pad on the leatherette reclining chair, so that your personal space would never share vital fluids with someone else's personal space.

At a much later venue, in Connecticut, I had to do it in a room that shared a wall with the staff break room, and I could hear them making jokes, talking about their shifts, thinking aloud about what to do for the weekend. It made it very hard to get to the point of no return.

For a sexually compulsive person who had taken a vow of chastity, who had grown out of arrested and adolescent self-destructive sexual longing, who had grown into a long-delayed adulthood that was antithetical to these things, I had a lot of trouble adjusting to masturbation in various doctor's offices, and to the massive vitamin diet I was about to go on, which was intended to get me to a much more fertile state. As I also had, as guys in their fifties sometimes do, prostate difficulties during all of this, I was also going to Freelancers Medical, and having fingers stuck up me, by an extremely good guy called Dave (I never called him by his honorific title). At one point, Dave even said, "I feel something!," which are the ominous words you don't want any doctor to say when he has his finger up you. To put it another way, he definitely was feeling *something*, but maybe he could keep it mostly to himself until a more definitive ruling was being given by a urologist. I did in fact have to go to a specialist, a guy who probably had his finger up the asses of men literally hours of the day, and his office was particularly rich for its melancholy. I had to give a sample there too, a urinary sample, and in the men's room, I could hear a guy in the next stall straining to pee. He sounded like a goat in the rut, straining and straining but getting nothing out. Eventually his daughter, who reconnoitered with him out in the hall, brought an empty sample jar to the nurse at the front desk, set it down, and said that her father couldn't do it. To which the nurse said, "Well, he can just sit there until he can then." I believe it was suggested he drink more fluids. Eventually the bodily productions *would* issue forth.

The urinary specialist told me I didn't have cancer yet and that I should come back later. Instead I just had pain, and lower back pain, and these, according to Dave the doctor, were some kind of lower pelvic something or other, which might be occluding the size of my sperm sample. There were a lot of things going on that were more important to me than the size of the sample. I was more interested in my writing, more interested in my teaching, in my daughter, in my wife, than in my sperm sample, but if you want to be on the team you do what the team asks of you, and that means you take the foul-smelling fish oil vitamins. You take the vitamins, you get accustomed to the heavily thumbed pornography in the little closets, you comfort your wife through the wild mood swings of her meds, and you pray for a quick end to a thing that is not going to end quickly at all.

We waited, waited through the long nights of winter, waited through, for example, the jackhammering in the Park Slope apartment next to us, where the new neighbors' renovation was proceeding into its last phase. There had been months now of the intense environmental degradation owing to the renovation pursued by the short lady and her gigantic Flemish or Belgian husband, and our only hope was to get out of town to Dutchess County as much as possible, except on teaching days or days when my daughter was with us.

And let me tell another story from the same period, that same January, that same wintery indoors of 2014.

Though this story began in 2010, at the Rubin Museum of Art in New York City, when I participated with the physicist Melissa Franklin in a public discussion about "nothing," and in particular about the way "nothing," as a creative limit, informs the work of Samuel Beckett. I always like talking about Samuel Beckett! He was a writer I was so obsessed with in college that I didn't talk about much else in sophomore year. It is rare that I meet people who are *more* obsessed with the topic than I am. Melissa Franklin, however, knows a lot about Beckett, and she knows untold amounts about physics. As an interlocutor, she was an artful dodger, and I ultimately felt set up for failure at the chat, which took place at an institution where thoughts about "nothing" are likely well integrated into the Rubin's Eastern and Buddhist-inflected programming.

As a result of this talk, however, an online study group on Beckett sprang up among friends of mine. In particular, we started reading Beckett's trilogy: *Molloy/Malone Dies/The Unnamable*. These were books that I had read in college (except that I never finished *The Unnamable*), and about which I had a lot of passionate feelings. When we, the group of my friends in this very loosely organized group of friends in my online reading group, finished the Beckett trilogy, we determined we should read all of Dante's *Divine Comedy*, the structure of which was aped by Beckett in his work, and Dante was followed by *Don Quixote*, which was followed by Chaucer, after which the reading group fizzled.

It was the shelter in the storm for me, in my period of great change, with my new wife, and my bountiful trips to reproductive endocrinologists, to have a work of literature that I was reading slowly, at my own pace, in the few available moments I had to do so. And the reading groups, whose membership ebbed and flowed, were often full of committed nonspecialists with real insights on these classics. People worked hard and brought a lot to the discussion. No unusual angle of engagement was turned aside.

The point of bringing this all up, however, is less to mention Beckett and Dante than it is to talk about one of the participants among those of us I'm going to call the Beckett Study Group, which was the first iteration of the book group. This group featured a mathematician, a painter, a musician, me, and M.J., who was a blogger of some kind and a freelance editor and a person who seemed to have as much if not more of her life online than in the fleshy "actual" world of humans. This made her a perfect heroine of the Beckett Study Group, which acknowledged the ways in which the body, as a warehouse for the self, was complex and difficult.

M.J. wrote to me not long after I began writing a music column for an online magazine called *The Rumpus*, for which I still write. She wrote to me, in part, I believe, because she liked my music columns. But she also had this way, an extremely persuasive way, of getting you well integrated into the world of her online self.

Very quickly after writing to me, M.J. came to send me her poems, which were not necessarily poetry as I understood poetry in the contemporary academic sense of the word, meaning not fragmentary, free, political, containing traces of languages that were not English, or concerned with the works of Emily Dickinson, but rather which boasted old-fashioned features like rhyming and meter. (Though later on she wrote original and moving collage poems, some of them made out of lines from Wikipedia, but much transmuted, like this: "the monks and lacan found themselves on / the same train to Paris. / they did not interact except to smile, except to / share cheese sandwiches and tea. / a passenger sketched the scene, which / might have been one of a kind.") She would send links to her online stuff, and while she was not institutionally literary in the way they might have thought about literature at the Associated Writing Programs convention, she kept up with the Beckett Study Group, which was fine with me, and seemed thoroughly to enjoy it.

There was something strange going on with M.J., though, that seemed to have to do, for example, with her being mostly indoors, perhaps agoraphobic, and more internet-connected than face-to-face. Her parents, as she recounted it, were not well. Her dad was depressed, and her brother was *depressed*, and she felt responsible for them all. I think the family lived in the Middle Atlantic part of the East Coast, and occasionally M.J. would go from her native San Francisco (where she was married to a fellow we infrequently heard about) east, to try to stabilize whatever difficult situation had recently come up among her parents and her brother. M.J., I believe, was considered the most competent person in the family.

When M.J. got back to the Bay Area, one thing she did, and I think it was a long-standing tendency, was to *eat*, as people under a lot of stress do on occasion, myself included, and as a result for a very slim woman (the M.J. I saw in one photograph was thin and wry and beautiful) she had become a bit obese. She was open about this. I asked, at one time, a poet friend of mine in San Francisco if she would read a couple of M.J.'s poems and evaluate them for her, but that friend wrote back, after meeting with M.J., that she was never going to progress as a poet until or unless she dealt with her personal problems, chief among these a food addiction. She needed, my friend said, to start there.

Curiously, it seemed to me then, M.J. was also preoccupied with the founder of the website where I published my music columns, and with other well-known writers online. She said that there were people trolling her online, and that she was suffering as a result. I had no reason not to take her words as entirely credible, though something also seemed wrong to me, as though a misapprehension lay at the heart of her point of view.

As gently as I was able, mindful of my own privileged position in the writing world and mindful of a desire not to presume that whatever the scale of that privilege was it did not mean that I knew more about the kinds of relationships that people had with others in an online setting, I tried to alert M.J. to the possibility that maybe what was happening online wasn't quite as she imagined, and very quickly M.J. decided that she had, for the time being, had enough of me.

In my experience, even the most troubled people often tell the truth, often a very revealing truth, even if layered in metaphor or allegory, and according to this way of seeing it, I decided that I hadn't quite done a good job with M.J. When she tested the waters of being back in touch a few weeks later, I was glad for it. I was responsible for many people, in those days, Laurel and my daughter, and my extended family, and my students, and so on, but I didn't feel comfortable with letting M.J. down.

Why did she want to talk to me again? If she associated me with a cabal of successful writers online keeping her in obscurity or otherwise harming her? I wasn't sure. Nevertheless, M.J. seemed to declare our difference of opinion null and void, and went back to writing frequently, with the same warmth.

The same problems were still a part of her life, she was taking care of a dreadfully ill family, and not really finding a lot of freelance editing for herself, and not getting that much prose written, or poetry, and so on. And I tried to help, but I also recognized limitations on my ability to help, for being 3,000 miles away from her, and busy with my own portfolio of difficulties.

It was in this period, perhaps in the middle of reading *Purgatorio*, or very nearly, that M.J. started to send me spam messages that she'd gotten via email featuring that sort of *word salad* that one occasionally received in those days. "Take sharpness filling soda cans wetness smooth dancing sheep horse paper handbags skipping forests play together in worlds with pencils, schools page drink slime loving living nectar of bees of pollen and butterflies amok children bikes cars sliding." You know the type. Like many other admirers of process-oriented and collage poetry I had much loved computer-generated word salad when first exposed to it, and I definitely tried to evolve some collage-oriented work of my own from it. But over the course of time I had come to feel that the automatic writing component of spam, so redolent of the computer in the process of underestimating poetical writing, was too easy to simulate. It only glancingly related to the philosophical mission of poetry. What I mean is: word salad got boring for me.

But M.J. instead, even years into the advent of machined word salad, had decided that the word collages were specifically targeted at her, and that the bots, or the frauds, or the identity thieves, who were sending this stuff to her, had somehow invaded her computer, and were now privy to her information, her life story, or were using other means, and would I mind looking at the enclosed and offer my opinion on the subject?

Usually, the word salad enclosed by M.J. would mean nothing in particular, but would just have the contoured, postmodern look of arbitrarily formulated word salad—not the Antonin Artaud kind of word salad, but the "buy Vicodin online!" kind of word salad. That was as much as I could see. Reading M.J.'s forwarded word salad was sort of like reading the phone book, or a compendium of weather-related data. You could give the text a few lines, and admire an inadvertent poetical phrase, but otherwise there was nothing to say. Often what would happen with M.J. was that she would become exasperated if I refused to endorse her interpretation of a spam explosion, or whatever it was, and she would then lurch prosaically back into her tirade about oppressors online, and start in on how I had, it seemed, betrayed her and her needs, by

refusing to renounce these miscreants, who had sullied
her reputation, and so forth.

Here's part of Mandelbaum's translation of Dante's *Purgatorio*, from Canto XIII, Virgil's apostrophe to the sun:

> "O gentle light, through trust in which I enter
> on this new path, may you conduct us here,"
> he said, "for men need guidance in this place.
> You warm the world and you illumine it;
> unless a higher Power urge us elsewhere,
> your rays must always be the guides that lead."

In the Dante reading group, which followed the very
difficult and dark reading of the Beckett trilogy, I found
myself finally at a threshold with Dante in which I was no
longer struggling with the text, and in which I could turn
to the thematic arc of the book, and accept it, and live with
it, and live in it, and not expect, any longer, Dante to be a
dramatist and nothing besides. As Virgil extols the sun
itself, and as *Paradiso* comes to turn to the orbits of light
in the concentric heavens, I wanted to make the journey
of the whole of Dante this time, even as much of the Dante
reading group fell away the longer we spent on it. M.J. was
one of the people who fell away. Canto XIII, quoted above,
goes on to catalogue how the eyes of the envious are
stitched shut in the *Purgatorio*, for some long duration,
because they cannot rightly see what is in front of them,
and thus they stumble around the mountain of Purgatory
for hundreds of years, until they are redeemed of the

envy that has caused them to suffer in this way. Was this "stitched shut" quality more an aspect of my character? Or of M.J.'s?

While it would be too judgmental, and too reductive, to say that M.J. was somehow envious, as are the sufferers in the passage from Dante above, or that she would map onto the purgatorial journey of Canto XIII, which I don't believe she elected to read with us, I did sort of feel like there were ways that she wasn't entirely seeing what was happening to her and around her, and that this was, after a fashion, a choice she made. Or this is how I thought about it then. She would lock herself into a vault of her self-designed torments, and refuse to come out for a while, and she had an answer for every route out. Now, I am extremely well acclimated to the conviction that mental illness is not a choice, that it is an *illness*, and that the torments are real. I know this firsthand. This self-inflicted but unavoidable misery was my own recollection of major depression, that you were locked in with the dread, and that you had a hundred answers for why the treatment that might work would work for everyone but you. The whirlpool of delusional thinking makes it so hard to clamber up the mountain of grace and there to begin to attempt to see, at the summit, the light that is all around you.

At a certain juncture M.J.'s insistence on the hermeneutical meanings of the random messages she received online went from being a sort of funny, plausible interpretation of gibberish to being mystifying, and unyielding. She could mock herself and her deteriorating circumstances for a while, and then gradually she couldn't mock her circumstances at all, and the whole story became dreadfully serious.

This I grew used to, but with increasing discomfort, a discomfort owing to the mental illness in my own family, and the fact that Laurel and I were trying to deal with incipient dementia and worse among those in the generation that preceded us, and with vast sums of money that we were beginning to pay into treatment for infertility, and with problems of my child custody agreement. Eventually, I wrote these words to M.J.: "You need to consult a mental health professional."

It is perhaps a comprehensible fact of life that nobody ever seems to like the sentence "You need to consult a mental health professional." M.J.'s response was very unhappy and immediate and personal, and she wanted nothing more to do with me, and a great silence opened up between us. I have used the sentence with other people occasionally, over the course of my life, and this is often the outcome.

Ours was a bifurcated friendship in the first place, in that M.J. often seemed to write to a Rick Moody who had only tangentially to do with me, and who stood for something from her point of view, and this made me uncomfortable, and put me in a curious position. But on the other hand, as Laurel might say of me, I expend real effort on difficult people, and I come, because of expending the effort, to give them reserves of time and appreciation, and sometimes I do this to the detriment of people I most care deeply about and live with. It's true, perhaps. I like the genuineness of really troubled and bereft people, and I end up giving them a lot of time. In this case, I experienced some grief, from the sudden absence of M.J., who, in a curious twist of millennial culture, I never ever did meet in person, not even once, and whose own reports of homeliness I can neither confirm nor deny, for all I know of her was the one or two photographs I have described.

Her last letter to me, from summer of 2013, is heart-rending in the extreme. It is both lucid—

> but you do have my sincerest apologies if i've
> added to your already large burden of hurt

—and subtly full of a distraught and erroneous belief:

> if you wanted to humiliate me, to show me up
> as less than your intellectual equal i could
> have spared you the time. i humiliate myself
> daily, as does the universe. it's just the way
> things are.

(Capitalization as in original.) Already, of course, the email messages of deepest concern behind M.J.'s back were circulating at an enormous rate. Though most of the Dante reading group constituents were on the East Coast, there was a real effort taking place to try to find a way to reach out to M.J.'s husband, through email or snail mail or telephone, to try to let him know what we were being told, if he did not already know.

It was my wife, Laurel, who suggested that we *had* to do something about M.J. And this she felt in part because her mother was going through related crises, and because she had close friends and family with problems, some of them people she had worked with in her videos. Laurel knew, and knows still, a lot about this kind of suffering, the loneliness, the exile, of delusion, and the way that it becomes a responsibility that isolates the sufferers and drives away everyone who might help. Laurel, though she wasn't reading Dante with us, was a powerful advocate for the group doing something about M.J., just to make sure that we had been responsible and alerted others who were responsible. And so we did, though for my part, I did it while no longer speaking to M.J. directly, because of the implication in her last note that I was somehow involved in the conspiracy against her, or that in some way I didn't care or worse wanted to hurt her, when these were the furthest from my wishes for her peace and equanimity.

As I have said, what I know about delusion, from having lived with schizophrenics and bipolar sufferers when myself an inpatient at the psychiatric hospital in 1987, likewise from being related to any number of mentally ill people, both through marriage and by blood, is that even delusion often tells a very human truth, if read properly. I had to let go of M.J., because of email messages like this:

do you know what's happening and why?

are you angry because i posted in the
rumpus comments of your music column?

angry because i contacted you for help?

angry because i wrote poems?

i am a person, first.

a person.

But if I had read the notes carefully, perhaps I shouldn't have let go of her at all, even though she was someone I scarcely knew; if I had thought more clearly about her initial difficulties; if I had inquired further, perhaps I could have done more. The only way I can comfort myself now is to think that she had closer family and close friends, and it is my understanding that they were doing their utmost too to try to stem the tide of woe closing over M.J. But the pain was significant then for me, and it is now too, the pain of thinking that more might have been done.

Not long after this upsetting sequence of events, I learned from various members of the Beckett/Dante Study Group that M.J. then began to struggle with frankly psychotic delusions about messages being delivered to her through the electrical system in her apartment. I remember reading a few Facebook posts—expunged now, appropriately—that featured comments of the "I hope you are getting the help you need" variety. Loving, but direct.

We watched M.J. collapse in some way, and we watched

it happen in microns. I have always opposed light psychiatric terminologies like "psychotic break" and "nervous breakdown" that frame these transitions into mental illness as cataclysmic and sudden, when, in my experience, they are a lot slower moving, and more holistic, and they certainly were slow-moving with M.J., not to mention (for point of reference) myself. I do not, that is, consider myself *cured* of the depression and obsessive thinking and alcoholism and self-destructiveness that afflicted me as a younger person. I consider myself to be in remission to greater and lesser degrees, and possessed (for which I am grateful) of a number of extremely useful tools and approaches that allow me to head off problems. But I am, while much changed, still myself, and M.J., while performing an excellent facsimile of upstanding (and extremely funny) citizenry, was, it seems, in tremendous discomfort. The longer I knew her, the longer my circle knew her, the more difficult it became for her to pretend otherwise. If there were tools at hand, which I think there were, she failed to see them herself, or to know how to employ them, or they failed to work.

In short, I became one of M.J.'s delusions. I was, it seems, one of the people attempting to control her and her thoughts, and this was apparently the case because she had never entirely overcome the fact that I was a successful and somewhat well-known writer myself. In the end, this felt particularly disquieting to me, and it was one of those delusions that, if repeated enough, starts to feel like maybe it *should* be accurate somehow, that I was an online oppressor, if only because it has been repeated so often.

By winter of 2014, the silence, and the determination to let others nearer to M.J. lead the charge, made her death harder to take (and I'm forecasting here, slightly, in that she didn't pass away until a couple of months later). That she took her life sank in *after* the shock that she was no longer living, this person with whom I emailed at least once or twice a week, if not more, for a couple of years. The suicidal part settled in like a howling in the night. I don't know, didn't know, probably never will know how M.J. did what she did. And in a way that's just and right, in that the silence between us, which could still be intimate and (at least for me) supportive, does not inevitably suggest a discernible or interpretable death. That is her affair. It is an intimacy of her life. My friend Iris, also in the reading group, asked her if she wanted to rejoin when we got to *Don Quixote*, which came later, and the reply was *thanks but no thanks*, which is a remark free of distorted thinking, but also one that wants for the warmth that we had all felt for her.

Her poetry was really warm, sometimes it had an Ogden Nash quality, funny, charming, surprisingly antique, and as a mood it overcame her only occasionally, but it was the writing I liked best about her. As a prose writer, as she herself would have said, she *could not lie*. In a way it is a dangerous habit for a writer, as a capacity for editorial intervention is self-protective sometimes, and allows us to pass by topics and narratives that would require too much of us, or that could even endanger our well-being.

I'm still circumambulating around her death, especially on a day like today (for I am setting down these words on the anniversary of her death), and can find no end to the agony in it, even in the light above purgatory.

February

There were years in the nineties that I went *north* in February, having stayed at an artist's colony north of Albany in the deepest winter months, but that kind of crackpot thinking I had come to leave behind. I was instead this February to go south, to lead a so-called "master class" at the Atlantic Center for the Arts, in New Smyrna Beach, Florida. This oddly named berg, New Smyrna, celebrates an ancient Greek city-state that is now part of Turkey. I believe the site of "old Smyrna" was multiply conquered, and the site of tribal conflicts. Why New Smyrna, Florida, wanted to summon up that legacy is unknown to me. The Floridian Smyrna is not that far from Daytona Beach where, as you might suspect, you can drive your car on the beach. The region has excellent citrus and some slightly seedy pockets hidden away. Serial killer Aileen Wuornos apparently frequented a bar in or near New Smyrna.

The part of town where the arts center is located is dense with mangrove and canals, and, one presumes, gators, and the arts center itself is constructed with boardwalks and informal hangouts, and we were there with Dana Schutz, the artist, who was already friendly with Laurel, and who is a lovely and unpretentious and funny and thoughtful person whom we came to love without hesitation. She was pregnant with her son at the time she was there. The other "master artist" was jazz pianist and composer Marilyn Crispell. Marilyn is a truly unforgettable person, mild-mannered and easy to talk to, a bit like some of my sister's friends, well acclimated to the counterculture and its iterations. But then when you talk to her about music and the people she has known and played with, Marilyn takes on a dense and powerful importance that is as if she were concealing inside a second self. I don't think I have ever seen anyone play piano live the way that Marilyn plays it, in a kind of luminous possession.

You can go through life listening to jazz, and knowing a lot of jazz players, as I have done as an adult, and still never really get an idea of the fundamental principles of jazz—for example, what improvisation really summons or requires. How it might feel to take the idea of improvisation to heart, and to make it a principle of being, a kind of art-making that is more broadly important than simply: it's going to be flavored like New Orleans and have sevenths and ninths in it. Or: it's going to genuflect in the direction of Louis Armstrong or Miles Davis. Marilyn

Crispell truly composes the music on the spot, and it comes from wherever Coltrane came from, which doesn't mean that it sounds like Coltrane (or perhaps more accurately like McCoy Tyner), or Coltrane's music, but that it comes from the same idea of what music is, a set of procedures that rain down on her like ions from above.

So the three "master artists" were as just named, and then there was a group of students, handpicked by each of us. I had given applicants to my "writing" class a description that indicated that I didn't need for people to be "writers," that my class was interdisciplinary, and that anyone was welcome to sit in. I have always wanted to teach this interdisciplinary class. I have always wanted a class that was in no way a traditional writing workshop, and in which I didn't teach fiction writing, but rather some impulse to compose literature, or to use language, in a way that was not normatively inclined toward genre at all. I wanted to make a class that was about using language to arabesque around the traditions of contemporary writing instruction, that was spacecraft in an era of train travel where traditional writing classes were concerned, or maybe I was just trying to make a class that was like one Marilyn Crispell would teach, except that it was made out of words, and finally I was going to have a chance.

Does it sound preposterously idealistic? Maybe! I know and can feel, at this point, having been teaching in one capacity or another for nearly thirty years, that teaching is not about the dispensation of information. Teaching is not about a professor giving you information that she happens to have available, in which process you consume the information, as though it were comestible, after which you are then in some fashion ready to teach yourself. And teaching writing is the teaching that is least like this. French pedagogy often involves lecturing, and I could therefore no more teach writing in France than I could teach physics. Teaching in my mind is about an exchange of human values, an oscillation between teacher and student in which the roles are dynamic, and the subject matter in some ways is a matter of indifference. The listening that is required for teaching is omnidirectional, and the talking is omnidirectional, and it's perhaps more like playing jazz than it is like preparing for an SAT. The more I teach the less certain I am that I know anything, but the more I can feel the future of the student in and around her or him, and the more I know how to get there without undue time-wasting. I know nothing, but I can feel the personalities, and, in a way, I can love the personalities, no matter who they are, who the student is, love in this case meaning respect and esteem and compassion in a rigorously pedagogical environment, I can practice the kind of transferential esteem that works in psychoanalysis to make it possible for students to see their own way into growing and changing, and challenging themselves. I wanted to teach this class at the Atlantic Center for the Arts, in which you could bring *anything* to the class. One of the assignments was: I read aloud Shakespeare's sonnet 73 ("That time of year thou may'st in me behold"), we discussed it for a minute, and then they had to rewrite it from memory, after which we all read our results aloud *at the same time*, in various different configurations, and recorded the results. This was the class I always wanted to teach.

Laurel and I were trying to have a baby the old-fashioned way in February, getting ready for another full-scale IUI when we got back in town in March (because the prior one had turned up nothing), and therefore we were using thermometers and attempting to do what you need to do to bring the whole thing to fruition, but at the same time I was having a lot of the aforementioned issues, prostate and pelvic floor pain, and feeling like an old, fat, irritating white guy.

A poet and photographer friend of Laurel's who, with his wife, had also gone through infertility, had suggested to me, on a number of occasions, how awful the whole thing had been. They had recently adopted in 2014 (indeed, their son had been at our house at the wedding, and had memorably rolled down the hill in the backyard quite a few times), and their having done so enabled them to put the infertility treatments aside. Laurel's friend had written a song about how much he hated seeing other people and their children, how much he hated the children, and how bad he felt for hating the children. Or for being envious of the children and the parents to the point of hatred.

I didn't know what to make of this feeling, then, but now in a way it was my feeling and it was Laurel's feeling, too, and it was my job, and responsibility, and duty, to try to understand and feel what Laurel was feeling, and to try to help. There was one contextual difference between us, of course, and it was that I already had a child. And she did not. I had, in a way, backed into being a father. I might have put it off even longer. But by the time we were in New Smyrna, my daughter was five and was well on her way. Laurel had the role of stepmother in hand, and had known Hazel, my daughter, since she was very young, but she had no child of her own, and her frustration with the meager pace of our fertility got to her.

Park Slope was to fertility what Wisconsin is to dairy farming, what France is to unpasteurized cheeses, what the Gulf of Mexico is to red tides; everywhere you went in Park Slope was occluded by breeders demanding that you accommodate both parent and spoiled brat while the parent reached over you for his kombucha. The park near us was gummed up with the 10% and their offspring, if not the 1% and theirs, and they were awfully hard to watch sometimes. In fact, Laurel and I had a jokey, not-at-all-funny gesture that we had borrowed from our friend who wrote the howl-of-pain lyric about children when he could have none, a gesture that we used when we found ourselves in particularly dense sidewalk traffic with some battalion of Park Slope parents, and that gesture involved miming the act of pulling the pin out of a hand grenade with one's teeth and then lobbing the device into the crowd. We winced at the gesture when we first knew of it, and then we adopted it too.

This is an indication of how great was the pain we were in.

The hatred of children, when you are desperately trying to have a child, is explicable to me now, and the desire not to gloat about one's child because of the other people out there who are suffering with infertility, and in enormous pain with their suffering, is obvious to me now, and in a way it dates to the education that I got during our long period of involvement with the medical community.

There was a musician at the Atlantic Center for the Arts, in New Smyrna, Florida, who was simultaneously chatting up a number of the younger visual artists there, and at least one of my writing students, and I could remember well the time in my life when I would have thought of that preoccupation with the germinating youth of the colony as a worthy strategy for the weeks ahead, but it now seemed like some sepia-toned and antiquated approach to life. The personal lives of the other colonists seemed to be happening behind some scrim, and in front of me was the next move in our long, crushing path toward parenthood.

At the same time, Laurel had embarked on this photo project that involved trying to take portraits of people, at night, who were distantly related to her through DNA. She went online, to sites like 23andMe and Ancestry.com and located people who were listed as cousins or distant relations of some kind, and then she approached these people and asked if they would allow her to take their picture. She ended up doing hundreds of these images. In 2013 and 2014 she, and sometimes we, drove all across America taking these photographs. I think I went on about half of the total volume of DNA photo shoots. Laurel ended up traveling 50,000 miles in the United States of America taking these images, all of people on her mother's side of the family, because her dad, being third-generation Japanese American, had far fewer DNA matches online. (In Japan, DNA research had not yet had its moment. But it's also true to say that there are simply far fewer Japanese Americans than Americans of European descent, only about 1.3 million, and thus fewer of them to participate on this side of the ocean as well.)

In New Smyrna, therefore, one thing we did to keep to ourselves and to avoid the rabble with its youthful enthusiasms was to go on little field trips to take photos of people for Laurel's work. It's worth saying here how much I revere my wife's work. It is a great revelation, being in a relationship with someone whose work I passionately love, and whose work continues to challenge me, and which causes me to learn new things. Laurel's early videos, a sequence of incredibly difficult-to-watch videos that she made in collaboration with strangers (men) who stopped her on the street, is *world class*, and enormously important, but it is not now the work that I think about when I think about how much I admire her as an artist. I admire the entire span of the Nakadate canon, but also the work that doesn't call attention to itself immediately— for example, her second feature film, *The Wolf Knife*, which was made for the ridiculous sum of $5,000. (She did spend a little bit on postproduction later.) There are moments in *The Wolf Knife* where Laurel's eye, what she sees through the lens, is the subject of the story, not the characters so much as how the characters exist in space and light, *l'amor che move il sole e l'altre stelle*, the love that moves the sun and all the other stars besides.

In her photographs and her videos, Laurel tends to see

into space and how people are in space in ways that I never am able to do. This is talent, like Gregory Crewdson shooting the best photograph of our wedding on his iPhone, but it's also looking carefully at the world. Because I have cared about photography and have been related to photographers, because it has always been at the margins of my family and among my close friends, I have taken many opportunities, even if I had to be photographed in the process, to watch photographers perform their magic—Gregory Crewdson, Tina Barney, David LaChapelle, Sylvia Plachy, etc. Like these others, Laurel thinks with her utmost clarity and power when she's looking through a lens. She's a great writer (she studied with Robert Stone when she was a graduate student at Yale, and with Deborah Digges at Tufts, when she was an undergraduate), and when she has time to write, it is invariably interesting and gets somewhere that I really want writing to go, but it is in her photographs (and videos and films) that the visible world is made new, and where human emotions and human frailty are most evidently at the center of the work. I wish writing, as I experience it, were as good at documenting emotional frailty and the fragmenting of dignity in a consciousness, as Laurel's work has often been.

My question about her early videos has always been not *are you taking advantage of the men?* but: *how are you able to be vulnerable to all those people?*

Notwithstanding the fact that I am a mediocre photo assistant because I can never anticipate what Laurel is really going to want at a shoot, and can never duplicate exactly what she wants by depressing the shutter, even when she tries to explain it to me, I like going along on the shoots. She is on occasion expedient and admirably results-oriented on photo shoots, and because I am a person with various complexities myself, and I truly would chew my own arm off rather than be told what to do, by anyone ever, it is not always useful for me to be her assistant. But: I loved her DNA project, which breaks down ideas of race and family until they are no longer operative in the normally simplistic ways that we talk about them in our cultural discussions. Laurel's "family" as described by the DNA portraits transcended class, generation, race, political belief, region, and every other boundary you could erect in which to wall off your "family" from those other people out there at the edge of your property. She photographed gun-toting Republicans in the South, and Democratic African American union guys not too many states away. She shot Mennonites in Oregon. She shot Jews in Queens. The American family, in Laurel's project, could be anywhere, at any time, and the responsibility to love them and treat them with respect, therefore, extended outward into the unexplored expanses beyond home, until home was in every direction.

In New Smyrna, first we had a DNA relative visit us on the Atlantic Center for the Arts campus, a guy from elsewhere in Florida, and he gave us a whole spiel about particle physics, and the new accelerators coming online. He was clearly a little curious and inquisitive about what he'd gotten himself into, especially as Laurel liked to shoot the DNA portraits at night, and she would never really talk to the subject until she'd gotten the photograph out of the way—so that the image really corresponded to her very first impression of him or her. The physicist, for that was his job description, didn't know what to expect, but neither did we. We never knew what to expect. With the Christmas tree farmers in Oregon, for example, we were asked to stay for dinner, and in the midst of this feast, their youngest child pointed out that our host, his dad, had himself shot the venison we had been served, on the porch, one morning, still wearing his pajamas.

Later on, when this work was displayed quite a bit, it was hard to fathom what the subjects might have thought of what they had participated in. We shot another family in Florida, a little later, a truly lovely and exceedingly warm family, where there was a boy with some learning difficulties, who definitely knew a ton about the theme parks in Orlando, had all the facts at his command, and this boy had a grandmother in a motorized wheelchair, and we shot him and his mom and uncle, and then we shot the grandmother, and the poignancy of those images is overpowering and hard to describe.

Laurel's single-minded drive toward the truth of an appearance, her refusal to idealize or to shape the subjects, was like unto her personality in other ways. I had learned long ago that there was never any profit in trying rhetorically to appeal to Laurel for peace when there were interpersonal problems happening between us and others. Laurel was going to speak the truth, for the sheer idealism of doing so. The photographs were the commission of this philosophical style in an aestheticized container. I admired them immensely. They were lyrical, beautiful, frequently otherworldly with their narrow alien columnar light (as if the subjects were about to be levitated up into paradise), they were sometimes funny, but they always told a truth about people, about individuals, about family.

In a way, the impulse feels novelistic to me, because novels, to me, are where those really complex thoughts about the truth of humanity get stored to best effect. The field of characterization in Laurel's photographs is like the field of characterization in the best novels—rich, complex, new. I loved watching this work get made, even when I didn't do a good job as the photo assistant.

In Orlando, Laurel was also to photograph a woman for the project who was more nervous than almost any other subject of Laurel's DNA portraits. She kept calling and waffling about whether or not she was going to show. The subjects were often encouraged to come up with the locations for the images, the only requirement for which was that the location should be dark. Laurel's only light source was an old handheld flashlight that I had given her some years before. Laurel used that flashlight throughout the project and would never tolerate a replacement. On this night in Orlando, we were driving through some parts of town that stood in distinct contrast to the theme park monoliths outlying, and all the stylized Harry Potter worldliness of Orlando. This town square downtown, among the people. Laurel and I wandered around beforehand, looking for any setting that was dark enough for a shot, but there was light pollution no matter where we turned. The subject continued to call and say she was a block away, and then more than a block away, increasingly nervous.

And if you thought about it there was really no reason why we did not sound like we were going to bludgeon her or dismember her and bury the body parts in various swamps outside of the greater Orlando area. Eventually, however, she turned up, the woman who was to be photographed, and she was an incredible addition to the project in every way, human, self-conscious, exceedingly shy, not like the America of fashion inserts or living below Fourteenth Street in Manhattan, but of the America that has no power, that lives in exile from power. It was easy to see, while I watched the photograph happen, and the halting conversation got traded back and forth between photographer and subject, that she, the subject, was not going to get entirely comfortable, was marked by a great discomfort. Laurel asked her what prompted her to agree to be part of the project, and she said: *I just wanted to be part of something.*

I lost another friend besides M.J. that winter, too. A close friend, Maggie Estep, a spoken word artist, a horse-racing enthusiast, a serial monogamist nonpareil, a nicotine gum addict and former heroin abuser, a yoga expert with a titanium hip, a prose writer given to slang, a performer at the twentieth anniversary of Woodstock who turned up on *Beavis and Butthead* once, a punk, an inveterate curser, a would-be real estate agent at the end of her life, a New Yorker who had decamped to Hudson, a traffic-stopping but unconventional beauty who was also beautiful in life experiences, a sober person who was once on the cover of *High Times*, an unrestrained laugher, a musician and singer who never really sang, a study in contrasts and paradoxes of every sort, someone who bulldozed through a lot of cherished encampments in the writing and art and music communities of my youth and made everyone think more carefully about what they made, and someone who literally everyone I knew downtown in the eighties loved in a way. Her vitality and her enthusiasm for life was the quintessence of having lived well, though she never had much money and was often chasing a book contract, and it made no sense, of all the people I knew in the eighties and early nineties, some of them self-destructive in the most baroque ways, that Maggie would be the person to die of a heart attack at just fifty years old. The only possible rationale for this was that she had already used up a lifetime of events in the short time she was on earth. Her death was a terrible shock for a lot of people, and I missed her badly, like many other people I knew.

While Laurel and I were at the Atlantic Center for the Arts, there was also a satellite launch at Cape Canaveral. And we all trooped out to the beach to watch. I have always found that going anywhere in a large crowd of artists or creative people most reminds me of when I was in the psychiatric hospital in 1987 and we were allowed out for a walk in Hollis, Queens, usually to go to buy a soda and candy at a bodega. I don't know why we were allowed to buy candy, exactly, and I imagine that the neighbors must have gotten very tired of the dual-diagnosis fuck-ups wandering down the hill, past their houses, to the bodega. Anyway, trips with artists are not at all dissimilar. People struggle to get a conversation going, are frequently awkward, and it's hard for the group to behave like a group. On the beach in New Smyrna, the light started to fade, and the conversations became more atomized, as though the things driving the artists apart were far more profound than what bound them together.

But just when it appeared that the group might be terminal somehow, or that it was all about who could do the best job of impressing the slightly vague but very beautiful dope-smoking painter women, the satellite was launched. Somehow, perhaps from watching footage of the Challenger disaster, I expected these rockets to go straight up, and then to vanish into the crepuscular skies, but the rocket, instead, careened horizontally out over the ocean, toward the Bermuda Triangle, perhaps a bit like MH370 lurching free of its appointed course, and it felt intensely military, and ominous, or as though the military applications of the rocket should be obvious, as they clearly were since World War II; the rocket and its payload traveled out horizontally for quite some time before abruptly lifting up into whatever sweet spot of earthly orbit was required. There was something nearly spiritual and thrilling about the way the satellite pierced the twilight, the magic hour, there on the easygoing and faintly louche seaside of the Daytona Beach environs. The satellite launch showed us a little bit of the military-industrial complex, a part that could not be hidden from us, because the mere launching of the rocket and the satellite could not pass unobserved. It *had* to be observed. All those alien-bearing unidentified flying objects must be similar, I suspect, they must be the military-industrial complex doing best what it does, mixing expensive weapons for mass murder in with a media blackout. In the desert of New Mexico, this combination of forces always mixes in with the febrile imagination of the delusional, the unrepentant alcoholics, the rugged individualists.

We watched the satellite launch, and then went back to the arts center, a little more dazzled, and a little less impressed, by the project of advanced rocketry.

At the Atlantic Center for the Arts, you're supposed to sign your name inside the closet of the faculty apartment (which, it bears mentioning, is a serene and wonderfully isolated little pad down at the end of the boardwalk), and it didn't take long to see that the closet contained the signature of my friend no longer living, Maggie Estep.

March

Laurel's mom was failing. It was a fact unignorable, and yet our difficulties, our sense of constant crisis and mounting difficulty, from longed-for child lost to miscarriage to the loss of Stella, from the haunting by M.J.'s troubles to the death of Maggie, the struggles piling on, of the kind that is so often at hand that you don't really know which way to turn upon getting out of bed in the morning, often made it impossible to attend specifically to the problem of Laurel's mom. She had been living alone for some years in downtown Ames, Iowa, where Laurel grew up, and she had almost everything she needed, excepting peace of mind. There was a really great food co-op in town, of which she had been a member since it first existed in the late seventies. And there was a church, a Unity Church, that she went to on Sundays, and where she tried with the

utmost effort to keep the demons inside from comman-
deering too much real estate. The dignity of her attempts
was easy to admire.

Things had never been quite right since the period in
which she lived off the grid in Port Townsend, Washington, where her shack was in the woods and had no plumb-
ing, a time she referred to as the best in her life. Reality
had shifted to some parallax orientation for her, different
from how we were understanding it. But there were also
specific physical problems, which may or may not have
been manifestations of the same paradigmatic change.
Laurel had had to intervene to bring her mom back from
Port Townsend to the Midwest for treatment. For a while
this seemed to work, and the major project with Mary was
to eliminate stress and keep her life as simple as possible.
She had enough money to pay the rent, to get some gro-
ceries, and to send some money to Laurel's two somewhat
unconventional older half-siblings.

But then, all at once, things started to decline seriously.
The particular eruption of hardship, as it was relayed to
us by her friends on the scene, was that she started leaving
things outside in front of her apartment. In the hallway.
Some of these things were of real monetary or emotional
value. There was no talking to Mary about why she was
doing this exactly, because Mary was either incredibly
loving and kind, or else she was clearly anxious about
something that she wasn't going to tell you about in any
rigorous way, because she didn't trust people not to mis-
understand. There was often a person or persons who she
believed was oppressing her, usually a *man*, and it was easy

to read these oppressions as metaphorical transformations of difficulties that Mary may have had when younger, when a child in Texas.

A friend of Mary's from Ames, whom I'll call Jeanine, came to take Mary in, part of the time, and tried to help her with the anxiety and the more complicated battles she was waging. At first this seemed like a good thing, but then it quickly began to seem as though it might be less perfect than we would have wished.

Mary then had some kind of sudden, overpowering aphasia, in which she lost a great many words and had to resort to elegiac but impractical work-arounds like: *the deep plate that you put food in* (bowl), and the like. Sometimes these work-arounds were poetry, and sometimes it was just hard to figure out what she meant. Many doctors weighed in on the difficulties she was facing, and at first it seemed obvious she'd had a stroke, but not everyone agreed, and there was also always, in the background, the discussion of the car accident she'd had earlier in her middle age, and of the coma that followed, but after a few days of casting about for a diagnosis, a social worker friend of the family suggested that Mary might have an infection, which sometimes, in older people, manifested in cognitive impairment. Mary was then prescribed a large dose of antibiotics for a few weeks, and this did, in fact, help a bit with her aphasia. Words started to come back some.

When the independent living facility where Laurel had placed her got wind of Mary's aphasia and middle-of-the-night wanderings, she was ejected, even though she was paying for the right to live there, and though she was no trouble, and never had been. It was the kind of injustice that really causes one to doubt the system and its ability to care for the elderly and indigent. Thus began a desperate sequence of addresses for Mary in which her physical situation always grew worse, never better, including hip trouble, maybe knee trouble, and then, ultimately, a brain tumor. An inoperable brain tumor, as it turned out, but maybe a benign one that would, at least, have the virtue of being slow-acting.

A battery of tests followed Mary's infection, which was perhaps gram-negative, or E. coli in a site not specified, and these were not conclusive. She got an EEG at one point, and the MD, when she read it, said that Mary had significant dementia, and that within a couple of years she was going to be seriously impaired. This turned out to be the one piece of reliable and honest medical advice that Mary got in this span.

Mary's ability to struggle through the difficulties, and her absolute failure to complain, no matter how bad things got, was nearly overwhelmingly poignant. The fact that Mary had not always been present while Laurel was growing up didn't seem to affect how Laurel felt about her mom. On the contrary. Laurel was incredibly fierce about trying to protect her mom, and you did not, no one did, want to get in the way when Laurel was pursuing some reasonable fix on behalf of her mother. Laurel and her brothers had to plead and yell and threaten legal action in a great variety of settings over the years, and they did it without hesitation. The cost for Laurel of all this pleading and hectoring was not clear until much later. She would never allow any of these midlevel social workers and medical dysfunctionaries see her as weak or irresolute. The vibrations of despair and woe about her mom came only when no one was around but me. She was grief-stricken, and often overcome about what to do. Mary kept moving around from one short-term address to another, and at each there would be a moment when Mary's prognosis was self-evident and she would be too much for the facility taking her in. For a while during her episode of aphasia, she was shipped to a nursing home in Ames, and when Laurel visited her there, she found her in tremendously undignified circumstances with no nurse anywhere around. You would not have wanted to be among the nursing staff that day, when Laurel got to them. But this story doesn't find its relevance in the amount of yelling you can do at nursing home staff, but in the way calamity engenders deeper feeling. And the way it ultimately draws people together. There's a powerlessness that I felt about Mary, as the mere husband of Laurel, but I could love Mary and Laurel both, and the great intensity of their bond made this easy to do. It was perhaps an aspect of the matrimonial long accomplishment that I most needed to develop: listening and helping, and otherwise not needing to do much in particular. Even at her sickest, Mary still managed to be a loving and generous person, and so she was a model for just how to be with her in her hour of need.

In March, I had been asked to teach for a week at the University of Alabama, where I had once also been a finalist for a teaching job in 1994. I had passionately disliked Tuscaloosa the first time I'd been there. I didn't then and don't now care very much about football, I think football is a brain injury delivery system, and in 1994, during my campus visit, the University of Alabama had a grand parade for the members of the Crimson Tide football team, which was a parade of American things I don't understand or admire. Somehow, when I didn't get the job, I felt like the Crimson Tide was responsible, that I was not *their man*. Going back to the school twenty years later was meant to exorcise some of the feelings from that earlier time, when I had been in my early thirties and was generally willing to undertake employment in any rural portion of the nation, even if no such employment materialized.

I was invited by Michael Martone, a writer and professor with impeccable experimental bona fides, and also simply one of the nicest people on earth. Martone, among his many strengths, had also been (along with his wife, the excellent poet Theresa Pappas) Laurel's occasional babysitter, back when he taught at Iowa State with Laurel's dad. However, once our trip to the University of Alabama wheeled into view, after months of thinking it was impossibly far off, Martone's own father became ill, to the very precipice of his mortality, and Laurel and I took off for Alabama without much expectation of community. It was, in effect, just another short-term teaching gig, one I was lucky to have, but one that was going to have a certain relentless sameness to it.

Luckily, Laurel had a number of photographs she was going to take in the Deep South. And with our rental car, we chased DNA portraits into the deepest of the Deep South, and we ate a bunch of grits, and we watched the

fraternity and sorority boys and girls of a southern state
school amble around in what was already spring weather,
many of them sporting what we had come to think of as
the *no pants* look, meaning shorts with a long baggy T-shirt
whose hem fell only an inch or so above the lowest mar-
gin of the shorts. There was something infantilized about
the fashion decision making, as if they were all giant tod-
dlers, in their brightly colored onesies.

By the end of the time in Tuscaloosa, with a few new
photos in Laurel's project saved on the relevant hard drives,
we decided that Mary Ivie was at a point where some
supervision was urgently required, and therefore we just
took our rental vehicle and started driving, a thousand
miles or so from Tuscaloosa, Alabama, to Ames, Iowa.

In a way, Laurel and I were made to travel, to do this
kind of turn-on-a-dime traveling, and it's both a blessing
and a shame these days that we don't have as much time to
do it as we did formerly. Laurel was in Estonia for a bit
the first year we were together and in Poland a couple of
times, and she had to be talked out of a trip to South Korea
in the same interval. And the two of us, when feeling less
satisfied with what was in front of us in the way of work,
were perfectly happy to get in the car and drive a thousand
miles. (In fact, we'd just driven all the way from Brooklyn to New Smyrna, Florida, and back.) Listening to the
radio, and watching the miles go past. I think it was a
problem-solving technique in some ways. We had similar habits about travel—bring nothing, book cheap tickets, don't stay more than a day longer than the absolute
minimum, always try to go to places you haven't been to

before, make the travel serve the work—and there were no questions asked when either of us wanted to go. We'd just go, as long as we were willing to take the other.

It was in this period that I really became interested in writing about travel, in trying to make all of our travel pay off aesthetically in some way. I became interested in trying to write in the worst circumstances—not at a desk with all my precious books around me, and with a fountain pen, and photos of my family before me—but in the not-terribly-good hotels that we were often staying in on our journeys together. Often Laurel, whose thyroid problems were about to be diagnosed in our journey of fertility, such that she would, shortly, no longer have to sleep *thirteen hours a night*, was often asleep long after I was awake and ready to face the world, or, more exactly, ready to face the oatmeal tin at another somewhat lackluster complimentary hotel breakfast, and in the hours when I was waiting for her, I would conceal myself in some corner of the room where the illuminated screen of my laptop would not bother her, and begin the fictitious hotel reviews that became my novel of 2015, *Hotels of North America* (while failing to deliver the work I had agreed upon with my publishers, the book with the conventional heroism in it). The trips with Laurel were invaluable for the novel, and they became such a shared concern, and an area where our work seemed to be influencing each other's. The hotels were a by-product of Laurel's photographs, and the hotels in turn became the centerpiece of my project.

The mutual influence, artistically, in our marriage, runs deeper than this suggests. Because Laurel's tech-

nique, for the DNA portraits, was something she perfected one night in Tucson, Arizona, when I was reading
there, and I took her out toward Saguaro National Park,
to a high desert pass I liked over there, and we sat for a
while and gazed at the night sky. There was a passage in
my novel *The Four Fingers of Death* about the stars as one
perceived them in the Sonoran Desert, and I used to read
it aloud on tour every night, or almost every night, when
I read from that novel. Laurel came on a lot of those events,
and when I took her up into the mountain pass overlooking the city, she began trying to perfect a way to both shoot
the stars above Tucson and shoot us at the same time. It's
not that the book influenced her directly so much as the
stars of Tucson influenced us both, and the book was the
occasion of this. That's when she began experimenting
with the old flashlight. I don't know how many photographs we took of ourselves that night, the night of my
reading at the University of Arizona, or how many times
she flashed the flashlight on me, standing in the dirt pullover by the side of the mountain pass, but that's when
she started to conceptualize her own particular available-
light technique, because of the night sky. If I were scoring
it, I'd say: Laurel was tangentially influenced by the passage from *The Four Fingers of Death*, and my tour provided
the site-specific revelation about her photographic undertaking (the DNA portraits that she ultimately called
Strangers and Relations), and then I in turn conceived of
making a novel out of hotel reviews as a result of accompanying Laurel at the many roadside hotels and motels
that she stayed in while shooting her images.

Early in the period of getting to know each other, I wanted passionately to collaborate with Laurel on something, as I have often collaborated in my work. I have found the process of collaboration epiphanic and have felt some great surge of joy from making work with other artists. There is also a deep learning that can take place in these circumstances. In the context of our relationship, though, despite my innumerable offers to write a screenplay for Laurel, or to get mixed up into her creative process, it has turned out that it doesn't make any sense for us to collaborate specifically or directly. We collaborate on family. As Laurel is a person who likes to work alone, and who is an intense perfectionist along the axis of her creativity, it has become more rewarding to track subconscious pathways of contact, as I have done just now, the more organic and unplanned ways we have collaborated, the way influence has passed back and forth between us peripherally, unconsciously, without really having to talk about it at all. If it ever happens these days that I take a decent photograph (which is infrequent), it is because Laurel's ideas of framing have started to sink in, after seven years together. And, similarly, I noticed not long ago that she composed a piece with a lot of semicolons. A long run-on sentence with semicolons. It did look a little like a paragraph that I might have written, or, at least, a paragraph that I might have influenced slightly, even if its meanings were all hers. This influence, across the platforms of our work, is made stronger by not being interrogated terribly much, and our collaboration is more comprehensive for not being driven by one or the other of us. It just is. It's a measure of time spent together, and in the company of each other's work. In a way, our individual tendencies are still there, but they have become less individual, because in each case the other is helping out in ways large and small throughout the production of the work. *It's all collaborative*, just not in the way you might think, not project oriented, unless the project is life.

Connecting up the ligaments of the South and the Midwest was just not something I had done, really, so going through Mississippi, and Arkansas, and the whole length of Missouri, and then up into Iowa satisfied some wanderlust, some inner need to avoid stopping at all costs, especially when we were outrunning a lot of stress, a long list of nearly crippling events.

We ended up stopping for dinner in Iowa City, because one of Laurel's best friends, Dora Malech, had graduated from the writer's workshop there, and had stuck around in town. I hadn't been in town in fifteen years, since a reading at Prairie Lights bookstore, and couldn't remember that much about it, but we were landing in town on a Friday night, and like Ames, Iowa, where the college president had just canceled an annual homecoming festival because of drinking and vandalism, Iowa City was noteworthy for the absolute abandon of its Friday nights. It was rare in my life (excepting maybe a Saturday night I had once observed in Reykjavik) to see so many kids so bent on reducing themselves to pedestrian-mall beer zombies, made only to stumble around and vomit up servings of beer so that they might have some more. I should not be seen to be in judgment of the drinking habits of the young, when I myself managed to become an alcoholic in my twenties. And yet: Iowa City on a Friday night was an abject and dehumanized place; the scale of drinking had a sort of factory-farming quality, like sows at a trough, and as we sat trying to eat a burrito downtown, a drunken guy slid repeatedly into our booth in a way both earnest and disheveled, while trying to pick up Dora, who, though she was a married person, tolerated his aimless and slurred conversational overtures, at least for a few minutes. Then we got the hell out of Iowa City and drove the last two hours to Ames.

Was this the trip where I noticed that Mary had a life-sized sculpture of Jesus next to her armchair? She did, and somehow it became a completely reasonable and even reverent appurtenance the longer we sat with her. I remember that it was my chore, because of good typing skills, to type up a list of names and numbers to put on Mary's refrigerator, so she wouldn't have to flip through several old date planners and a few scraps of paper, in search of an old friend and her number. These names and addresses seem like some effaced bit of quotidian life signaling through a receding past to Mary. No longer were the names and addresses written on randomized scraps, or bits of an envelope (Dickinson-style), or on a scrap of memo paper, or a Chinese food menu in the corner, now they signaled loud and proud on the front of the refrigerator, *This is my life, I can find what I need here.* Our only doubts being that a) she would forget that the names were on the refrigerator, b) that she would forget to whom the names belonged, c) that she would forget how to operate her flip phone, d) that she would forget how to talk into the phone. (There were a lot of other things we were worried about her forgetting, too, like her many accomplishments as an adult—her time as an EMS technician, her time founding a Waldorf school in Ames, her studies in comparative religion, not to mention her boundless maternal love.) We didn't know if any of these forking paths were the paths ahead, or which, and the names and addresses felt like an earnest attempt to keep these paths from coming into view, ahead around a bend, and so we typed in an effort to forestall what was perhaps inevitable.

The life-sized Jesus was so to-scale, and so Caucasian looking, and so mild and gentle in demeanor that it was hard to think of him doing anything *but* preaching about the kingdom of heaven while using a lot of exotic figurative language. There was no reason to assume that Jesus was anything but benevolent, though intimidating at life-size, and it was possible to tolerate him up to a point. He was the perfect Jesus for Mary Ivie in her hour of need, even if he was about to be returned to his rightful owner, Mary's old Iowa friend, Jeanine, who would also take Mary in anew while we attempted to find her next home.

I was teaching adjunct-style at NYU in the spring of 2014, as I had done for three years, and that year the topic was literature from Eastern Europe, one of the first texts of which was from the Romantic Era predecessor Heinrich von Kleist. It had been difficult for me, as a young person, to understand Heinrich von Kleist, because there is some kind of strange noncausal sequence of events in Kleist, many times. Things happen, but it's very unclear if they are *caused* to happen, or even if one event leads to another event. In Kleist, it's more that events take place, disassociatively, and we are at their mercy. We, the readers, impose an interpretation of events, even though their sequence is contestable, and thus it was Kleist, as you can see, all around us.

April

I mean, in the thick of 2013–14, in which Laurel and I were trying to be newlyweds, and human frailty was everywhere happening around us, it was easy on occasion to feel like we were in a Kleist story, in which nothing caused anything exactly, but there was poignancy at every turn, all of it obscure, hard to interpret, explosive. There were *explosions of poignancy*. It was an explosions-of-poignancy life. There was a deer carcass in the yard of our house upstate, for example, when the snow melted, and Hazel and I were out walking in the backyard, when she said, *What is that over there?* Meaning what was that thing protruding from the lawn over there in the corner of the yard by where the scrub stretched out luxuriously for a bit. *What is that?* Well, it turned out to be the upended rib cage of a deer in the yard, which had probably been taken out by some larger predator, but which larger predator in our neighborhood could *do* something like that?

We had seen coyote in the yard, we had seen fox in the yard, we had seen eagles in the yard, even the occasional turkey vulture in the yard. We had even seen a bobcat on two occasions. You're not supposed to see bobcat, at least not often, and in the spirit of Heinrich von Kleist it would be possible to see one and simply to wonder at its appearance without interpreting it or believing it emblematic. I would estimate that our bobcat was in the forty to fifty pound range, with big substantial paws. So different, in terms of the volume of menace, and chutzpah, from its distant relative: the domestic shorthair. It loped across the lawn in a way that did not quite say, for example, *I will disembowel you and not think twice*, it wasn't quite that brazen, but neither was it in any way afraid. I suppose only a bear or a mountain lion would cause the bobcat to feel afraid. Did the bobcat make piecemeal of the yearling?

And there *had* been a bear in the neighborhood. Our just-over-the-ridge neighbor, who had a single cow on the property, until the cow got made into a bunch of cuts of beef in the freezer, and who also had pigs, and bees, that neighbor had seen the bear, and I use the singular here to describe the bear though I am powerless to evaluate whether or not it is multiple. The neighbor even noted that the bear pushed over the beehive and helped her- or himself to all the honey to be found there. We might imagine that the bear didn't quite come over the hill and down closer to Route 22, because that would be unwise for the bear, and yet there was something large enough to bend our birdfeeder out back of the kitchen like it was a sapling, empty-ing all the seed out on the lawn and then pawing through it.

My point is we didn't and don't know exactly what killed the deer on the lawn, what killed the deer and left the skull and the rib cage twenty or so feet apart, all but entirely denuded of anything that might conceivably have looked like the soft-tissue portion of the deer. Hazel was in a phase where nothing much triggered revulsion in her (indeed she has often been in this phase), and she wanted to get closer to the deer remains. So we got right up close. The community of deer, in the first of the thaw, had this strange tendency to walk a particular way across the lawn, mono-directionally, as though they had a footpath. It was a rea-sonably large lawn (because this was all happening in poverty-stricken eastern Dutchess County), and there might have been many ways to cross it, but the deer crossed it in just the one way. The upturned rib cage, which looked like paleo-futurist lawn furniture for elves, was *right* on the deer path through the lawn, as though the bobcat, or the mountain lion, or the coyote, or maybe a drunken yahoo in the neighborhood with a firearm, had slain the deer right out in the open on its regular peram-bulations.

There's no particular end to my anecdote, which means that it's in the style of Heinrich von Kleist, except this: I dragged the rib cage to the edge of the forest, using a sturdy tree limb, and then I did the same with the skull, during which Hazel asked if we could take all the bones up to the house, bleach them in a vat, and then attempt to reassemble the deer, but on this point I demurred, owing to the partial qualities of the skeleton. It was not a full-sized deer, as I have noted, it was a yearling, and so the skull was not so large as to be truly the stuff of horror cinema. With Hazel, my daughter, we stashed the skull near the rib cage (and what of the remainder?) and then all three of us, Laurel, Hazel, and I, said a prayer for the deer, as we always do when dispensing with wildlife, like the pileated woodpecker that flew straight into one of the windows on the side of the house and then collapsed dead on the windshield of our car. My God, was that upsetting.

Nature, red in tooth and claw, as the poet Tennyson had it, and as in the struggle with infertility, which we didn't discuss with Hazel, and didn't much discuss with my family, but kept between the two of us, between Laurel and myself, because what was there to say to others, but that we were trying, and often failing rather painfully, and just sort of putting one foot in front of the other, and it was easy to allegorize events like the deer carcass in the yard, but how to come up with a coherent response, a kind of dramatic rising to the occasion. Laurel, for all of her sometimes hard-boiled feelings about the foibles of human beings, had boundless feelings of responsibility for animals, the more innocent, the more boundless the feeling. She regularly escorted bugs out of the house, even the ladybugs that had a tendency to blight the place in fall and spring. She resisted even my vacuuming and releasing when there were dozens of them. Spiders were escorted out. And she had a very practical method for removing bees and wasps that involved an overturned glass and an index card.

April ended with Maggie Estep's memorial service in New York, organized by the sterling poet and singer and human John S. Hall (of King Missile fame), and featuring just about everyone I knew from my misbegotten youth in early sobriety, and then a whole bunch of Nuyorican Poets Café types. It was a spectacle. Maggie took so many people to the racetrack for the first time, myself among them. It's possible she had taken every friend we had in common there, one day after another. She made me feel like it was our conspiracy, back then. At the memorial service, all these young addicts and alcoholics who had all tried to clean up together, going for endless cups of coffee (and nicotine gum in Maggie's case) and mulling over the gossip of our various sober dances, all revealed to be well into middle age, all lurching to and from the various explosions of poignancy, the stuff of daily living that Maggie would miss from here on out. We stood out on the sidewalk after, with one last story to tell, and then wandered around the East Village. Somehow I ended up with my friend Randy, the best man at our wedding, the witness, talking to Ann Magnuson, the actress and singer, in Tompkins Square Park. The scene was just as colorful as when I had woken up there thirty years before.

May

I had contracted to celebrate Laurel's brother's marriage in Houston in May, and this had resulted in my getting officially ordained by a certain permissive ordination outfit, the Universal Life Church. It's not that I didn't want a more formal ordination, I should say. I did. I really thought about trying to go to divinity school in 1992, until my first novel *Garden State* was accepted for publication by a small press. I had failed out of book publishing pretty well, I thought. And I couldn't seem to get my work published anywhere except, once or twice a year, in a quarterly magazine that inevitably paid in contributor's copies, and so I thought first about graduate school in literature, which seemed uptight, and then about divinity school. I went to a meet and greet at Union Theological Seminary.

Once I learned about the Universal Life Church, I ordered up the complete package of materials, which languished in the mailbox upstate just long enough to become completely overrun by spiders. The mailbox also houses mice in autumn. So my ordination pamphlet, with the offer that I could go to the Universal Life Church physical address and get some priestly training, was so full of spiders that they were spilling out the side when I got the thing into my car.

I wasn't sure, and am not now sure, about why I was selected for this particular duty, the duty of being marital celebrant. Nate Nakadate, Laurel's older brother (of the two siblings she grew up with), is a good-looking, funny, honest, heartfelt, guitar-playing surfer and fly fisherman, who has hair well below his shoulders, and who writes a frequent column on his far-flung angling exploits for a glossy magazine on the subject, and who also writes about guitars and music for a similarly glossy publication. He is a great and poignant writer. He is also, by trade, a public school teacher of English to high-school age kids. I like Nate a lot, though I do not fish anymore because of the hook-in-the-mouth problem, and am such a mediocre guitarist by comparison to Nate that I try, when in his company, not to bring guitars up too often. Nate seemed to want me to officiate, and I was touched and honored.

They'd had a whirlwind romance, he and his bride, a year or so, theirs was a paroxysmal love, a powerful thing, a surfeit of desire and love that swept into it anyone within orbit. It was hard not to admire how passionately engaged they were, even if it sometimes made me feel like Laurel and I were more about arduous collaboration on life-and-death matters. Anyway, I was happy to serve, and I went looking around for ideas about what kind of service Nate and the woman I'm calling Natalie were going to have, and what, after all, I was going to wear. Laurel was worried about how her mother was going to get there, to Houston, Texas, where the marriage was taking place. When Laurel's mother came east for our wedding, there were enough friends and family making the trip that there was someone on the same plane with her, but in the case of Nate's wedding, it was more complicated. You could almost drive to Texas from Iowa, if you could hack the long empty hours. In the end, Laurel's mom made it back to her Texas homeland without too much difficulty, on commercial jets, and then we made sure that we were across the hall from her hotel room, so that we could help when necessary.

Houston does not yield up its treasures easily. It requires a car, for example, which makes it more of a western city than I am used to. And it is divided into neighborhoods, separated by bayous and waterways, that are only connectable with psychic effort. It's hot, incredibly hot by northeastern standards, and humid, and while it's not quite as resolutely Texan as Dallas, it's still a big city in a red state.

That said, it is easy to forget that Laurel is from Texas, was born in Texas, and that great numbers of her mother's extended family still live in Texas. Nate Nakadate landed there primarily because he has an ex-wife in town there, who has family and connections in Texas, and he needs to be close enough to her for their teenage son to travel back and forth easily between the two of them. Nate left real seniority in the Florida public school systems to travel to Texas with his ex-wife (she was his wife then), and now he is duty bound to spend a few more years teaching in the greater Houston area, though with every free afternoon he is off with his canoe, which fits perfectly in the back of his pickup truck, to fish (the canoe was out on his front porch during Hurricane Harvey, in case it was needed), and to be in the rehabilitative solitude of a natural setting.

The fishing part of the Nakadate family story comes from Laurel and Nate's grandfather, a figure of striking importance to all the Nakadates, who served as a medic in the American military during WWII, while his family was incarcerated in Minidoka, and while his brother, who had returned to Japan for school and who was still there during the conflict, fought on the Japanese side. Later in life, while he practiced medicine in the Northwest, still carrying shrapnel from injuries he suffered for this country, Laurel's grandfather often fished, and found peace and reward in the same kinds of rivers and lakes that Nate haunts. The angling skipped a generation in that Neil Nakadate was not interested in the same way, but he now fishes with Nate periodically, honoring the prior generation and indicating the way the stories of family are honored by inclination and reiteration.

Let me digress just long enough, then, to note how much I too love and respect my father-in-law. It is not always easy being with one's in-laws, and in my first marriage I could feel everyone trying to bridge the significant differences by sheer will. Everyone tried, but there were times that the chasm was too wide. They lived in Florida, and, in fact, you had to cross a lot of bridges to get to their condo, in their gated community. I was all but obligated to watch televised college football on Thanksgiving, and this became a symbol of the difficulty with the in-laws, that there was great effort, and despite that effort, feelings of isolation and difference.

But that hasn't been my experience with Laurel's family at all. Neil, Laurel's dad, is interested in a lot of stuff that is easy to share with him, like major league baseball, and, more accurately, minor league baseball (because the Chicago Cubs' Triple-A affiliate is in Des Moines, Iowa, the I-Cubs), and also American literature, which was his specialty while teaching at Iowa State. Neil has taught all the books that my father read as an American literature major, for example, and what he hasn't taught, he knows plenty about anyway. He will send you a Virginia Woolf story in the mail, now and again, alongside clippings from the local paper of Ames, Iowa. Also, while he has written a lot as an academic, he has also written a memoir about the internment of Japanese Americans during World War II, which was and is his story; he has gathered this story into a tremendously powerful and important book. There is, as it turns out, a lot to talk about with Neil, who has also, naturally, spent a few decades around Laurel, and is full of good advice, and support, on that subject, as on so many others.

That all three of Neil's kids were married in an eighteen-month period was self-evidently moving to Neil, even though he is occasionally reserved. He tucks the emotional part of the conversation into it at the corners, and doesn't go on at length. There's a bit of subtlety and disinclination to showboat there that feels culturally Japanese American to me. He has the dignity and reserve that you associate with a Japanese American family that lived through the Second World War in this country, and who lost a great deal, but he's also funny and warm and down to earth. He wanted all the kids to land well, and he is not shy about saying so.

The first thing we did in Houston, when we landed, was a rehearsal of the service. We all went down to the chapel in Houston, the one that Nate and Natalie had rented at great expense, and the wedding specialist lady waited while we tried to go through the ritual at top speed. I had tried to keep the bride and groom focused on the vows, despite my own troubled relationship to this language, because in spite of everything I felt that sometimes language does confer change on they who utter it.

Generally, I think I'm a reasonably good reader. And therefore I naturally felt like reading the service of matrimony would come easily to me, because I think I know what reading is all about. But the irony at the rehearsal was that Nate really *didn't like* how I read it! He sort of stopped the proceedings and gave me some line reading alternatives, which had the effect of banishing any confidence I had about serving as the officiant, and suddenly we were all standing there uncertain if the thing was going to go off without a hitch. I should have asked first what Nate wanted! And not assumed that my professional capabilities were so admirable! Nate and Natalie's whirlwind romance, the kind you hear about in songs, that you associate with films by American directors of the sixties and seventies, was built on the language of desire. They knew what language they wanted, and how it should sound. But I think Nate was nervous anyhow. Who wouldn't be? Nobody sensible wants for nerves at the nuptial ceremony; if they are without nerves they're just not thinking ahead. Nate was sort of holding the whole ceremony on his back, Atlas-like, and a big posse of Ivie relatives were coming in, Laurel's mom's family—for example, all of Laurel's still-living uncles, who all lived in Texas, and of course Mary Ivie, who had managed to get on that plane.

If I say that I once wanted to be a minister, or a theologian, when younger, and that I take to heart the implications of, for example, a Christian model of pastoral responsibility, what does it mean for a moment like this when it seems I was not doing a perfect job? On the one hand, I have a long list of performances as a reader to my name, which would suggest that, at least, I have an idea why I might read a particular passage of nuptial language in a particular way. But why do this job, the job of celebrant, if in doing this job I was not there to serve? If the task was intercessory, if I was there to serve as the intermediary voice between the ideal of marital language and the couple before me, there was no room for self, for ego, for expectation, for a resting-on-the-laurels, for a discussion of conventions of reading. I stood before the intended couple as the gatekeeper of the institution of marriage, I stood for the language of marriage, and what I could offer, and what I *should* have offered, was exactly what the marrying couple wanted and nothing more. And the one thing they wanted was peace of mind in the context of the ceremony. The ideal of pure service, in this setting, is powerful and instructive. I was fortunate to be in receipt of that lesson, as I always am fortunate to be the recipient of opportunities for growth. And therefore I asked Nate for notes, and I made adjustments. Maybe I did a better job as a reader the second time, or maybe I simply got better at being the celebrant who modeled the celebration, the give and take and the joyous union of it all, but suddenly we seemed to be having a marriage.

It was pretty hard to figure out what Natalie's family made of it all. They were from the land of hunting and fracking, where the winters were long, the farthest north, and were perhaps unused to some of the features of the Nakadate and Ivie clans. Not many of them came over to chat.

And Laurel's mom definitely could not find a way to easily weather the bits of decorum that were integral to the wedding, and all weekend Laurel kept going across the hall in the hotel to make sure Mary had a bit of a grip on when and where we were going, and what she was supposed to wear. I was well into writing *Hotels of North America*, by then, and Laurel took a photo of me wearing the suit and hat I wore to the wedding in the hall of the hotel, and there's a somberness to the photo that I associate with worrying about Mary Ivie. It became the author photo for the book.

The next day we conducted the wedding, though Nate was still abundantly nervous. Maybe I was too. I thought he was great, honest, and true, his posture all vulnerability on display, a person truly in love, feeling the terror and confusion and desperation of being truly in love, feeling what being in love really means.

Mary sat at a table with her brothers Walter and Danny, and I don't think the three of them had been together at a table in a long spell, maybe ten or even twenty years. And I could see that Mary wasn't much talking to them at all, and that they didn't quite know how to talk to Mary, and it was no one's fault, it was the pain of all the time, the eons, the decades of hardship, and the gravity of Mary's decline. Maybe the silence, then, was something generous, and giving, and what Danny and Walter were doing was letting Mary be there, and in their company, but not needing her to be other than she was. Frail, wearing the same dress she'd worn at our wedding, quiet, burdened, but full of support for her children, even in her own time of hardship. There was nowhere else on earth she wanted to be on that day, even if she could do no better than she was already doing. For me the camera of these recollections wheels around in the reception hall, but always goes back to record Mary and her brothers.

I remember after conducting the ceremony chasing a bunch of kids around the yard out front of the reception hall, just taking off the top layers, the priestly garb as it were, and chasing kids, like it was exactly what an officiant should be called upon to do, getting behind a water fountain and waiting for a kid to run by and then springing up with some immemorial huzzah. Of such moments is the worthy life made. But worrying about Mary and at what point Mary was going to be unable to look after herself, that was more on my mind than anything else, as I'm sure was true for Laurel too.

We went off to shoot photos on Laurel's project after the wedding.

We drove farther west, in fact, to visit Laurel's great-uncle, Mutt Ivie, who lives out near Cisco, Texas. As far as I can tell, this is true bootlegging country, and some of the Ivies, or further-out in-laws of the family, really did do some bootlegging back in the day. But Mutt, like everyone else in the family in West Texas, is involved in the oil business now. In particular, he was until recently a foreman and technical expert on oil drilling rigs, and was known for his professional expertise. He couldn't retire, even in his eighties, because no one else was as good as Mutt was. Mutt has an honest forthrightness, and a warmth that is incredibly life-affirming, and his devotion to his wife, Bertie, now his wife of seventy years, is a thing that serves as a beacon for the notion of how decent people can be. Mutt and Bertie live in a tiny ranch house in the middle of the prairie in West Texas, and it took us many hours to drive there, and they were all incredibly beautiful hours of travel. We were sort of terrified by the majestic emptiness of West Texas, the severity of it. We drove back and forth past their house a couple of times, trying to will ourselves to find it easy to stop. And then we did.

It was so hard not to feel like the city slickers coming in and gumming up the smoothly operating country traditions of West Texas. But Mutt and Bertie, who knew lots of stories about Mary and her sister Katherine (who had died not long before our trip), welcomed us, no matter how unlikely it was that we were there, that we had come all the way from New York City to see them. Mutt has, it's honest to say, lost a few digits on either hand in the line of his work, on the drilling rigs, but he reaches out and grabs you and reels you in and there is no problem, there is only warmth, while you're there. I was just the college professor who married Laurel, and of no other significant interest, but they welcomed me just the same.

After we visited with Laurel's great-uncle, had some chicken soup, looked at yellowed black and whites, we drove toward the Oklahoma line, where we met some even more distant cousins on Laurel's mother's side. And then we went to photograph a further passel of extremely distant cousins, on a thousand acres in the dark of the Great Plains. A galaxy of stars above. It was a strange scene. Laurel has always thrived in these completely awkward and sometimes ominous situations. I will often find her marching off for a long conversation with a stranger, and even prolonging these conversations, really giving of herself to people she doesn't know at all. And so the Oklahoma scene, which involved, in my recollection of it, rather sweet and good-natured relatives of the southern variety, and the presence of guns in the house. My family had guns around when I was growing up, too, so I should not have been surprised, though having renounced firearms in my twenties and never having shot one since, I am often surprised by the fact that the guns are still happening, and even that they are flourishing throughout the nation. As a result, we were the strangers in that Texas landscape. And yet Laurel's persistence, and her friendly banter, wore everyone down, until we weren't just the couple from the dreaded New York City (*it's so violent, isn't it?*). At the end of the night, we were hanging out with one of the cousins, a long-haul trucker, and I think his wife and daughter, and I can remember some pretty strange, and sort of punch-drunk conversation, but also the sense that this was it, *this was family*, this field of utterly inexplicable outcomes, people whom you didn't know at all, who don't think like you or dress like you (all those things seemed to be decided *regionally*), but to whom you could apply the loyalties of family just the same, and by doing so earn something like an honorary place in family, just by risking some affection.

This was the lesson of Laurel's *Strangers and Relations* project: you could find family anywhere, and in it you could emphasize difference, if that was your wish, or you could emphasize affiliation, and that's what she did when she photographed the distant cousins. She created the affiliation, created the connection through which affiliation might take place, and it was always repaid to Laurel twice over.

Then we drove back down into Texas, from Oklahoma, to return our rental car and fly home.

From where I am sitting now, it's hard to imagine that we logged all the miles we logged that year, and the one that followed. And I only went on 50 or 60 percent of Laurel's photo shoots. She was often out in Montana or in Arkansas, calling me from the road, from some dangerous motel where they asked her in reception if she was a teenage runaway and if she was going to do drugs in the room. But I went on some of the harder and more unpredictable shoots. There was always a hard reentry.

After all of this—wedding, and photo shoots—we walked back into the apartment in Park Slope with exactly this kind of culture shock only to find that: the apartment smelled bad.

And I mean not that it smelled really bad, like we had left garlicky Thai food in the refrigerator for the ten days we were away, or like there was a dead mouse in the hall, but like there was an overpowering chemical of some kind dispersing in our apartment. Because I can *never* (I think it's safe to say) adjust to an emergency, or a crisis, immediately, but always seem to need a day or two to mull it over, to decide if the crisis is really critical, I was *mad* that Laurel was saying the chemical smell was dangerous and we should get the fuck out of the apartment. I had just come home, and I wasn't going to not be at home, and I wasn't going to accept that someone, somehow, had put us out of our residence in this particular way. But it did kind of smell awful. I persuaded Laurel to try to spend the night there, and we slept, the two of us, in my daughter's twin bed, because her room had the most windows, and we opened these and got fans blowing, and we both woke up with horrible headaches, at which point we fled out of town for our house upstate. And there we stayed for several days.

Upon investigation, it seemed clear that what had happened was this: the renovation of the palatial two-apartments-fashioned-into-one apartment next door, the renovation of the southern lady and her enormous Flemish or Belgian husband, had culminated in quite a bit of *varnishing* of the floor, which had been undertaken without proper ventilation, and which had then (because of the way the drafts worked in the building, which had resulted in our earlier cannabinoid contact buzz from the prior owners) ventilated almost entirely into our space. Our windows had been closed while we were in Texas, bantering with gun owners and other distant relatives.

It happened we knew the super of our building, the pretty excellent super who had replaced the guy with the drinking problem, and the pretty excellent super could, at least, be relied on to tell the truth to a somewhat financially overstretched artist couple as opposed to the one percenters who'd just moved into the building, and who subcontracted, it seemed, laborers who were perhaps being encouraged to cut corners. The pretty excellent super took up the matter of the floor finish, which the subcontractors insisted was "eco," despite the fact that they had dumped empty polyurethane containers down in the basement, right by the super's office, even though polyurethane floor finish was prohibited by the building, according to the rules of the co-op board, precisely because of the possibility of creating environmental problems with the neighboring apartments. That polyurethane is a neurotoxin is, I think, irrefutable, and easy to verify quickly with research, online and otherwise. And the effect of it in small quarters, in six hundred square feet, is hard to describe if you haven't had the displeasure of trying to acclimate to it in this way.

When in due course we again arrived back in Brooklyn, in order to spend a few days with my daughter, we really had no choice but to confront the truth: that we couldn't live in our apartment. Because Hazel, my daughter, was friends with a group of four girls her very age in the building, a girl squad, one other of whom was in her father's apartment only half-time, we had a place to stay for a couple of nights, while we put in four incredibly powerful window fans to try to evacuate the fumes from our actual apartment. My daughter kept saying, with incredible urgency, "Why can't we go home?" while standing forlornly by our front door looking in at the devastation as the fans blew. Because I am extremely stubborn in some ways, just ridiculously bent on doing things the same way I did them yesterday, I went in there regularly to get my clothes and to shave, and so on, but I often found that my knees kept getting weak if I spent too long inside, as if I were going to pass out. I was clutching the sink basin to get finished with a shave the second morning, wondering if I was killing more brain cells than when I was an active alcoholic. That the whole situation made us look bad, or so it seemed to me, made us unable to provide a reliable place for my daughter to stay while with us, made us seem like ineffective, bohemian, crisis-afflicted parents, and this caused real hurt for me, and remorse. Feeling I have let down my daughter is the worst feeling of all. And that was in addition to looking like people who were overreacting to neurotoxins.

And for Laurel, the situation was even worse, far worse, in that her family had and has a real sensitivity to chemicals.

They do not evacuate the toxins with the tumor-suppressing effectiveness of Moodys. Her aunt Katherine, she who had died not long before Nate's wedding, had been exposed to an abundance of chemicals while working as a receptionist or administrative assistant at a manufacturing firm in her youth, and had become increasingly neurologically afflicted over the course of her life as a result. She was housebound in her later years, had little effective immune system, had all kinds of mysterious ailments, rheumatic, autoimmune, and otherwise. Laurel is avoidant of chemicals and their odor both by inclination and physiologically. She literally cannot stand a minute with a powerfully industrial or chemical smell. And there we were, with our apartment that we could not use, but were paying for, next door to the more affluent professional types, who had smoked us out so that they could renovate their multimillion-dollar apartment for their own imminent baby.

This would have been funny if it were happening to anyone else, because it was such a Park Slope story. Now that we are gone I can perhaps take this moment to indicate why it was so hard to like Park Slope, Brooklyn, and why the changing face of Park Slope was bringing into relief features implicit in its sense of self-regard. Park Slope was the kind of place where whether or not to boycott products manufactured in a certain Middle Eastern country is of such urgency that friendships can end as a result. Park Slope is the kind of place where you live near not one but two private day schools that require (as my divorce lawyer suggested to me) a $600,000 annual income to be affordable. The kind of place where suggesting that you are not going to transition your preteen child, even though she likes boys' clothes, because she has indicated no wish to transition, gets you a death threat (true story!). And where abandoning the public school system because the middle school is integrated seems like the most normal thing you could do. It was the most natural place for us to live, because of all the writers who live there, and, as a result, the most depressing to me. The homogeneity, the blind acceptance of dogmatic approaches to contemporary life, were increasingly hard to fathom, or to live with comfortably, and I implicate myself in these crimes. Were I to attempt further to boil down my resistance, it would be in the following way: I dislike ideological purity, which doesn't exist in nature. No one is pure. Humanity is always corrupt in one way or another, despite its touching need for gold-plated and laudable ideals. Everyone's beliefs, when lived out, when activated, when embodied, are fungible, complex, contradictory, much more so than whatever it is they proclaim before a Park Slope co-op board meeting.

The polyurethane incident made all of this clear. I can tell you the day when our new neighbors moved in to their newly renovated home, because I came up in the elevator behind them, and I saw their shoes out in the hall, as they went to look at the finished renovation, and their lovely varnished floor. They didn't want to scuff. I am sure that in another context I would find these people tolerable, but in this context, while we were breathing the poison that would allow the husband to have a perfect floor on which to put his baby grand piano, they were extremely hard to like. She worked for a white shoe law firm. He was the CFO at a tech company. They definitely could afford one or both of the neighborhood private schools. Their apartment was probably four times the size of ours, if not more. It was a corner apartment with a view of Prospect Park; ours gave onto the interior and the apartments across from us. And once we began talking to them about *compensating* us for the weeks we lost in our apartment, it was clear how much they wanted to be rid of the problem that was the couple in the apartment next to them.

In thinking back on it, I wonder what we might have done differently; I want to try to fix the awful interpersonal stuff, as though it could be fixed. I feel awful, for example, about trying to get Laurel to stay in the apartment the first night, and for underplaying the significance of the toxicity of the smell. I did this in a way that is utterly in character for me. I *always* underreact at first in a crisis (more depressing examples to come). If a neighbor came running into my apartment with an arm severed but for a single strand of tendon, trailing a pool of blood, I would probably say, *Let's think about this for a second.* And then I would help my friend to the couch, and make us both a sandwich. I might do this before getting a tourniquet. This is a quality that Laurel dislikes immensely, I think, though I am putting words in her mouth. Perhaps it is even a quality that I dislike. I suppose I strive for an *accurate* response to crisis, but in attempting to assess accuracy I inevitably aim low. I don't want to seem like a complainer. And this probably comes from being told not to complain about my circumstances as a child, because so many people had it worse. I was a child of privilege, so I was to understand my situation in that light.

It was my underreacting that kept us in the apartment that first night. The only good thing about it was that the bed was tiny, so I had to sleep tightly curled around the wide-awake Laurel. There is almost no time when this is a bad thing. If we were living in caves after the North Korean nuclear assault, and it involved lying next to the warm body of Laurel, I would accept my lot for bringing about this closeness. So: I kept us in the apartment, and this in turn had me sleeping in close quarters with my wife, and I do not regret these moments of intimacy, and how deep they can be, and feel.

That said, the battle with the neighbors over how to settle the fact of their having polluted us out of our apartment went on for a long time. We suggested an amount in week one, but by week three that amount seemed insignificant, since it didn't include the dry cleaning, and the utility bill that included running four fans for three weeks, and, for example, the time lost when I had to send my daughter back to her mother's house. And the longer the battle went on the more we seethed about what bad people they were—like when they said they would apologize as long as we signed a document saying we and our descendants would never sue them. Which we would not and did not sign.

These were the people living next door to us, understand, in an elevator building, where we were liable to see them (excepting that they worked conventional business hours and we did not) two or three times a day. We could even be waiting with them for the elevator. In awkward silence.

Because Laurel is a person who will never *not* say what's in her heart if she knows it to be true, I knew that there would come an even-more-uncomfortable discussion with this couple. They did, it should be said, apologize in person to us at one point, though the extent of this apology did not impress me, in part because I sort of hate that European IMF-style entitlement, and in part because the apology seemed constructed from a public relations manual. And so the whole thing careened on, with our trying to avoid them, and feeling like we were being edged out of an apartment building that we had enjoyed living in at first.

It seems it *does* come down to money and power in the end, and that certain people believe the money and power comes to them legitimately, because of earnings capability, while certain people are embarrassed by their power. Their insurance company gave us $1,200, which was about a quarter of our expenses for the month in which our apartment was difficult to live in, and that they did not budge from that number was a telling illustration of what they thought: that we were making it up, that Laurel in particular was making it up, and that we can't possibly have been uncomfortable in our apartment for almost three weeks.

The pregnancy of our neighbor was not a value-neutral aspect of this little moral tale of Park Slope. She was pregnant, and wealthy, and privileged, and we were struggling to conceive, and trying to hang on, according to the shabby gentility that I knew so well, living in an apartment too small for us. We were working artists, adjunct professors, which felt frivolous in the context of a full-on war of public opinion. The other thing that was not value-neutral was that Laurel was (is) a person of mixed race. There were a few African American people in the building, but not many. None on our floor. There was an Asian American couple on the end of the corridor. But the building was exceedingly white. And the husband in that couple next door was Belgian. I have already told you how hard I was on the one European member of my family, my British stepfather.

It breaks the chronological flow, but let me finish this particular anecdote. So you'll know from what context I have written what I have written. There was a long, long stalemate about the polyurethane, notwithstanding the $1,200 and the bottle of wine they left for us, neither of whom drinks, and a voucher for a *massage*, and then they had their baby.

And the newly minted mother had a mother herself, who must have gotten an apartment in Brooklyn, because suddenly the mother, who resembled the kind of sinewy Carolinian lady that you might read about in a Southern Gothic story, was often in the building pushing the stroller of her grandchild, wearing an expression that clearly said: *My daughter has made clear that you people are insane and are trying to take all of her money and I will not be having any conversation with the likes of you.* On it went, with Laurel nursing the feeling that she was meant to think she had made it all up, as her poor, struggling mother was dying, and we were planning on leaving the building, because the vibes were so menacing and awful, and then one day I was at the apartment of the guy across the hall from us, the one whose daughter was friendly with my daughter, and suddenly, from the hall I heard *yelling*.

I knew instantly what it was. I had known for months that the day would come, and now the day had come. Apparently, Laurel had said to the neighbors just outside the elevator, beside our door: "You know, you never fully compensated us, and I want you to know that I know that to be the case, and I haven't forgotten." Which produced a torrent of invective from the Belgian guy, the apex of which included the words *Who let people like you into this building?* Laurel then really gave it to him, at length, because that's the way she is, and she resorted to a few zingers, which then encouraged him to intimidate her further, and as he is about a foot and a half taller than Laurel, he backed her up against the wall in the corridor (when they got out of the elevator, that is) and got right up in her face, and really cursed her out, called her a *psycho,* and his wife shouted from behind him, *You made it all up. It's all in your head, Laurel.*

What I was doing was standing in the apartment of my neighbor, trying to keep my daughter from going out there into the hall, because I was worried about the kids—my daughter and her friend from across the hall—getting caught up in the outrage of the battle. That this was a strategic failure is understatement. I was torn between which person to try to protect, and I should have gone out there and said, *Lay off my wife* and *Shut the fuck up, both of you,* but with the emphasis clearly on the fact that the big European knucklehead should return to paying an inhumane wage to Chinese motherboard manufacturers and get out of the business of physically threatening people. That I did not support Laurel, but chose to try to keep my daughter out of the scuffle, this may have been fruitful for my daughter, but was costly, for a while, in our marriage. There was a cooler-heads apologetic meeting with the neighbors in the hall the next night, where the Belgian guy apologized, said he behaved poorly, and Laurel did her best to walk back her own remarks, and we complained to the co-op board, and the co-op board said, *Your problem.* We put the apartment on the market.

That is to say we lost, in this particular struggle. Money and power were victorious. Admittedly, we did well on the apartment sale, and we were secretly a little happy when we heard that the apartment below our neighbors was renovating not too long after, and that this renovation caused some structural damage to the apartment of the Belgian guy and his southern wife.

That was all months later, but it is the tonal color in this account, acute feelings of having been pushed out of a community, of having been pushed out by people who would find it easy to say the words *Who let people like you into this building?* And perhaps most importantly there is the legacy of my having failed to support Laurel. What do you do about these things? I tell my daughter that saying you are sorry is the bravest thing you can do, and I am often a person who does it. I feel that I am more often the person who does it with almost every significant relationship in my life. But in marriage it is the best and most honorable way to demonstrate respect. Listen carefully and say you're sorry.

June

Relatedly, school choice is the horrible part of life in Park Slope and of life in New York City, and I could go on and on about school choice, about all the many schools that we looked at during this year, and my hatred, for example, for all the alternative schools, even though I am sure they are excellent. As a person who teaches, I feel I have an especial skill which enables me to look deeply into the soul of an educator who is telling me how excited she is to work with these kids, and to see in this soul massive burnout and barely concealed clinical depression. It was always the alternative schools where I felt this most clearly. There was always a Svengali principal, and then a group of teachers who looked like they could be swinging from a noose.

There is one very good public school in Park Slope, and my daughter was granted a spot, because of our address, and it was one reason we stayed and took the abuse from the neighbors. People have suffered worse to get their kids into PS321 of Park Slope. People have feigned addresses, they have borrowed the addresses of relatives and friends, they have used former addresses. They have moved to Park Slope simply to get into the school district, and so on. Of the four contemporaneous girls in our building, only two went to PS321, and though Hazel, my daughter, was granted her spot, her mother refused to allow her to go there, because she seemed, as I understand it, to find the school elitist. The conflicting opinions among the adults of Hazel's life about schools could fill a long tedious pamphlet entitled "On Co-Parenting," which would probably be on display at some of the storefronts of Park Slope, and I for one am not going to contribute more material to the pamphlet and will say simply that Hazel was also accepted into a gifted and talented program in Astoria, Queens, about an hour from Park Slope by train, and in June we learned that this would be her school.

There are the moments in life when you know change is about to assert itself, and that, in the main, you are unprepared, but that doesn't mean you can't ride the steed of change in the correct direction. Hazel going to school in Queens presented this entirely different idea about how to live in New York, and the idea was: Why not live in Queens? Besides going to the airport, and besides knowing that Mayor John Lindsay once ineffectively plowed the borough of Queens after a blizzard, and besides knowing that it had a reputation for being the most diverse of the five boroughs (sixty languages are spoken in the Queens public school system, I have heard it said), I knew not much about Queens. I suppose I was a Manhattan snob when it was easy, and then I was a Brooklyn snob when it was easy, and in each of these periods of my life, looking down on Queens seemed routine. Queens could scarcely defend itself.

But here we were thinking about where we would live, after we sold the apartment in the co-op building in Park Slope, and it seemed like maybe we would live in Queens. (Especially when we found out how long Hazel's commute was going to be. An hour, one way. To kindergarten.)

That Hazel got into the citywide gifted and talented program was therefore really good news, in that she could be in the public school system, which I believed in, and still believe in, and she got into the most permissive one, because it was brand-new, and she was going to be in an incredibly diverse school district. But ultimately we were going to have to think about moving to Queens, and that was going to be the way out of Park Slope.

Meanwhile, we went back for another round of IUI at the clinic on the Upper East Side, where there were now a lot of health insurance problems. The endocrinologist told us she would honor our insurance through the cycle, but didn't tell her associates in the front office, and at every stage we had to sort of beg for the arrangement to be as it was initially described. We could feel the business relationship on the verge of breaking apart. Which implied: finding a new clinic. However, we had the IUI scheduled, and once you schedule it, and go through the difficulty of preparing, you want to finish it up without having to interrupt care. In the treatment of infertility, every month counts, especially when the prospective mother is, as they say, of "advanced maternal age," which is to say in her mid-thirties or several years beyond, as Laurel was.

So I was going back into the closet in the basement, after the first IUI, which came to nothing, which was a big flop, and I was meant to produce more genetic material. The second time was not as awful as the first, unless you thought about it. Upon thinking about it, the second time, in its way, became far worse, because it was about normalizing this activity, the furtive medically approved spilling out of your double helixes into a little plastic cup with your name and signature on it. The signature part was particularly odd (though it should be obvious why it is a feature—so you don't get a rogue employee mixing up the samples, or, say, introducing his own into the plastic cup), and made the providing of the genetic material eerily similar to signing a book for a reader. Once you thought about it, you were sort of doomed. Self-consciousness of any kind could arguably result in die-off of the good sperm, or could create more of the two-headed ones. It had come to pass, though, back in March, that there was the sudden vitamin enhancement of my daily life, including the fish oil ones. I took a fistful of the various sperm count enhancers every morning, frequently gagging, and well aware from accounts online that a significant portion of men, husbands, partners, made a line in the sand and said: *I'm not taking your fucking vitamins.* By which they meant: I am uncomfortable about the child, or I am uncomfortable about our relationship, or I am uncomfortable about medicalizing our free and easy sex life, or I am uncomfortable about not being in control of this process, or I am uncomfortable that in the postmodern now being masculine means all of these things, means being *uncomfortable*, about all of the above. Treatment for infertility entails giving up one thing after another in the process, both little things and exceedingly large things, for both partners. For men, it's not impossible to feel that you are a shrunken vessel of the past, an atavistic biological entity, a series of codes to be mined for the project, who galumphs after the mother into this appointment and that appointment, easily replaced with technological devices and some frozen sperm if necessary, and there are many opportunities for depersonalization, unless you take a big step outside, and, for example, look for the capacity to support.

At the second IUI, we were still hopeful.

Laurel has a really amazing smile, which is something every married person should feel about her or his spouse, a billboard of a smile, a rose garden of a smile, a sunrise of a smile, and, like her mother, a completely unrestrained laugh, which, when really set off through some organic means, can gather force, and occasionally through this year, we lost track of the capacity to find that part of our conjoined lives, if only because of sorrow piled upon sorrow, and yet at each new episode of infertility treatment, we worked to muster some hope; I would find myself at her bedside hoping that maybe some good would come of all this. In particular, with IUI, the medical people go away for a while and centrifuge the sperm, and there's a moment therefore where a couple might take stock of where that couple is, and so we did that, amid all the swirling of difficulties, *together* in our struggle.

And in the days after the procedure, because Laurel had become an adept with pregnancy tests, and would use two or three different ones, the cheap ones and the less cheap ones, and knew exactly what the results looked like, and could look at even the faintest trace of a positive, more a ghost of a positive than a positive, a line signaling through a dense fog of grim outcomes, a faintest figure of a line, a hope of a line, we knew pretty quickly that something amazing had happened, namely *good news*.

Bear in mind that this was all going on in the midst of two lives that were pretending, in a way, that no pregnancy was coming, no child, and we were pursuing our professional ambitions as though we were younger and more heedless, and everywhere around us there was death and chaos. As noted, Laurel had been crisscrossing the nation on her DNA portrait project, and I was teaching and ferrying my daughter back and forth from day care on the days when she was with us, and trying to get the new novel off the ground, and there was no room for error. If a long-term plan didn't work, we didn't have time to grieve, really, nor room for it. There was too much to do.

And that's why the good news was sort of unfathomable. You build up a hard outer shell, and I know when I say this that there are people who have suffered far more than we have suffered, even among our friends, couples who lost pregnancies at twenty weeks, or had to terminate because of genetic problems or grave illnesses. The hard exterior can be a lot harder than ours was, but ours was plenty bad enough. To have a little good news, however unbelievable, was so *good* that we mostly stowed it away for the time being, allowing ourselves into the castle of familial dreams for only very short visits. We didn't purchase the crib.

This was about when my online friend M.J. took her life. As I say, I had known a number of suicides, for example, my friend Lucy Grealy, and my friend David Foster Wallace, and I expect I will know more. The really sad people are sometimes the very best writers. If there were a way to go back and prevent the suicide, you say to yourself, while acknowledging the faults in the logic. On my first real date with Laurel, as I've said, we had seen *Avatar* together, a truly execrable film, in my view, a true dog, and out of boredom perhaps, I forgot that maybe I wasn't supposed to hold Laurel's hand at that film, and so I did it without really thinking, it was just two hands behaving as hands are to behave, given enough time. I think people should hold hands all the time. I am given to lamenting the possibility that my daughter will no longer want to hold my hand; I think about it a lot. That I do not want her to stop wanting to hold my hand. Though parenting is a recognition that the day will come, and the child will no longer want to hold your hand, and will make some kind of joke about it, and that joke is the indication that you have done your job really well. I am not ready for that day yet, because I think people should hold hands all the time.

Somewhere on the web I saw a video of a chimp who had been held alone in a cage for a long time, I can't remember how long, some years, I believe, and then one day they decided to put *another chimp* in the cage with the chimp in solitary confinement, and you can see, in fact, and I don't believe I am imagining it, the astonished joy of the chimp in solitary confinement, and what he or she does is reach out her hand for the other chimp, whom she has not ever met, simply to hold that chimp's hand, and often Laurel and I, in a bad patch, will do an imitation of the chimp handhold, a handhold without opposable thumbs; we imitate the chimps, by which we mean that sometimes the handholding is sufficient, and if I could do it again, and go back in time, maybe I could persuade M.J. otherwise, maybe I could somehow prevent what she had done, or at least demonstrate that I personally was no threat, was just some slightly desperate guy trying to hang on and do his job now and again. I would just try to sell her on the handholding as a treatment model.

For the sake of the argument, let's say that we were doing the chimpanzee handholding when Laurel had the first beta pregnancy test and confirmed a heartbeat! Confirmed a heartbeat! Confirmed a heartbeat! We had never gotten to a heartbeat before, in all of our laborious efforts, and now we had a heartbeat! The endocrinologist was not exactly overcome with joy about it, but we had a heartbeat, and that was the main thing. Because I will never disbelieve a bit of good news if there is no reason to disbelieve. This was one of the days in which I began to see that our bad luck with conceiving had visited on the normally upbeat Laurel a kind of posttraumatic stress, in which she could not believe, not without air-tight reassurance that was multiply deduced in different ways and from different angles. She kept asking the endocrinologist about the heartbeat, was it the right kind of heartbeat, and, after the MD left, she kept asking if I noticed anything out of the ordinary in our treatment that day. To which I said, no, of course not, because I still wanted to believe.

There *was* the issue that we were going to get kicked out of the MD's practice, because she no longer took our insurance. Laurel was convinced there was bad luck just around the corner. We would have to wait ten days for the next scan to find out.

July 2014

It was the dog days, and we were heading back to Skidmore College, where I have taught for a couple of weeks each summer for so long now that I can't remember when I didn't. Perhaps it's two decades now. This was the first summer that Laurel got a legitimate ID card and cafeteria privileges. Such privileges retroactively confer monogamy on you, you know. In years prior she had always been denied the free meals because of our not being joined together in the eyes of the law. Somehow this came to be a feeling that we were used to, a feeling of constrained legitimacy, a feeling of being a team against the vast and immobile outside world. This year was different, therefore: we could eat soft ice cream from the Skidmore College cafeteria at every meal if we wanted to, and no one could stop us—we were married.

I take pride in professionalism. I am willing to do things that other people find ridiculous if I have agreed to appear at a certain festival or school. Once I say yes I don't do otherwise. I will drive four hours to teach a class and then turn around and drive straight home. Those stories of the really famous writers in which a college buys a house in town for this newly hired writer and then he simply uses that house as leverage for or against some other school, these seem like dreams to me, Scheherazade-like folkloric exaggerations. Even the time I got a vile skin condition in the now-demolished old dorms at Skidmore I tried to say nothing for as long as possible. Once, on the way to Skidmore, I knocked out most of a tooth getting into my car, and instead of panicking I drove up, taught my first class, drove down to my dentist in the city, capped the tooth, and then went back up to Skidmore. I will work under bad circumstances, and I will feel virtuous. Laurel sometimes puts it this way: *Rick likes it when it sucks.* I can't address the origin of this particular way of being, the professionalism just is. It makes it easier for me to wake up in the morning, because I know what I have to do.

Similarly, in July, we had to drive up to Saratoga Springs, and drive back to the city the next day for our second pregnancy scan, and on the trip back, Laurel was sure that we were facing bad news, maybe just because we had gotten used to bad news. Lately, the precipice of good news was the most worrisome place of all. I would have to find a way to read stories for class on Tuesday sometime after the long drive and the trip to the endocrinologist. Not to mention there was a wealth of ancillary responsibilities at my summer program at Skidmore, dinners every night, and readings after the dinners, and tutorials with each student. It was a whole *community*, which was part of why I went back year after year. It was my one chance each year to have a good chat with the poet Henri Cole, whom I greatly admire, and, in those days, to hear Mark Strand read. I think hearing Mark Strand read his essay "On Nothing," which may have been this summer, was one of the most important moments I have ever had at a summer writing conference. Strand was already ill, as I recall it, but he managed perfect comic timing, despite his illness: "I have no subject for this talk, no subject except nothing, which is both a subject and not a subject." These were part of our life in Saratoga Springs in July, and we had to try to do our best to participate, no matter the hardship.

In the office of that Upper East Side reproductive endocrinologist, the dread was a feature like the wallpaper was a feature. The dread that was on a lot of faces in the waiting room, lots of women, lots of them with extremely bad news to come. Nobody goes for doctor-assisted reproduction without a problem. No amount of wait-and-see optimism could paper over the dread, and the up-tempo "mellow rock" station in the waiting room could do nothing to help us either.

Laurel lay on the table, therefore, when it was her time, and the reproductive endocrinologist and her assistant went about trying to find the baby, which they had managed to find just two weeks before, and then they started attempting to locate the baby's heartbeat, and there were a lot of silences, and the silences were a perfect setting for

the accumulation of dread, and though I can often feel
like the sound of HVAC is the sound of God, that day
the silences were an oppression, each more garish as it
extended around us. *Say something! Say something!* The sec-
onds ticked past, unremarked upon, and every moment
brought its gymnastics of certainty and uncertainty. The
dread as oppressive as the air quality of Manhattan in the
summer months, waiting for the pronouncement, with
the waiting, after a point, hoping *against* the pronouncement, knowing that it was going to be bad, and back into
the gymnastics and hoping otherwise. So now you know
that our good news had become bad news, and the embryo
had not grown since the last exam, in fact, the "embie," as
Laurel's online fertility community called them, was less
robust than it had been before, and that meant that there
was a *problem*, and the particular problem was no fetal
heartbeat, and, said the RE, we should not consider this a
pregnancy that was going to *progress*. And in fact the products of conception would now have to be removed.

If we were going to try again.

As I have said, I know Laurel well enough to know
when she is dissembling, for the sake of social require-
ments, or I know that the face of real hopelessness is not a
face that is made available for the world immediately, but
needs rumination, needs a gathering of force, while the
mind whittles away the possibilities for hope, and finding
none, gives up. Laurel was not about to betray these inner
workings at the office of the reproductive endocrinologist.

Once we got out the door she was absolutely distraught.

And how can one be the husband of the mother who

has just lost her child and still somehow not know, not feel, exactly, what your wife feels, what a mother feels? Why wasn't there some mechanism so that we could know exactly, so that we could take on some of the disconsolation and thereby help? Why always this philosophical distance, the masculine difference, a gulf of recognition, that to know what a mother feels is impossible for all of those who have never been mothers and who will never be mothers? Laurel and I came to know a woman who lost a child (much further along in her pregnancy) and had to terminate, to safeguard her own life, and who was then told by her employer that she could not have maternity leave, because her child had died, and thus was never *born*, and thus, according to her employer, she was never a mother. That the truth was otherwise was unmistakable in the agony she went through in the aftermath. We have felt her pain, I have felt her pain, and feel it still. So how to pierce through this feeling that was the insulation against feelings, that was the feeling of covering up from further blows, so as to hold the hand of a weeping woman, with tears of rage, and tears of abject loss, how to get through with the dead part of the self to the part of the self that wants to help? Why so much easier just to walk down the Manhattan streets belittled by scale and glamorous emptiness, just waiting, waiting for something more, some undeniable good?

It was nearly impossible to fathom that this particular thing was happening again, that we were going through another loss, and that we knew all the treatment options for treating a missed miscarriage, and that we had been told we had pulled it off this time, but in fact nothing of the sort was happening, and now we had to drive back up to Saratoga Springs, and pretend that everything was all right, when it was anything but all right. And then we would have to come back down the following week for a D&C, after my two weeks at Skidmore, and then Laurel would have to recover from that, and then we would see where we were.

Laurel's sobbing outside was matched only by her rage. She had known the week before! Why had I tried to convince her otherwise the week before? (Because I know no other approach than the optimistic approach.) Why didn't anyone *believe her* when she already knew? And how the hell were we supposed to get through two weeks in Saratoga Springs? And what the hell were we going to do now that we no longer could use that Upper East Side reproductive endocrinologist, because she wasn't taking our insurance anymore?

We did drive north again, and I finished my class, because of the myopic style of professionalism I have already alluded to, and we told no one of our plight. We told only our friend Amy Hempel and one other friend in Saratoga Springs what had happened. And I didn't do anything in the classroom I would not have otherwise done, excepting that every time I *went* to the classroom, or did individual meetings with the students, I was leaving a distraught Laurel alone in the dorm.

It's an experience of *being* that one has in the most spiritually destitute of times, where the extraneous is cleared away, and suffering is exposed as a really unique and critical approach to knowing that you are in the world, because you are a *being* who does not know when the suffering is going to end. Laurel got into bed for a while in Saratoga, and if she made a few appearances in public, they did not require her entire person, because the majority of her person was engaged in suffering.

The silliest and strangest thing that was the only outward manifestation of my own loss, in all of this, was that my *floaters* suddenly got dramatically worse. I tell this story only because it's an example of the condensation and displacement that adheres to human events amid a repetition of losses and high-stress occurrences. I couldn't really talk about my own anxiety, because it needed to be significantly less important than Laurel's, in order to keep us moving forward, and so instead of worrying about Laurel and miscarriage, I worried a little bit about *my eyes*. I've always had a little bit of sludge in the visual field of my eyes. In my thirties, I got my nearsightedness fixed, through laser surgery, and all was well for a while, and vanity was preserved, spectacles foresworn, but then the floaters really began to achieve a certain colorful density. While gazing on any white background, now, I can see what sort of looks like one of those environmentalist advertisements about petrochemical flotsam in the ocean, and the horror thereof. The floaters, those bits of my own vitreous material, have become the flavor of much of what I can see. Occasionally, these days, they affect my reading a tiny bit, and despite all of the literature—which suggests *You'll get used to them over time! Your brain will correct for them!*—mine only get more numerous and larger.

And there are some flashing lights too. Which of course means: retinal problems. Or scintillating scotoma! I really came to love the description of scintillating scotoma, which if you haven't read yet you owe to yourself. With scintillating scotoma, which is either predictive of a migraine (I have only ever had a couple of them) or its own otherwise asymptomatic migraine, you see these very carefully arranged light patterns. Some people get *teichopsia*, which is when you see a *star fort*! So excellent! Mine isn't as good as a star fort, though I have seen the psychedelic equivalent of a flashing pink, red, and blue parallelogram in my field of vision in both eyes, and while it's happening I can't read, or drive, and it doesn't matter if I close my eyes. I still see it with eyes closed. Luckily, it only lasts for forty-five minutes or so, or that has been the case so far, after which I do not get a headache, although I feel sort of dizzy and weak.

While Laurel was suffering, therefore, I was also worrying about my eyesight, or about having to have my retina stapled back in, or about macular degeneration, which afflicts others in my family. I went to the eye doctor, who subjected me to a battery of tests, and suggested that my visual field test was awful. He gave me three chances, and eventually I passed a visual field test. "It's really just a baseline reading," he mumbled. He celebrated this accomplishment by sending me off to the retinologist.

There were a lot of visually impaired people at that practice. People being helped inside by others, people with canes. As my job is the writing of books, and, in parallel, the joyous reading of books, I didn't want to be one of the people being helped into the practice.

And the retinologist must have been a reader, because he was very interested in my profession and wanted to talk about it, and how he was stuck inside in a darkened room all day, and he'd *really* like to write a book someday, and by the way my retina was fine, and don't do the *floater removal* operation, it's like the old needle in the haystack, he said, and *there's nothing that can be done now,* and you'll probably get used to the floaters after a while! Your brain will correct for them! He subjected me to another battery of visual field tests, and said that if I didn't do better next time I'd be shipped off to see if I had a brain tumor.

This was the couple in July, the emotionally distraught couple, one of whom was prostrate with PTSD from pregnancy losses, and the other who was grief-stricken and two and a half years sexually sober and worried he was going blind, the couple who then went to yet another clinic to do the D&C, after our missed miscarriage. We had been effectively ushered out of the foregoing practice where we did the IUI, because of insurance, and were now embarked on a third practice, well-known as the cut-rate infertility choice in New York City, but in the meantime, we had to terminate the pregnancy. So we went to another place in Midtown. The *pregnancy removal* operation was noteworthy for a lot of younger women, who had perhaps collaborated in the employment of unreliable contraception, or who were involved with guys who were careless, *or worse,* and many of whom had come here by themselves, and it reminded me of times in my life decades past, whose shadow of grief is the shadow looking back into you, the shadow colonizing you, the shadow occluding the visible and perceptible. At least I had come out of the low days in search of opportunities to support and love, and now was my chance.

Before they would do the D&C they did an ultrasound, to make sure Laurel was pregnant, and that was when the following sentence was uttered:

"Neither one of the fetuses has a heartbeat."

To which Laurel said, "Neither one of the *two*?"

"There are two, and neither one has a heartbeat."

Twin boys, reader, they were twin boys.

In my heart, I always assumed I would have another daughter. Or, rather, I assumed this, because I really liked having a daughter, and felt great infinite waves of love for my daughter, couldn't live without her, no matter how challenging I found being a dad sometimes, and how ill-equipped I believed myself to be, short of the requisite patience and sometimes the reserves of compassion.

But my sense of the moral architecture of the universe is such that my preference for a girl was definitely, it seemed to me, going to be rewarded with a son. So certain was I that I sort of knew, somehow, that there were twin boys in there, twin boys lost to the world, now, or in the process of being reabsorbed into the first spark of the universe, to be reclaimed at a later date. I honestly don't know how I could have taken care of twins, nor do I know how Laurel would have done it, with our elderly and in some cases infirm parents. But I knew that the loss of two was an enormous loss, a sort of accretion of losses that no one should have in one year, and that the reabsorption was going to take place, someplace out beyond Alpha Centauri, and then we were just sort of going to *move on*, but this did not seem possible.

Total up some of the hardships, reader, and ask yourself how we could possibly continue. We were two people who had been married less than a year, and we had already dealt with multiple losses, a dying mother, a dying stepfather, the deaths of acquaintances, suicide, the loss of a six-year-old girl in our community, and we were supposed to be successes well known in our fields, but we felt more like a traumatized couple, battered, and worn, and bruised.

Laurel, like the incredibly strong person that she is, went through the procedure somehow, because there was nothing much else to do in our desolation, and then we were out the other side, without a clue in the world about how we were going to do in vitro fertilization cycles, not in terms of the money, which is astronomical, nor where we were going to do it, nor when. And in addition to those considerations we were supposed to go visit my parents for a week.

August 2014

The staging of memories in a marriage, it seems to me, is vitally important. A marriage is a sequence of stories you tell about yourselves, to yourselves sometimes, in order to encourage the marriage to signify, to stand for something. The stories support the marriage itself, and perhaps sometimes they support the very idea of marriage. They are effects of the marriage and causes of it, too. And therefore I'd be remiss, especially in the month of August, a holiday of a month, and a month of grief, if I didn't tell you a couple of the stories that I have left out of this account so far.

The first involves the moment in the summer of 2013, the summer before the October when Laurel and I were married, the summer when a former student of mine wrote to me about a theatrical experience she'd had in which she'd been the only audience member for a performance by a theatrical entity called Odyssey Works who design performances for an audience of *one*. That is, they design a theatrical experience just for you. My student said her *life had been changed* by her experience of Odyssey Works. I definitely did not have to be told twice, as life-changing experiences with art are (by definition) rare and formative. I immediately began looking into the matter of Odyssey Works.

Why did I do this? I did it because my divorce had just come to an end, and I felt bulldozed inside, inert, depleted of meaningful reserves of the human, and I wanted to do something with myself, in the months before Laurel and I married, to restore my faith in creativity and in artmaking. That is, I totally saw the Odyssey Works experience through the lens of creative selfishness. I wanted to refill the tank a little bit, in the same way that I went to Burning Man while finishing my novel *The Four Fingers of Death*, or in the same way that I went to a Meredith Monk vocal training workshop at the Omega Institute. Being offbalance, uncertain, baffled, challenged creatively, these often resulted in the kinds of experiences that I like to write about. (Another example would be giving a reading at an ashram on Lower Broadway.)

Laurel has slightly different impulses. Her interests initially, as an artist, were partly in documentary work, when she was an undergraduate, and she really believes in depicting what *is*, and in the daily struggles of people, and the nonnutritive New Age stuff, the whacky spiritualism, really irritates her. I think her mother's fascination with alternative spiritual systems when Laurel was young may also play a part in her resistance to adventures of these kinds. Her attitude about Odyssey Works, especially when, in the intake period (I was accepted as the audience member for summer 2013), they called her to talk over how the odyssey experience was going to work for me, suggesting briefly (though *only* briefly, as I understand it) that they were thinking about throwing me out of a plane—with a parachute—her attitude was that it would all be a ridiculous amount of time spent away from my family, meaning herself and Hazel, with nothing much to show for it.

I cannot deny that it did result in a lot of time away from my family. My odyssey ended up taking a not-insignificant portion of three months, and it began, one night in May, when I went to the Russian and Turkish Baths in the East Village. It had been a long time since I was there, so long ago that the last time I'd been there, for someone's bachelor party, I still wore glasses and therefore could not see a thing in the baths and kept running into naked people. I did not quite understand, and never have understood, the allure of the public bath, although I suppose I liked them a little bit when I was in Iceland. I have also been to the Roosevelt Baths in Saratoga Springs, where you get your own room. In Saratoga Springs, the baths were a lot like being in the psychiatric hospital.

But Abe Burickson, artistic director of Odyssey Works, who was and is an architect, and taught architecture, loved the idea of the public bath and was interested in trying to think up new ways of designing baths, or that is something that he told me while we were sitting in the baths, and losing body fat, and then occasionally diving into the cold water, only to lose some more pounds in the steam room thereafter.

Abe, it turned out, had been a Sufi spinner when young. Not a Sufi spinner at Hampshire College who was pursuing a major in *Proto-Industrial Conceptions of Religiosity in Modern Byzantium*, but an actual trainee with professionally and spiritually legitimate dervishes in Istanbul after he got out of college. Abe's mother is a painter, and I think Abe was looking around for something like a meaningful, epiphanic, transportative spiritual experience apart from the history of painting, and the answer to this search was found among the whirling dervishes of Istanbul. I think he worked at Sufi spinning for some two years.

It happens that though I cannot dance, cannot remember any kind of choreographic routines, I dated dancers almost exclusively in my later college and graduate school years, and on one occasion I appeared in a dance, a dance in which a certain text of Gertrude Stein's was recited, and during which the movement of the piece consisted entirely of Sufi spins. So, at that time, I undertook for several weeks some training in how to do a Sufi spin, which involved looking only at my hands, and retreating into some deep space in myself, and not turning my eyes until the last moment in a certain 360 degrees. This involved a lot of interfacing (this was my particular solution) with the music of Steve Reich and Meredith Monk, and some hoping that I would not throw up. I think the piece was influenced by Trisha Brown, who was a choreographer I loved then, and I think in our campus environment it was original and provocative.

I told Abe about this, but Abe's story about training with the dervishes was far more interesting than my college experience in dance. Abe's story was about spiritual awakening and Sufi spinning. While I believe in spiritual experience, while I believe that spiritual experience is the kind of thing that enabled me to stop drinking and which undergirds some of my work, and which has brought order to a life that was in no way orderly in prior years, I am also a skeptic, and sort of want to make everyone with a spiritual awakening *defend* their story, because the defense, in the first person, is often very moving. I was, as you might be, somewhat skeptical about the ability of a guy from the United States, whose only qualification was that he had studied some architecture and written a few poems, simply to enroll in a class in Istanbul, after which he would experience what Sufi spinners have tried to have for centuries. Why Abe? What was so good about him?

If it were a short story, instead of an encounter from the year of the Charles Manson autographed postcard, I would instantly push Abe Burickson to the most dramatic recitation of his story, and I certainly tried that. I don't know why, because when I talk about being redeemed by sobriety, or the moment when I was in a James Turrell skyspace piece in Santa Fe and the light did something that I had never imagined light could do before, I try not to tell the story in a way that exaggerates it. I try to allow

epiphany to happen without overselling it. And this is
exactly what Abe Burickson achieved, he slowly teased
out the long and solitary nights of practicing over and
over and over, not really knowing much Turkish, not
knowing anyone much in Istanbul, constantly doubting
the validity of the undertaking, constantly thinking he
might as well go home to the United States and figure out
something else to do. But then his story rose to some peculiar and uncanny climax, and I can only imagine that it was
this way because we were in the baths, and perhaps all the
relevant electrolytes had been sweated out of my system.
Abe, it seems, had the requisite experience of God, while
doing some extended bout of dervishing, or, if not God,
the infinite, or, if not the infinite, the numinous and unex-
plainable, the beyond words, and perhaps because it was
beyond words Abe could not fully explain it to me there in
the baths. He said only that something spooky and unex-
plainable happened, and that after that time he left his
training in Istanbul and came back to the United States
and, presumably (or so I was led to believe there in the
baths), started Odyssey Works. I don't think it actually
went that way, but I think Abe led me to believe it in the
baths, because it would seem appropriate to the performance we were about to collaborate upon.

Because of the James Turrell skyspace epiphany I've just
mentioned, which I had shared with Burickson during the
long Odyssey Works intake session, along with my pro-
nounced fear of heights, and my feelings of tedium about
dreams, dream recitations, and dream work, I expect that
Abe understood that this idea of epiphany, and of achieved

meaning in the area of the arts, was somehow essential to me, and maybe the Sufi spinning story was itself *spun* in order to have the desired effect or to be predictive thereof.

In any event, on the way out of the baths, I ran into a guy I knew from recovery circles, and from having jointly participated in a student film twenty-five years ago. I ran into this guy in the locker room, and he was lying on a bench with some hot towels on him, apparently mummified, or so it seemed, and groaning loudly in a way that was somewhere between torture and erotic release, and for a moment I thought: *I wonder if this guy is a plant, if Abe has somehow arranged to have this guy here at this moment.* Except that I couldn't even remember his name (his name is Gary, though I couldn't think of it right then), and I didn't know him well, and, in a way, kind of steered around him some.

Next, Abe and I went down St. Mark's Place for a burrito. It felt strange to eat in this tiny burrito joint with someone I didn't know that well. It felt like an earlier epoch of life, when I had sufficient time at hand to just go out to dinner with a stranger and get to know him. What I noticed about Abe was that he had incredibly involved dietary needs, and in the course of our eating together he did explain that he had an aggrieved case of Crohn's disease, and that he was trying to eat very simple things (he was on a modified paleo diet) to keep himself from having an outbreak of Crohn's. When he talked about this stuff, he looked both wise and crestfallen, and I felt bad for the guy. Just when I felt like I was getting to know him, though, he laid out a few calendar issues he needed to go through with me. He'd need me to set aside a weekend in

September, and also some time in the midsummer, a day or two, for odyssey-related performances, which, because these dates were a long way away (it was May), didn't sound difficult, and then he abruptly got up as though about to leave, which in fact he was doing, and said, "I'm going to leave now, and, by the way, the piece has now begun." And then he was gone.

What happened, thereafter, slowly at first, but with ever-increasing frequency, was that I would have these experiences in my life with strangers that had an eerie quality to them. Often I didn't understand at first that there was something off about the interaction, and I wouldn't really feel the reverberations of it until later, but then it would hit me, with the force of epiphany, that the interaction had been part of Abe's magic. For example, coming out of a reading in Saratoga Springs in 2013, there was a woman in red doing a sort of a modern dance piece outdoors, and she turned out to be a plant. And once I was having lunch with my friend Randy Polumbo, when a guy sort of busted in on us at Pain Quotidien in Tribeca and said he knew Randy from Burning Man, and soon we were having a long conversation with him about his grandmother, and her loneliness, even though I had never seen the guy before. It took me a couple of days to figure out that he too was part of the piece.

There were many more of these picayune but oddly numinous coincidences, and amassing them here is less important than simply putting my finger on the effect of the odyssey on my person, namely that it caused me to look at everything in my life as though it had narrative value. That is, if you start to think that *every* interaction in your life is part of a performance piece of some kind, with a resultant emotional purpose, then it stands to reason that *all* of your life has thematic weight. You begin to read your life as though everything in it is *important*, not something simply to be sped through (*this checkout line sucks!*) to get to the other more high-impact sections.

There was a big culmination of all of this, which lasted for three days in the end of August or beginning of September, and which partly involved a house party in Prospect Heights, clown training, a dance performance for me on the Brooklyn Bridge, a story written especially for the odyssey by Amy Hempel,* and many other choice bits, but all of this was reiteration of the core principle of the odyssey, which I have just expressed above, namely that life, experientially, is a thing you can value generally, rather than episodically.

However, I do want to preserve one particular episode of the odyssey for the marital import of it from both Laurel's point of view (time consuming) and mine (profound),

---

* "When I left the house it was still dark. A friend, before he died, said, 'Home is waiting in the dark for us to come home.' But what if you don't recognize your home? And what if you feel at home nowhere? Or is a better question: What would it take to make a place feel like home? It would be nice if there were blueberry bushes lining the road, and maybe, in a nearby field, raspberry canes. A girl could learn to pick them without getting poked. A father could show his young daughter how. That would be in summer, of course. In winter: the pond out back of the house would freeze over, and a girl would ice skate with her father to the music one plays while gliding on ice—Stravinsky the obvious choice, or anything that makes a body lean to one side, then the other, in concert across a pond."

namely the day on which I was kidnapped by Abe Burick-son and flown out of the country.

For a time just before this kidnapping, Abe had asked me to go to a certain empty storefront in Brooklyn and hang around for a little while, for a couple of hours at a stretch. In this storefront, there would be clues about things that were going to happen to me, as well as ethe-real drone-based music (with a bit of Morton Feldman around the edges) playable on a boom box there, and cos-tumes that I was supposed to wear. I really did not like it in the storefront. If loneliness is a problem for me, if being alone is contrary to good mental health (as they always told me back when I was in the psychiatric hospital in 1986), then the storefront was a bad spot for me to be awakened to my odyssey. Nevertheless, on the day of the kidnapping I went there for an hour or so, per instructions, and I brought a backpack, and a change of clothes, because I was told to, and I took leave of my wife and child.

I had on my street clothes by the time I met Abe and a driver (a young woman) out front. He told me to get in the car. I got in the car. I asked where we were going. Abe said to the airport. He'd told me to bring my passport, so I'd brought my passport. He wouldn't tell me where I was going other than the airport. I didn't even know which air-port, though the route indicated JFK. I was flying some-where internationally, apparently, but where? Wherever it was it wouldn't be for long, because I hadn't set aside much time. I was personally hoping (and this is where the ody-ssey process is odd, in that it somehow encourages really ridiculous fantasizing) Greenland, or maybe Prince Edward

Island, or maybe Iceland again. I think I had told Abe about my outsized love of Iceland. What made it reasonable to think such things? Maybe the isolation of being in a hardware store by myself, listening to incredibly bleak music, and wearing the clothes of a Samuel Beckett character.

We got out at the curb at JFK, Abe and I, and he told me he was just walking me to the check-in console, and then I was on my own. I swiped my passport as usual, and then I waited. An itinerary came up. It was for a ticket to Regina, Saskatchewan.

I had sort of been interested in Saskatchewan as a kid, because of how interesting the word was. Canada, to me as a child, was peculiar, because it had many superficial differences from the United States, but was reliably similar, too. I thought of the northern prairie of Canada as being remarkable and strange, similar and dissimilar, totally empty, totally impressive in scale, and different from the United States of America. And now I was going to get to go—for about thirty-six hours.

Yes, I had very little with me, and this is important for the story. Since I was only asked to prepare for one night, I had packed light. It was easy moving around the airport. But it's strange getting on a plane when you have no idea where you'll be staying, so everything about the trip was mildly stressful, ominous. I assumed that there were other people on the plane associated with the odyssey, but I couldn't identify them at all. The trip had meaning, resonance, even though, in a way, it was precisely banal. I was flying to a place that most people, most North Americans, would avoid just on principle. Flying to Regina is sort of like flying to Billings or Fargo, or Omaha, an economically relevant city, surrounded by great undeveloped expanses. As with the cities of the American prairie, the city is a little bit rundown and has a criminal aspect (it's Canada's most crime-afflicted city, I believe), but I didn't know any of this at the time.

Owing to my experience with traveling for readings and public events, I have a sort of a space that I can get myself into for flights and trips where the unexpected is a regular fixture. I suppose I would describe it like this: I completely stop forecasting about my circumstances, and I just deal with what is directly in front of me. Abe Burickson told me to bring a copy of *Moby Dick* with me on my trip, and so I had *Moby Dick* on my tray table, and a movie to watch, and I wasn't thinking about Saskatchewan at all.

As night descended on the jet, just when I'd settled down into some kind of reasonable compartmentalization about the nature of my trip, I heard a guy coming up the aisle behind me, saying, *Sir, sir, sir, I think you dropped this!* And before I knew it, he had dropped a manuscript in my lap. There was one other person in my aisle, and he didn't pay any attention, and I was, initially, so focused on the strangeness of something being dropped in my lap, and on the fact of it being a manuscript, that I didn't have time to give my liaison a look. I really should have, but I didn't. I thought I got a quick glimpse, but no matter how I tried to find him later on, on a stroll to the back of the jet and the restrooms, I couldn't find him again. It was a classic bit of Odyssey Works dodge and feint. I just had this manuscript, which turned out to be a musical score.

A musical score of an unusual kind. Instead of written out in staves, as might have been done in a conventionally classical piece of music, this score was a flow chart, with small boxes indicating bits of melody, and spots where instruments were free to improvise, or to react to things happening elsewhere in the piece. It was a thoroughly postmodern score. And it could have been a map for the odyssey itself, where the possibility of static interactions with performers, with a reversal of performer and audience, such that I was performing for an audience of my cast—seemed possible somehow. I read the score for a while, and found its blankness at once appealing and daunting. I didn't know what to make of it (or the suggestion that I bring *Moby Dick*), except that these forecasted future events in the very way that an infant's face does: it tells you exactly what a person is going to look like, except that you don't know yet *how* it does so.

I was filling out my landing card, later on, when I realized that I had a real shortage of information available to me about my plans in Canada. There was an unspoken agreement between Abe Burickson and myself that I wouldn't use my phone to text home about stuff unless there was an emergency, but I could sort of feel the itch to text at that point (I was still using a flip phone in those days, in my intense desire *not* to capitulate to the checking-mail-twenty-four-seven culture), to ask Laurel what I should do about my lack of information about where I was staying in Canada. I tried to maintain a studied commitment to the *art* of it all. This was the point of the project—to be off-balance, to be seeing the world as an adventure, a voyage of discovery.

The airport was tiny, as I recall. Did I change planes? I did, in Minneapolis, which gave me a chance to walk around a bit, and by comparison, arriving at Regina's airport was like flying into a tiny regional landing strip. The customs area was tiny, just a couple of lanes, one for Canadians, and one for the rest of us. Though in the old days, I had flown into Canada having forgotten my passport and somehow talked my way in and out, it was no longer the old days, and when I told the guy at passport control that I didn't really know where I was staying in Regina, nor what I was doing there, he gave me a curious look and told me to go wait by a certain door. I waited there, it seems now, for a long time, until they had cleared everyone out, the entire flight.

Except for one pretty and self-possessed blond woman in her thirties (my guess), who was carrying a tote bag from the New Museum, or some similar arts institution. She too seemed to have none of the requisite information, or that was my guess. She took no interest in me, at all, and seemed utterly assured about her fate, and they worked her over first. I could see her in an office lined with windows, and she sat in the corner, as animated as if she were discussing stock futures, or annual crop yields for the Saskatchewan provincial government. Unperturbed! However, I was getting more unsettled as I waited. I texted Abe and told him that it didn't seem to be going so great with the immigration people. Indeed, eventually, a functionary called me into his cubicle. He said: *What are you doing in Canada?*

I said, *I am part of a performance by an avant-garde theater company, and as part of this performance, I am going to be in Regina tonight and tomorrow.*

He said, *Where is this performance taking place?*

I said, *I'm afraid I don't know that.*

And where are you staying?

I'm afraid I don't know that either.

And with whom are you doing the performance?

Well, it's in the nature of this theater company that I don't exactly know that part either.

I tried to leave out the part about it being a performance for an audience of one, because that just sounded preposterous.

So you're doing a performance in Regina with a theater group except you don't know where it is, where you're staying, or who's involved?

Then we went through it all a second time and a third time, and he asked me my profession, and why I didn't have any luggage, and the more I talked the more indefensible the whole thing sounded to me. I kept looking over at the blonde in the other office, and I could tell that she was having a similar discussion.

While the functionary was talking to me, he was typing a lot into the computer, and at some point I surmised that he was feeding me into the Interpol databases of known terrorists and outlaw types. Now and then in my life I have really disliked the fact that my first name, Hiram (of Hiram Frederick Moody III), is often assumed by the less informed to be a Muslim name, and this was one of those times. While I look about as much like a Muslim terrorist as your average Irish pub hound, I did and do have a name that is Turkish, or maybe Lebanese (look it up!), and it's only natural that it would give a constabulary person something to inquire into.

At one point, I said, *Look, I'm pretty well-known in my business, you can just look me up. I would give you one of my books, but I don't have any with me, but if you go on Wikipedia you'll see my photo and my bibliography.*

To which the functionary said, *Wikipedia pages are easily falsified.*

He had me there.

I texted Abe: *What's the plan if I get sent back to the US?*

I texted Laurel: *Abe didn't consider what was going to happen at the border. I'm thinking I might get sent home.*

Her text back featured a lot of cursing.

I'm thinking I sat there for half an hour, maybe, and it just got worse and worse as far as my faith that I would ever see Saskatchewan. But just when I was convinced the blonde and I were getting back on the plane, the guy said, *Okay, you're free to go, have a nice stay in Canada.*

And with slightly shaky knees, I walked out through customs, and looked for the person with the sign that said "Rick Moody."

The guy who picked me up was chatty, but I had little appetite for conversation at that point at all. It was night, and the outskirts of Regina were like the outskirts of anywhere, and they had picked a decent enough hotel, because they knew I'd be exhausted, and the art in the hotel was these etchings that made little pictures out of the word *dream*. I doubt that Abe Burickson ever got to see this feature of the establishment, but it was sort of what the odyssey felt like, of course, to the adventurer, like a dream that kept inserting itself unpredictably into the here and now.

In the morning, the landscape revealed that Saskatchewan is flat. Per its reputation. Flatter than just about anywhere else, and flat in all directions, and as far as you can see. I recognize that its flatness is part of the same flatness that gives us the Great Plains of the United States, which I have also seen and admired, and I recognize that there are other flat places (like the interior of the Netherlands) that have a similar effect. I am sure if I ever see the Mongolian steppe I will be impressed. But the landscape of Saskatchewan was at the limit of what I have seen, in terms of flatness. I was driven out about an hour or so into the great expanses beyond Regina by another driver in the employ of Odyssey Works, and I was told nothing, just driven out in fairly abstracted silence punctuated by a few polite words here and there, and upon parking I was shown a certain footpath, and directed to follow this footpath, through a waving field of grain, out about half a mile to a small adobe hut out in the middle of nowhere. Then the driver left.

To restate: I was to walk out into the middle of the grasslands in a foreign country, into an apparently uninterrupted agrarian landscape, mostly unperceived, or so it seemed, and wait. If the Odyssey Works people, for some reason, wanted to take my life and dispose of my body where it might be undisturbed for a long while, in a ditch in Saskatchewan, they had found a really good way to do it. I was now an hour from Regina, my last known address, and even that one was a stretch, being 2,000 miles from home and across the northern border. Nevertheless, it wasn't that I felt worried about my kidnapping. The Odyssey Works people didn't summon up feelings of endangerment. It's just that I felt really lonely. At every turn, in the process, given the opportunity to pause and reflect, I felt most cut off from the nourishing part of my life, which was just being around people whom I knew or cared about, like my soon-to-be wife, for example. In this way the odyssey they had constructed for me was very Odyssean, the more so the more I experienced it. But I wouldn't know what it meant until I was done.

At a certain point, as I walked through the field of waving grain, I could hear cello music coming from the small adobe structure to which I was bound. That is, as I marched through this racket of crickets, across waving fields of fallow scrub, I could hear a cello. That sublime sound. And indeed when I finally made it to the structure, which was rounded on the inside, with an opening into the ceiling, some windows that looked from the edge of an escarpment into a valley (about the only disturbance in the plains of Saskatchewan that I had seen since I got there), there was a cellist present, alone, with some sheet music, which I could see now was either the exact sheet music that had landed in my lap during the flight the night before, or cut from the same larger composition as that piece, with the same cells and open-ended passages.

I also noticed that the escarpment, the steep sloping down into the valley out the window, had been in the photograph that I had seen at the hardware store the day before.

The cellist, who was tall and trim and fair-haired and purposeful, kept playing, gorgeously I might add, with lots of open strings, and pregnant silences, and somehow the live quality of the music enabled it to have a mournful impact that I had not always gotten from the music in the hardware store. Same composer, different result. I lay on the floor listening for a while, and then I watched the score for a while, and then I went outside and listened for a while, and at some point while I was doing that I noticed that there was a person burrowing out in the fields just beyond the little hut where the cellist was performing, and that person was, it seemed, photographing the proceedings. She was trying to avoid being seen, but her way of avoiding being seen had the paradoxical quality of helping me feel a little bit less isolated in the tale of my odyssey. It didn't take that long to realize that she was the same woman who had been harassed by the border agents at the airport the night before.

In due course, the cellist finished the piece. I'm going to say it was a forty-five-minute solo, and she played it with great and lucid commitment. When she was done, I whispered a few questions to her at first, because the immense stillness, and silence, the intermittent sounds of nature that were the noisy silence of the Canadian plains, at first seemed to suggest that whispering was the reasonable way to go. But the cellist answered aloud some questions about the piece, about how much of the piece was improvised, and so on. She was really patient with me, and she didn't realize how desperate I was for conversation right then. I would have gladly taken her for dinner in whatever backwater we were near, just to hear her talk about her food allergies, or her trouble as a child with long division. But after five or ten minutes she said that she was going to leave me alone now, and she packed up her cello and walked off. Back the way I had come, through the field, to the dusty dead end of the road down which I had traveled.

I assumed that the photographer was still out in the field, but in the meantime there was only myself and the vast, barely disturbed expanses of Saskatchewan for another hour or so. This was like my regular life in no way at all. And, on paper, it was everything I wanted and couldn't have in my ordinary life—no playing with paper dolls with my daughter, no divorce meetings with the lawyers, no writing student recommendations, no bills to pay, no civilization to get in the way of the spiritual growth that I believe I wanted and from which I was frequently cut off by the responsibilities of the day—and yet though it was everything I felt I wanted, the last hour and a half of it felt demanding, even beyond my capabilities. Maybe Abe Burickson, who spent years learning how to perform a Sufi spin, would have known how to fill the two hours of prairie, but I somehow could not do it, and I couldn't shake a nagging perception of failure, as if a dozen people had volunteered time and energy to give me this feeling that my life was significant, but coming 2,000 miles somehow did not make me less insecure.

When my time was up, I hiked out, and a driver met me there, and took me back to the airport. I think he was the romantic partner of the cellist, or at least he knew the cellist. How Abe Burickson (who, I found out later, had never been to Saskatchewan, and still has not been) had selected this place, these people, this cellist, etc., for this part of my odyssey, I never quite found out. Only that once upon a time, when I was fifty-two years old, I was kidnapped by a bunch of actors and transported to one of the most empty places in North America, and it was incredibly beautiful.

I made it back in one piece.

The end of the odyssey, just so that you know, had to do with taking me out to Sandy Hook, New Jersey, and then bringing me back the following morning, in the company, at various points, of nearly every one of my dearest friends. It was delightful. But the very last scene involved seeing my mother waiting for me on a park bench in Soho, all by herself. Seeing her there was forlorn and sentimental, perhaps *she* was forlorn, or, more likely, she just had no idea what this theatrical thing was, and what she was meant to be doing. But she rode back with me on the subway, until we arrived in Park Slope, whereupon I came up from underground to find Laurel and Hazel awaiting me. After the on-and-off three months of strange, uncanny occurrences, in ever-increasing frequency, it was easy to see this last bit as a ratification of home, the idea of home, exactly like in Homer's *Odyssey*, where one returns home after ten years of traumatic adventures. What was important was *being present* for it, being present for the moments of being, and the turning away from adventure in the safe harbor of home.

Just before the last part of the odyssey, though also in the summer before the autumn in which Laurel and I married, one other very memorable event came to pass, namely our joint in-flight magazine travel piece about Ireland. This was right after I proposed to Laurel in Cannon Beach, Oregon. Laurel was very interested in the *ring* portion of the marriage proposal. Early in the process of agreeing to marry, she was bidding on used engagement rings from the turn of the last century, for an art project, until she had a great number of them, all bought on the cheap, and she liked to take them all out and look at them on the bed, and evaluate the bands and the stones and the settings. We found a ring in Millerton, New York, one I liked a bit, one that passed muster, and I sort of filed it away as the ring I would use when I proposed. There was no real mystery to any of this, like there is no mystery about the advent of the first perfect day of spring, and so she knew I would propose someday, and I knew I would propose, and we already knew more or less how the words would go.

I put the ring from Millerton, the one I liked, from the store next to the good diner in Millerton, in my suitcase, and we headed out to Cannon Beach. As usual, there, we didn't have that much time, just a couple of days, and there would be a lot of family around. Laurel's dad's house is just a couple of blocks off the beach, on a street heavily lined with summer cottages (and with signs marked "Tsunami Evacuation Route"), but lovely and quiet just the same. As with a lot of the Pacific Northwest, the tides are dramatic, and whole rivers and inlets are made and erased in the six hours between high and low tides, and we were always watching for the lowest of the low, because then you could get the farthest out toward Haystack Rock, where the swirling disturbances of gulls and terns above were nearest at hand. There were little sandbars, and heavily barnacled rocks, all of them looking like they were designed by some Hollywood backdrop painter with a flair for the dramatic, and that was where I wanted to do the asking that I was going to do. If, in a way, the purpose of the Odyssey Works odyssey that spring and summer was to restore a sense of purpose and meaning to some months that had become intensely painful and joyless, having a little bit of occasion about this moment, not overdramatizing it, but understanding it to be *of this place*, this beach, among this family, Laurel's family, was important to me, buoyed up on the rippling of the chilly Pacific.

We crossed the main drag, and went down toward the beach, and I suppose I was silent, with some kind of intentionality, not dramatizing, and Laurel asked what I was thinking about and I said something noncommittal, and then she looked down at my hands, which were in my pockets, and Laurel says that she noticed there was something *large* in my hand, a box in my pocket, and she knew, instantly, she says, what was in my pocket, that is to say the little jewelry case that hid the ring from view.

Laurel broke into some sudden rush of excitement and laughter, all done without any words at all.

The Pacific crashing down upon the enormous foggy microclimates of Cannon Beach, in which pedestrians (and their dogs) or riders on their recumbent bikes, emerged from backdrops of *sfumato*, and then disappeared back into them, notwithstanding that it was actually sort of a *sunny day*, and so forth, this was the day. And so we hiked down across the beach toward the rock, and the rock, as with all large-scale geological formulations in the West, seemed to recede the closer that you got to it, so that it was both near and far at the same. Over the years, I had made as to seem impervious to the cold of the Pacific. I had been dared to swim in it, and I had swum in it, so the waves were no matter to me, nor were the eddies around Haystack Rock, and so I took her down by the hand, and when we were near unto the rock, I knelt in the water, and she knew I was going to do it because I had to take the ring out of the box, of course, and I just mumbled what was the obvious, without wanting to get all *Bachelor Nation* about the whole thing,

Hey, Peaches, what do you say we get hitched and spend the rest of our lives together?

She said, *Sure.*

And then off we went to Ireland.

Three nights on the Aran Islands, one night on each, and in each the desolation and antiquity of the islands, their absence of vegetation, the ornate, nearly baroque complexity of the stone walls that subdivided up tiny immemorial plots of the islands for grazing, mostly unused at this point, the tiny fishing villages. The lingering shadow, like some whiff of an eclipse, that was the primeval Hibernian land of clans and warlords, the good-humored Celtic mythology, it was ever present. It was hard not to get brilliant photographs. But it was Inishmaan, the middle island, that had the most impact. We stayed, while there, in a sort of souped-up brutalist *cuisine destination* lodging, which was about as much characteristic of the Aran Islands as a chicken farm would be in Beverly Hills, and though it didn't have the word *folly* in the title, it should have, and the fact that our room was paid for by a council on Irish tourism made the proprietor dislike us somehow, us *rich entitled Yanks*. But how invalid were we, in wanting to come here to this land, for a mere span of days, to learn something about our Irish heritage in the *Gaeltacht*? That some coward a hundred or more years ago couldn't live through a bit of a potato famine and shipped off for New York City, leaving behind his poor and meager family, failing to send back American currency now and again, was that our responsibility? Was he not still Irish? And here we were back again wanting to take a few photos of the locals, and yet not willing, by virtue of congenital alcoholism, to go to the pub, did that make us less Irish?

Look, the whole mystique of the Aran Islands, an exporter of Irish speakers to the Irish mainland for more than a hundred years, is owing to one writer, really, and that writer was J. M. Synge, the playwright of *The Playboy of the Western World*, who first came to the Aran Islands to perfect his Irish in the mid-1890s (after his first attack of

Hodgkin's disease), and then every summer thereafter for five years, he stayed mainly in Inishmaan, in a little cottage, where there is a sort of J. M. Synge historic tour that you can take. It's sort of the only thing to do on the island, by way of an official tour (unless you want to see the sweater factory, which we did too). There's a woman whose family owned the Synge cottage after Synge did, and she gives you the whole spiel and points to the fireplace that he used, and maybe that's the bedpan that he used, and so on, and because I had been reading the very extraordinary *Aran Islands* by J. M. Synge on the trip over, I was very interested in all of this local detail, but, in truth, it was a tiny little cottage in which no more than six or seven could comfortably sit and be lectured, and it was hard for me to believe that the vast majority of Irish or European visitors (most of whom went to Inishmore, the big island, and called it a day) felt that the lecture at Synge's cottage, however well-meaning, was much more than the tourism equivalent of cod liver oil. We stayed till the end, and I introduced myself to the lady who did the lecturing, who was very kind, and who, I think, mainly came back to do the tours in the pleasant part of summer, and it was she who told us that Synge actually had a sort of an aerie up on the cliffs; Corough, I think the area is called, from which you could see, across a turbulent strait of water, Inishmore, next over, and there Synge betook himself to work, presumably on days that were fair enough, and no one bothered him at all. This I can assure you was true. No one bothered you on Inishmaan at all, *anywhere*, but especially not on the aerie of J. M. Synge, a sort of limestone throne, surrounded all around by loose rock and the thunderous assault of waves, and nothing else, nor man nor beast.

The lady at the cottage further alerted us that from there you could walk down the coastline of Inishmaan, to the completely unsettled far end of Inishmaan, and you could find at the end of the island, where the limestone was most pitted by the eroding action of saltwater and nonstop rain and dispiriting temperatures, *blowholes* in terraces of rock there, through which, if the ocean cooperated, there would be these geysers. You didn't have to tell me about this twice.

All the best places I have seen in the world—Iceland, the Southern Alps of New Zealand, the Four Corners of the Southwest, Marfa, Texas, the farthest-out coast of Maine, the White Mountains of New Hampshire, Wyoming, the Sonoran Desert—have been places that have the fewest marks of civilized humankind, and most geological activity, but the irony is that I never feel like I have truly seen them if unaccompanied. I need my desolation to be experienced in tandem, which is to say, I suppose, that desolation is a thing best experienced in love. It's too bad about J. M. Synge having to go up on the cliffs by himself every day. I was much more glad that I had a confederate in Laurel, a fellow adventurer, and the farther out we walked, and the more we wended around completely unfenced cliffsides, the more we watched the restless waves lash the edges of Inishmaan, the more I loved doing it with Laurel. We had been through a lot trying to get our Irish trip to cohere with what we imagined a travel magazine would want of our trip, and now, in walking away from the chic gastronomical resort, we were avoiding our professional responsibilities, and getting, instead, in the very limestone of Inishmaan, not only the true story of Ireland, its Irish and Celtic stony despair, but also a founding moment for our upcoming marriage, this trip into unspoiled perfection.

It was hard to know, from a distance, if you had really seen a *blowhole*, because there was no sign that said *blowhole this way*, in either Irish or English. Nor were there any roads, down which the cottage lady might have directed us. No, the directions were something like, *Go all the way down to the southernmost end and there are some blowholes down there.* The accent sort of made the word *blowhole* difficult to evaluate at first. It sounded almost prurient. But we made this long journey, and every so often, a half a mile ahead, or so, we'd see a pair of Norwegians, let's say, with backpacks, who had also decided that Inishmore, the big island, was *too easy*, and they wanted to know where the real Ireland was.

I cannot exactly describe the *blowhole* phenomenon in a way that will do it complete justice (inexpressibility!), because what this kind of odyssey is is to a place that's without language, in the sense that, like Abe Burickson pursuing his dervishing in Istanbul, if you can call it by a name, it's not exactly a complete spiritual experience, but upon the southerly plain of Inishmaan, a tiny island to the west of Éire, where they still speak a beautiful old language with a lot of silent consonants, there is a spot where the very fabric of the island itself merges with the waves, in the sense that the waves and land become one undulation of the material world, a mutual interdependence; the wave travels up against the coast, and then it disappears into the mottled limestone, and, at a completely different spot, suddenly there erupts another convulsion of saltwater, and it's not that it's as grand as Geysir in Iceland, or any such phenomena in the Rocky Mountains, that's not what's perfect about it, it's not that it must be for such a vast majority of the year unobserved. It's that the sea and the islands are heedless of Ireland and all of its heartbroken history, its violent convulsions of independence, its frequently conservative religious ideals, its small-town enmities, its alcoholism, its big-hearted bonhomie, its hospitality, its unparalleled enthusiasm, its capacity for mourning, and its music. The sea and the islands don't give a shit about Ireland, or about American tourists, their action is far too ancient and regular for all of that, and for a split second, on a blustery, perfect, and sun-dappled day, I got to see that with the woman who was shortly going to be my wife, to watch it, to watch it again, to watch it reproduce its immemorial show, in a way that would still be happening long after we were here to watch.

These are among the memories that we tell, and retell, sometimes altering them perhaps, sometimes doing our best to clear away the artifice and leave them as close to the truth as we can get them, each of us sometimes wanting to be the weaver of tales, each of us occasionally letting the other do the work. Stories are the thing, sometimes, that distracts, and leavens, and mollifies, and comforts. Maybe in this way the marriage is created by the stories, rather than the stories being created by the marriage. Maybe there is no marriage until there are the stories of the marriage, an agreement about what are the narrative contents of the marriage, what are the valuable tales, rich in laughter and sobbing, which reflect and construct the participants of the marriage, define them in relationship to one another. If you can't *tell* of a marriage, it doesn't yet exist.

September 2014

We hadn't even paid for one IVF cycle, and we were already in the red, just for all the testing and the medication for Laurel's IUI cycles, and we had been looking at various new clinics, and we knew that unreimbursed IVF cycles were many, many thousands of dollars, it was going to become astronomically more difficult to pay thereafter, with the later cycles.

Neither of us had the money.

I decided that I would inquire into whether my father would help us fund the first IVF cycle.

It would probably take an entire book to detail in full why I dislike asking my father, or anyone else, for monetary gifts, so you will simply have to believe me when I say that it's up there on the list with calling the Internal Revenue Service, or defending religion from its critics.

Were I to say that I simply like standing on my own feet, that I have done so since I left my full-time publishing job in 1991, I would be understating the intensity of my feeling. I don't want anybody feeling like they can call the tune. I don't like being patronized. I don't like owing people favors, I like the feeling that I somehow figured out how to get by without help, even if I only *just* got by. In the later nineties, when a certain muckraker liked to publish *gossip items* about how I was just a rich banker's son, I never bothered to point out just how underfunded, just how barren was the larder, at the home of the rich banker's son; the enmities of class are a thing that keeps people sharp, and protesting about them has never won a child of privilege a single ally.

But there was sort of no other way that we could afford the IVF cycle. It was give up on having a child together, or ask for help.

It happened that it was the weekend we were visiting my family, in August 2014, and Laurel was intensely uncomfortable, distraught even, after what we'd just been through, and in lieu of weeping all day was sort of ghostly, as if partway into another dimension, a shimmering indigo-hued dimension of loss. She was a hologram of herself. Trying her best, but racked with sorrow. It was my fault for thinking that she could trust my family to comfort her, because there are kinds of hardship that are too hard for any but the most intimate of friends and family. My family was most experienced at the stiff upper lip, and offering a few scabrous jokes about how awful things were.

Comfort was in distraction, not in any specific language of comfort. In fact, Laurel is and was best comforted by her mother, in my experience. My family, however much they cared, and I think they do, were going to have a hard time helping her.

I determined that I would take a walk with my father to describe the IVF problem with him, and this I must have done, therefore, by leaving Laurel to fend for herself for an hour or so. At that time I didn't really like leaving her alone at all. It was not our way to leave each other alone that much. I think in the years that we have been married, that I have failed to be in Laurel's company overnight no more than five or ten times, and they were all in 2013–14, and not very many since at all. We just spent most of our time together.

But I took the walk with my dad, around the airstrip on the west end of Fishers Island, a neighborhood near the ferry dock that is mostly quiet, and somewhat overgrown with wild raspberries and poison ivy. We talked about this and that, nothing serious, for a long portion of the walk, and then I finally had to bring up my particular problem. I went into some description of what our problem was, that we deeply wanted to have a child, but for some reason continued to be unable to do so. I told my dad about the twin boys, and the girl embryo before the twins, and all the surgeries, and so on, and then I told him that at this new clinic we were looking into they had a three cycle package for about the price of a new car, not a domestic model, for a slightly reduced fee. This fee was exclusive of medication, some of which would be covered and some wouldn't. I told him our statistical likelihood of getting pregnant on one cycle was roughly 30 percent.

I asked him if he would help us pay for the first cycle.

It was possible to do all this, to have this conversation, and at the same time to be very uncertain about whether this was the right thing to do. Why allow one's parents into this anguish? Why not, when they were in their late seventies, just let them go along thinking most things were mostly all right?

My father said he didn't think the odds were so great.

He said he'd be happy to help, but that the odds weren't so good.

It wasn't that we hadn't thought about the odds, of course, it was that in our fervent wish to try to get to a pregnancy as the possible way to overcome the missed miscarriages, the repeated losses, we didn't dwell on the statistical likelihoods. We did what was next, though sometimes a question might have been valid; but like a gambler on the table chasing the one big payout, we kept at it. I didn't know how to put this into language for my father exactly. Some of it was hard to talk about. He said he would give us the money. Or, at least, he would give us what he could.

The trip was worth it for this conversation, but it wasn't easy for Laurel. Neither of us liked spending too much time in my former house, on Fishers Island, now my dad's house (because he'd sold his and bought mine from me when I bought in Dutchess County). There had been a period when she and I were first dating, first spending real time together, when we made absurd numbers of trips to Fishers Island, just the two of us, in the deepest of the off-season, and wandered around there almost entirely ignored. (No one is completely ignored in the off-season, especially not if you are a "summer person" by association who has the temerity not to confine your trips to the warmer months, but still.) It is a time I really look back on with wistfulness. Not only because our lives are more encumbered now, or because there's a way that all of our trafficking with the medical establishment made us less carefree, but simply because it was the beginning of knowing Laurel, and as with all such things, there was a storied quality to the beginning of the time with her that has to do with a different Fishers Island, a Fishers Island with different coordinates, and going back there now feels disappointing, because it doesn't conform to the memories. I suppose, at this point, it would be accurate to say I can no longer bear Fishers Island, its pink and yellow and green, its loafers without socks, its privilege, its insularity, its political conservatism, its alcoholism, its ethnic and religious monochrome, its shortage of human kindness. I wrestled with Fishers Island, for twelve years, and then I moved on.

In the meantime, in September 2014, with enough money for one cycle in hand (and the intense gratitude that one would associate with such a gift), we decided to try a new reproductive endocrinologist. Specifically, we went with a guy attached to one of the really high-end clinics. We didn't know if we could possibly find a home there. But the doctor came highly recommended from a friend, and there was already a whole online group dedicated to nearly profane worship of his skills and kindness. The story of how this friend recommended him goes like this. One night I was performing at a gig in Westchester with a bunch of people, including the friend, who is a pianist and singer-songwriter, and Laurel and I needed a ride back from the gig, and she offered. Her car, it seemed to us, had great character, and definitely more than a hundred thousand miles on it, and at many points along the journey I worried if the car was going to make it. At last she dropped us in Park Slope, in front of our building, and then, when she attempted to restart the car after we got out, the car did nothing at all. The engine failed to turn over. We somehow helped to slay our friend's car.

She was nothing if not resourceful, though, and called a car service in Brooklyn, and asked if they could send someone to find us with jumper cables. Who knew you could call a car service and ask them to bring jumper cables? It was a brilliant solution. But the car service took a while. And somehow because I knew or had been told about our friend's manifold problems having a baby, somehow we got on the subject.

If her car had started easily, we never would have found our doctor.

(By the way, the jumper cables worked.)

The clinic she sent us to had quotations from Gandhi and Nelson Mandela on the wall in the waiting room, as though their desire to have people *relax* in the reproductive process was so immense that they would do anything to keep you calm and reflective. I think Laurel had to have a couple of exams by herself at first, while I waited in the lounge and compulsively ate these European tea cookies that they kept there for the patients. Laurel did in fact come out from these initial appointments raving about Dr. W.

If there is a passage of unalloyed joy in this account, a moment when the suffering is commuted unmistakably, so that we might reflect on good fortune in hard times, this is that moment, and it has to do with our doctor.

Simply experiencing in treatment a modicum of human dignity at this point would have been immense. Because the vast majority of news in a fertility clinic is bad news, you would think the medical professionals associated with such a clinic would have been educated into the nuances of dealing with people who have gone through many instances of bad luck, and who are reeling from it. And yet as the simplest possible way, the most convenient way, is to deny the full expression of consciousness to another human being, in order not to have to feel what another human being is feeling, we had grown used to this, used to peremptory and unfeeling examinations and consultations with the doctors in the fertility field, many of whom couldn't remember having seen us before, or had nothing new to say about our case, and whose utmost accomplishment was to be found in a bland and emotionally detached professionalism.

And then we met Dr. W.

As a practical matter, one doesn't really understand some particular kinds of suffering, indignities verging on episodes of suffering, or indistinguishable therefrom, until the indignities stop. And so with Dr. W., who is really good at breaking down the highly complex world of assisted reproductive services such that it is manageable and doable, we didn't understand entirely how much pain we had been in until he opened his mouth. He just manages to seem incredibly sympathetic without showboating, without overstating the case ever.

He always referred to Laurel as "Mizzzzzzz Nakadate!" Like it was a euphonious name that should be undertaken with great care and jovial, avuncular respect. And he always spoke really slowly, and looked her in the eye, and came up with plans for treatment in a collaborative way. He was young (by my standards, maybe in his early forties), with short brown hair, and occasional eyeglasses, and he looked far younger. He was skinny, and always in scrubs, spoke with a certain kind of offhanded med school grace, but always with the indication of sympathy and an understanding of the traumatic events that brought the people to his door. He was, is, a relentless empiricist, all about the numbers and angles and probabilities, and at the end of the day this might have been his genius, the numbers and probabilities, but with us, and, as far as we can tell, with all of his patients, he manages to keep the numbers and probabilities offstage, in what is primarily a human interaction, sort of in the way that Oliver Sacks always understood the struggle of neurologically afflicted people to be a struggle for self-respect and dignity. Dr. W., in our particular case, always referred to a successful pregnancy as "our goal," meaning the goal of himself and the team of Laurel and myself, as when, for example, a certain test might answer some questions "but will not get us any closer to our goal." And the objective for treatment, every appointment, every day, for the many months that we worked with Dr. W., was always getting closer to "our goal."

He had a wife and kid himself, and was often flying back to Taiwan to see parents and relatives; also, he had and has one of the most unimpeachable reputations in fertility treatment in New York City, where there are a great number of people receiving treatment. And despite all of this Dr. W. never failed to answer an email message, no matter whether day or night or weekend or otherwise. This is perhaps to get him in hot water for people out there hoping to get in touch with the guy, but Laurel frequently would become anxious or have a question during off-hours, and while trying not to overburden Dr. W. would sometimes ask him a question when he might have been home with his family, and not one time did he ever fail to answer. No question was unreasonable, and no feeling was unwarranted. As Dr. W. told Laurel on one occasion: "My patients often have posttraumatic feelings." He said it like he said everything else, with irreducible clarity. Excepting the original intake meeting, he didn't belabor appointments, but, at the same time, he never failed to have a complete interaction, and never failed to manage the easygoing charm and the sly wit.

To wake to a practice like this after three different practices where we felt like we were being treated like petri dishes that unfortunately had human anatomical bits attached was to feel waves of hope.

Without going too far down into the nuances of IVF

treatment, it's fair to say that Dr. W. had one particular area of expertise that most or many reproductive endocrinologists think is debatable, and that is autoimmune disorders. In short, Dr. W. felt that Laurel had an autoimmune problem wherein her body treated the embryo like a foreign body and very quickly wiped it out. It may have had to do with her thyroid, which she began treating more aggressively while under Dr. W.'s care. Whatever was causing the autoimmune difficulties, he wanted to treat it, and so Laurel began with a certain medication well-known to television viewers, where it is frequently advertised as a treatment for a great variety of autoimmune disorders. She later tried a different medication of a similar cast.

Throughout August and into September the only way to work through the ache of what we had gone through with the twins in July was to turn ourselves over to the reproductive endocrinologist called Dr. W., and to let the process take place, including the barrage of testing and the medicating, and to see what happened. We stopped talking to our families, who knew better than to ask, after the twins, and we stopped talking to our friends about it, and this is the way that infertility becomes a disease of silence, because it doesn't do to get too hopeful publicly, and because every individual fertility event has its potential for failure. It's stupid to encourage other people to try to encourage *you*, by giving them ammunition for their vacuous if well-meaning encouragements. We stopped talking about it, and in fact this is the first time I have talked about our time in the wilderness of fertility treatment in any detail.

Even in the context of being married there was some hurt in the process of fertility treatment that didn't always get expressed, because it was sort of in the category of things that we knew about each other, and so why get into it? Ideally, marriages should make room for this pain, should include discussion of this shared pain, but I like to think that holding the other person is good enough. Maybe just *hold the person* and talk about it all another time, so that there are moments of relief from the obligation to confess. But sometimes we were both so hurt that even bringing it up caused further pain. Looking back now, I wish I could have done better at listening, so that it was easier for Laurel to talk, and I'd be remiss if I didn't catalogue that among my regrets.

It was somewhere in this becoming of autumn that I decided I had to sell the Charles Manson autograph. Or get rid of it somehow. Whatever it took. It is true that I never totally believed the Charles Manson autograph was cursed, because what kind of curse is transmissible from party to party? You could make an argument that anyone who was stupid enough to keep a Charles Manson autograph in the house deserves to be cursed, and there may be validity to this point of view. I suppose I don't believe in curses at all, excepting the completely literary sort that you see in the Gothic novel. Those seem like oneiric representations of a feeling that a person might have about her or his life, that life is a sequence of bad luck events. In literature, *time* will do all of these horrible things to you, because time is no respecter of individualism, or even human subjectivity.

But the whole punitive concept of a curse related to the Manson autograph wouldn't keep me from getting rid of it. I was, because I had obtained the Manson autograph in a trade, intending to trade it to someone else, perhaps someone who would appreciate it. And so there was a week of perusing these websites that are set up and maintained by people who collect autographs of mass murderers and serial killers, in an attempt to ascertain the market for my autograph. And it seemed there were a lot of his autographs floating around out there. Maybe it's a prison thing, and maybe he obtained some advantage in the interior of his prison space, for doling out a certain number of autographs annually. Whatever the reason for the proliferation of Manson autographs online, the fact was that my Manson autograph was not worth that much, and I would really need to find just the right collector in order to get a reasonable return.

I could have just thrown it out, of course, and then in this chapter I could have reflected upon just the right place to throw it out.

But it seemed more sporting, given how I obtained the autograph in the first place, to try to find someone else who wanted it. That would thrust me out into the world of people trying to own paintings of Twisty the Clown.

However, Laurel did have a friend who worked at Amoeba Music in Los Angeles, possibly the best record store in America, and this friend, who knew everything about music, seemed to want the Charles Manson autograph. He was a collector of serial killer memorabilia. I don't know how the subject came up, but this friend did want to get just the right piece of vinyl for me from Amoeba Records in return for surrendering my Charles Manson autograph, and eventually what he came up with was a comedy recording from the beatnik period called *How to Speak Hip*. The album is pretty rare, despite being important to Brian Wilson, who gave the album a shout-out during the *Pet Sounds* sessions. It's a comedy album about beatniks, really. The copy I got was missing the inner sleeve, I think, and was lightly foxed, as the book collectors say. But what I got for it was the privilege of ridding myself of Charles Manson and his autograph.

As it happens, this week, three years after the trade of the Manson postcard for *How to Speak Hip*, in a class I now teach at Brown University, we discussed the differences between fate and magic, and whether fate presupposes a controlling hand, and an author, in order for it to take place. When Oedipus is fated in Greek drama, we know that the gods have made it so. But what about elsewhere? Does it make any logical sense in an empiricist present, or even in a liberal Protestant present, to believe that there is a destined quality to the turn of human events? Isn't it sort of unrealistic to think this way? Baseball teams often seem to want to be the team of destiny as long as they're winning, but what if they're not winning?

There's a moment in Boccaccio's *Decameron* where a certain nobleman is riding along the road one night, accompanied by a trio of blackguards who are about to deprive him of his clothes and his riches, and they ask him to whom he prays when traveling, and then they discuss these prayers for a while, before the nobleman is robbed by the blackguards, at which point they say something like: *What good are your prayers now, sucker? We didn't pray at all, and we're going to have a good time tonight with all your money!*

In August, or was it early September, I traded away the Charles Manson item, and got the *How to Speak Hip* album, and at that point if I were legitimately cursed, or if Laurel and I were legitimately cursed, we might have ventured to believe that our luck was finally to improve. Or that fate would turn in our direction. That September, my daughter first ventured into the New York City public school system without incident, and then I started back at the NYU writing program where I taught in those days, and we did a lot of medical testing for an upcoming IVF cycle, and I took a lot of fish oil vitamins, and Laurel took some immune suppressing medication, and we lived life for thirty days, and it was fine. Maybe sometimes autumn *is* simply just another season.

October 2014

October, when you come around now, you're like a houseguest I don't like very much. There's a dread when the weather turns to you, when the leaves go past their peak and amass on the lawn, when the seasonal migration passes overhead and leaves behind a hush in its wake, when the crickets fall silent, when there's the first frost. It's four years later now, and I still hate the sight of you, October. Going back to the year in question, to the beginning of the second year of our marriage, even now, brings about your dying off of leaves and vegetation, brings about your chill, and an anxiety about your grim and whispered secrets. I wish I didn't have to compile (in this longish chapter) all that you brought to the surface.

In the midst of this routine academic year that began in the fall of 2014, with all the driving to New Haven to teach at Yale, and back to NYC, Laurel was beginning our first round of IVF, and we did all the preparation in the first half of the month. There were so many pieces of paper to sign, and so much talk with nurses. We were back and forth to the clinic, as they showed us how the shots were supposed to be administered. I mean, they actually had us depress syringes, in mock preparation. Laurel was keeping up with it all, with the flows of acronyms and prescriptions and treatment protocols, but it was a big tightly wound ball of worry for me, especially the shots. I was supposed to be helping with the shots when the time came, especially the booster the night before transfer, which had to go into the muscle of her shoulder. Laurel was more uncomfortable with the ones in the stomach, which we started then, in October, and for a while I administered the shots in the stomach. It's both horrifying, and, after a point, mundane, to be jabbing needles into your wife's abdomen. I think we kept it all secret from Hazel, my daughter, and would wait for her to go to sleep or until she was off to school. Then all the medical paraphernalia came out, spread on the kitchen table like we were hitting the opiates hard. Laurel was trying to stay serene on all the meds, and the immune suppressors she was on, and we spent a lot of time watching mindless television at night. I have never seen as much of *The Bachelor* as I saw during that period. For a while, I was fully informed about *The Bachelor*, *Bachelor in Paradise*, and *Teen Mom*.

We owed my mother a visit in October. My mother was still in Bucks County, and we hadn't been out in far too long. I got a distress call from my brother asking if we would make the trip, as my mother had been asking for me, and I agreed. Laurel was willing to accompany me on what was going to be anything but an easy trip. My brother said my stepfather was not really able to follow a conversation anymore. He quoted my stepfather as having said to him, "I know you're in charge now . . ."

Despite my lackluster recent performance as my mother's firstborn son, which I normally attributed to my constant travel and my young child, I had and have now a significant emotional bond with my mother. My mother's situation, her immobility by reason of caretaking, causes me great heartache when I think about it too much, it is like a frozen subterranean aquifer of despair in me, and I was worried that the trip to Bucks County would just be too difficult for me, and for Laurel in a delicate moment. I suppose that was why I had put it off. Where they lived, in a subdivision in Doylestown, right near the highway, in one of those condos that seem designed to appeal to twenty-somethings with 2.2 children and minivans, inevitably made me feel like chewing my arm off and dashing into the woods to do some kind of naked, bloodcurdling self-sacrifice. The two feelings orbited around each other like roosters in a cockfight: intense protective feelings about my mother, and the desire to avoid her situation wherever possible. Even getting there was horrible, there was no interstate to Doylestown from New York City, you could go only partway, and then you had the endless slog through county roads for most of the last third. Inevitably you were driving behind a truck bearing a load of hay bales. This was my heritage, this was the woman who brought me into the world, and this was where she lived.

So we headed down, intending to meet my brother there.

The dinner the first night was not without its challenges. We went to a perfectly nice restaurant in downtown Doylestown, where the young and energetic professionals and the affluent families of Bucks County went to find others of their kind, but it was in that location that the scale of my stepfather's disassociation was now apparent. He would occasionally bust into the conversation for a balefully incoherent rejoinder, some tangle of grammatical units that seemed to resemble syntax but did not entirely, and then just as quickly he faded out, which would leave a fault line of muted shock in the discussion where he had been. He had to be coached through the menu ordering and didn't entirely know what to do with the silverware and the other tools of restaurant-visiting. And I could see my mother buoyed by our presence, and trying to make the most of it, having both of her children at hand, in the midst of this hardship. But it was impossible to keep the conversation going, as if we were all hiking on one of those incredibly steep hikes in which you have to keep quiet to manage the task. Periodically, from amid the lapsed banter, Laurel would venture a question, like: *Peggy, what have you guys been watching on TV lately?* Or something equally innocuous and preliminary, and we would head off trying to lasso a few sentences around the topic before giving up. But I found myself losing a grip on the necessity of talk, so overwhelming was it.

When we got back from dinner, Ken, my stepfather,

was exhausted, and we were exhausted, too, and we all hit the pillow fast, in my case only to spend most of the night unable to sleep.

The next morning, we determined we should take my mother's rambunctious golden retriever on a bit of a run to the park nearby, and this was in part to get some fresh air and some change of scene. But the second we slipped out the door with the dog, we noticed that Ken, my stepfather, was making a beeline after us. Not to be left behind. I think he was so attached to the dog that he didn't want anyone to spirit away his esteemed companion, and he therefore wanted to make sure we were to be trusted with it. I should add that he had no idea who Laurel was, though he had been introduced to her multiply over the last three years, and he had been at our wedding. And he didn't have any idea what my name was anymore, though he seemed to recognize that I had something to do with my mother. The dog was the only one going on the walk he knew at all well, but he seemed to want to go with us nonetheless, so out we went into the dewy October morning in the subdivision, over to the park—my wife, my mother's ninety-pound golden retriever, and my very impaired stepfather.

That was one incredible park. Enormous, first of all, and it had a bunch of discrete ecosystems, a variety of outdoor opportunities, including this children's play area that was an *actual castle*. It was one-quarter scale, let's say, but otherwise it looked exactly like a castle. We took the golden retriever out to the meadow by the castle, where I tried to run him around until his tongue was hanging out. Ken stood there, perhaps anxious, but waiting. He said almost nothing. Laurel and I were in one of those situations in which we became even more closely allied as a team, in which no one is really going to be able to find the prover-bial daylight between us, and that was just kind of how it was. I felt lucky to have her there with me, because I had mostly treated my familial pain as something that I had to deal with by myself. But she came, and helped, and she didn't ask for anything in return, which is the definition of a legitimately excellent partner. We walked back from the park with Ken, had some breakfast, hugged my mom, and bantered a bit, and then we got in the car.

Because: it happened we had to drive to Saratoga Springs that night. In fact, it was destined to be a long day, because we were supposed to drive to Saratoga Springs, and I was meant to do a performance at a club there, and then we were going to turn around after the gig and drive back to Dutchess County. It was something on the order of six hours of driving or so over the course of the day, with a performance in the middle.

It was like this. I was asked if I would perform with this band called Cuddle Magic. (Performance, in this case, meant: would I read some stuff with musical backing.) I had written about Cuddle Magic before, and there were a number of reasons why I really liked Cuddle Magic. One of the reasons was that the lyrics were mostly written by a photographer I really liked, who has occasionally been mentioned in these pages, Tim Davis. He was Laurel's friend too. They went to the Yale School of Art together, where, as the legend goes, the crits were so cruel that even

Tim Davis cried at one point. This is perhaps apocryphal. You would know how improbable this is if you knew how admirably tough and resilient is Tim Davis. I don't know if this is true, that he cried, or if it's just to prove how hard the crits are, but that's the story. Tim was a poet before he was a photographer, and there is a conceptual brilliance to his work that emerged in his poetry first. And he's married to one of the best painters of her generation, Lisa Sanditz. They have a son who is just a bit younger than my daughter, and we see them now and again. Once we all trespassed at the Omega Institute upstate and swam in their pond.

Tim's brother Ben is one of the main songwriters in Cuddle Magic, and Tim and Ben collaborate on the lyrics. Tim's lyrics are both beautifully composed and acerbic, but somehow Ben, maybe because he's Tim's brother, can really sing them with real conviction, even though they are emotionally complex and sometimes circuitous. The rest of the band is remarkably inventive too. Ian Spiegelman plays winds and does a lot of the business stuff, and it was he who asked me to come along and wrote some music to go underneath my few short things. And then they have a singer called Kristin Slipp, whose range of skills is sort of not possible to itemize, so vast is it. She can sing jazz, standards, new music, anything else, and has extended vocal technique at her disposal too. And Christopher McDonald and Dave Flaherty and Cole Kamen-Green fill out the ensemble, and they all seem to be able to play anything and everything. They all met at music school and their original ambition was to play as quietly as possible. They had, at the time of this event in

Saratoga, just released an album collaborating with a toy pianist called Phyllis Chen, and she was to play on the bill as well. Everything about this group of people was what I loved about music at this point, shifting time signatures, rhythmically complex pieces with simple arrangements, lots of analog instrumentation, complex vocal arrangements, and just really great songs. I would have hurdled a great number of hurdles to be on that stage that night. Just being around Cuddle Magic when they played amounted to some of the most fun I've had as a performer.

That the gig happened the same weekend as this trip to see my mother and stepfather was not ideal. The drive from Doylestown to Saratoga was really long, and I felt so down about my mother's situation that mainly what I wanted to do was crawl underneath a rock somewhere and brood. Also, I had this inkling that the ticket sales for the Cuddle Magic gig were not as good as I had hoped, and Laurel had to have an injection in the stomach that night, and it was unclear how everything was going to get done and at what hour we were going to get home to our place in Dutchess County.

Because I have a lot of friends in Saratoga Springs, I knew we could expect to field a decently populated dinner at the all-natural café in town, and after sound check we went over to this health food joint, and we were having a quiet dinner with our friend Marc and the rest of the band, when we realized, or remembered, or had it dawn upon us, that it was time to give Laurel the shot. We reminded each other covertly, meaning we were not exactly going to broadcast it, and then we got up from the table and we snuck into the bathroom in the Four Seasons Café together; it was around a corner, hidden away, so I don't think anyone knew exactly our strange purpose, but we went into the tiny bathroom together, and I stuck the hypodermic in, depressed the plunger, as I'd been trained to do.

The concert I was in town for was, it's true, poorly attended. It was one of these cases wherein I realized, yet again, that often many of the things that are really important to me are only admired by groups of twos and threes. I remember being on a book tour once and a media escort told me that a certain popular writer of that moment had expressed great outrage when a reading he gave had only a hundred people at it. Many have been the readings when I have yearned for a hundred people! A sense of entitlement about audience gets farther and farther away the older I get, and I repeatedly find myself moved and delighted in crowds that are only modest at best. There were maybe fifty people at the show, that night, and we did the first set, and the promoter fellow urged us not to take a long break between sets, but we kind of did anyway, and there were even fewer people for the second set. As far as I was concerned, there were a lot of people I liked personally there, and they were dancing some of the time, even to the challenging time signatures, and I felt like the bits that I performed, especially as contrasts with the excellent music of Cuddle Magic and Phyllis Chen, were reasonably successful and didn't really sound like anything else. I felt like it was one of those nights on which my only real regret was that I didn't get to do it again the next night, and the night after that. I caused Laurel to stay till the very end, and she was cranky about it, but then we thanked the band, said goodbye to all our Saratogian friends lingering around the doorway to the venue where this was all taking place (a former church), and then we got back in the car to drive to Dutchess County.

My greatest fear, at night in the Northeast, was another deer strike, and by *another* deer strike, I mean that we'd already had one, in the summer of 2013, driving back from a radio fund-raiser in the greater Hudson, New York, area. There was a full moon that night, and maybe the deer were experiencing ecstasy over the lunar display. I remember that Laurel was leaning out of the car window trying to take a photograph of the moon with her iPhone, though everyone knows that is impossible, but we were on one of the two-lane stretches that crisscross the forest-and-agriculture section of Dutchess County, and I think I was not going *that fast*, because if I'd been going fast, Laurel would have had a doe's head in her lap. As I wasn't going fast, I saw the deer at the edge of the underbrush, and shouted *shit!* And I had that moment in which I debated whether to turn hard right to get *behind* the deer if it ran out into the road, or left to try to speed around it before it decided what to do. This is the age-old question of driving on country roads at night. I bet that the deer would not walk out in the road, which means I swerved left, at which point the deer did in fact walk out into the road. I was braking as this happened, and so I think I was probably not exceeding twenty-five miles per hour, or thereabouts, at which point, with the right front headlight and bumper, we gave the deer a rude shove, which caused her to do a sort of double axel on the county road, over and over, scraping herself up horribly, no doubt, after which, pausing only for a moment, she got back up on her feet and with a couple of mighty leaps dove headlong back into the underbrush from which she had come. We pulled the car into the next parking lot, a couple of tenths of a mile down the road, and called the police, who came and ascertained the truth of our story since: a) Laurel had a photograph on her phone of the moon, and the deer coming out onto the road, and b) there were bits of deer fur in the smashed headlight. The highway patrolman said he would have to go look for the deer, and, if she were suffering, dispatch her. We were told by certain friends that deer, even if able to walk away from the accident, sometimes died in the woods of their injuries or from fright. It was the kind of thing I did not want on my conscience ever again.

Accordingly, I was in a panic on this occasion, which is to say driving for two and a half hours in the dark in forested latitudes for a majority of the trip. I have a whole set of rules under which I will drive at night in the country now, and here are some: drive next to the median, not in the right-hand lane. There are fewer deer on the median. Also, use your horn to frighten the deer. They get spooked by loud noise, thus all those deer whistles. And constantly scan the brush at the side of the road. These rules are doubtless ways of feeling falsely reassured, but they are how I get myself home when I have to drive at night. I can remember feeling really horribly tired on the drive in October, seeing a deer in every shrub by the road, with my glasses on, which I almost never wear except at night in the car: *Is that a deer, right there? Is that a deer there?* Grabbing the wheel hard, and letting go, grabbing hard, letting go, trying to keep myself reasonably awake.

We pulled into the driveway about midnight. I was dead on my feet, as the saying goes, when I got out of the car.

Here's an engrossing detail: we'd been having this problem where the garage door occasionally opened by itself. The automatic garage door. This was on the long list of first-world problems, problems that have to do with privilege, with having got a lot of things right with life. But it was also on the long list of things I was somewhat incompetent to fix. Because I am a liability with tools, and am also phobic about telephone calls to anyone handy or construction-oriented, I had not yet ascertained if this problem with the garage door opener was a myth, or something that could be fixed. I didn't yet know if I simply forgot to close the garage door. I pay very little attention to the practical, on-the-ground issues in my life. I can go a month without thinking about whether I should water a plant, or change a sheet, or take a vitamin. I just don't think about these things. Is there a dead limb on the tree in the yard? I might get to that at some point in the next *five years*. And it's not that I expect someone else to do these things for me, because that would horrify me; it is more that my relatively minimal capabilities in the areas of practical world skills just don't improve, as I grow older (though I wish they would). Thus: it was very possible that, when the garage door appeared to be open, as it did from time to time, I had forgotten to close it on the way out of town. I had occasionally pondered whether someone in the neighborhood had a garage door opener that worked with a similar frequency, who was somehow inadvertently able to open ours. Or maybe the guy who cut the lawn somehow triggered the garage door. Or maybe the garage door simply malfunctioned from time to time. I just was far more likely to be thinking about Flaubert, or Virginia Woolf, or that obscure British prog band called Gentle Giant, than I was to think about why the garage door was occasionally open. Since there was really no one in the hamlet of Amenia, excepting a few trailer park residents down the road some, I never worried particularly about the garage door being open. There was a bike in there, maybe two, and some rusty hand tools, a rake, and that was all. There was nothing to take.

Therefore on the night in question, dead on my feet, I noticed that the garage door was open, and I made a mental note to do something about the garage door, though apparently I had made that mental note before without following up. The list of things I had done nothing about (the lightbulb at the top of the second-floor stairs, the mice in the mailbox, the roof tiles on the shed, the rusty metal pipe that protruded in the backyard, the dribbling outdoor faucet whose shut-off valve I could not ascertain) was very long.

Laurel was still in the car when I reached the door that led into her office from the garage (it was the mud room, in effect, but also her office, which was sort of a sore spot as far as she was concerned), and noticed that, oddly enough, there was the male end of an extension cord protruding through the very slightly opened door into the house.

All of this next moment is slowed down with the retrospection that one brings to bear at these critical junctures. The next moment is like one of those dreams that mix up cause and effect. Interminably, then, I was having that instant of recognition: *There's no way I left that extension cord like that, hanging out of the door.* I am capable of any number of completely stupid and vacuous episodes of being in my daily life, as you no doubt know by now. Nevertheless, I have a bunch of rote activities that are performed with a stolid sameness, and one of these is closing the door carefully on the way out.

I looked at the male end of the extension cord, which I think was yellow.

I looked at the slightly open door, which had that quality that I associate in memory now with that famous Samuel Beckett stage direction: *door imperceptibly ajar.*

I pushed the door open slightly.

I pushed the door open slightly some more. Whereupon I reached up and turned on the light switch on the wall, and the room, Laurel's office, was illuminated.

The next garbled thought that occurred to me was something along the lines of: *A hurricane has blown through the house.* And when that seemed improbable I tried on the following: *A wild animal has gotten into the house.*

Because I could see through Laurel's office down the hall past the bathroom and into the kitchen, these things being in a straight line from where I was standing, I could see that everything that had been on a shelf or in a closet between myself and the kitchen had been liberated from these spots of stowage, and was now strewn onto the floor of the house. The technical term forming in my mind was: *ransacked.*

And that was when I called to Laurel, who was just emerging from the car:

"We've been robbed."

She said, "What?"

I said, "We've had a break-in."

I pushed the door open farther and started up the steps. Laurel, who was now behind me, said: "Where are you going?"

I said, "I'm going in to look."

And I can't tell you exactly what I thought that meant, because I sort of depersonalized at that moment. I stopped having any terribly rational motive, and instead I was having that very writerly thought, which was something like: *Wow, this is kind of exciting, I get to see what a robbery looks like,* as though the robbery had not taken place in my own home, nor involved my own personal effects.

Laurel said, "Get back in the car, we're calling the police."

I paused over this for a long time, because I guessed that the robbery was not taking place in the present instant—the perpetrators had already made off with what-.ever they had wanted—and I couldn't see, really, why we should call the police. I wanted to sort of think about it, and maybe go to bed and call the police in the morning, and, because I try to avoid using the phone, I didn't really *want* to call the police at all. But all of these perceptions were happening at once, were contradictory, irrational, and were an attempt, on my part, to deny or otherwise obfuscate what had clearly taken place, even in this preliminary view, namely that it was not a minor case of someone sneaking in and taking a couple of pieces of electronics before leaving discreetly.

I said to Laurel, "How are we going to do that exactly?"

"You just call the police. That's what we have cell phones for. Get back in the car."

So we got into the car, and locked it, and called the police. It was a sort of homey, rural state police troop two miles down the road that we'd had occasion to enter once, not too many weeks before, when trying to figure out if it was okay to *shoot*—using firearms—some of Laurel's monographs of her photos out in the backyard (though we had no guns with which to do this), and, well, we had been there just eleven months before to find out if it was okay, during our wedding, to park out on the street. On this occasion, we called that very same police station, and then we waited in the car. Within five minutes, because we could see Route 22 from the house, we watched the flashing lights of the police race, at a high speed, in our direction.

Those were moments in which our lives truly changed, in ways never entirely to be undone. Some last bits of trust emptied out of the car into the chilly autumnal night, some ideas of the rural, like that the rural was a welcoming place where life was simpler, these ideas vanished clean away, as we watched the cops barreling up the hill toward our house. Our sense of peace in the house was in the process of being violently obliterated, though we didn't yet know the scale.

A second police car from some other jurisdiction also converged on the scene, and followed the first into our driveway, and then the authorities got out of their cars, and the first thing they needed to do, they told us, was to secure the premises, and they were going to do this by going around the perimeter. So they walked around the perimeter. I don't think any weapons were drawn. Although I remember wondering whether they put their hands on the *outside* of the holster at a moment like this. How did they know the perpetrators were not still there? The one guy with the flashlight walked the perimeter, and I think he presumed that they were gone, but he didn't really know. And then he had to go up to the studio, about thirty yards farther up the hill, to make sure they weren't up there, and it was sort of a long, silent wait while he was off in the woods.

Eventually, the perimeter was secured, to use the procedural terminology, and we were told that the door to the back deck, a French door manufactured by a certain extremely popular maker of such things, was swinging wide, and that this was either the way in or the way out. But we ourselves ingressed through the door from the garage, where the male end of the extension cord was propping open the door imperceptibly ajar, and from there it was into the maelstrom of our unpawnable possessions, which were now *floor items*.

It was frankly impossible to take in the scale of the destruction in a single tour. It was impossible to determine, even, what the motive was, whether it was sheer mayhem, or something more picayune and explicable. It was impossible to determine because *shit was everywhere*. Laurel had a lot of clothes in the closet in her office, for example, because she has a lot of clothes. The closet in question was completely emptied, and all of these clothes were now on the floor. We had to get *over* those clothes just to get to the kitchen. And one of these items, to bring close the heavy reverberations of irony in this moment, was Laurel's wedding dress. It was on the floor in her office.

And the kitchen, once we reached it, was especially appalling. There was an obvious conclusion to be reached upon entering the kitchen, namely that the perpetrators had used the kitchen to make some food for themselves. While visiting. They had cooked a lunch or an early supper for themselves consisting of chicken nuggets. They had gone into the freezer, taken out the chicken nuggets (a food, let me hasten to point out, that neither Laurel nor I ate, as we were both vegetarians, so finding the nuggets must have been hard work), located a frying pan, and then put the nuggets in the pan (instead of microwaving) and heated them conventionally (despite the nearby presence of a microwave oven). The frying pan was still out. They burned something on the electric range, some portion of their not hastily assembled meal, and it had cooked on there, never to be completely erased, and then they threw a bunch of leftovers, leftover nuggets both cooked and uncooked, on the floor, as though, having cooked the nuggets (on the range, not in the microwave) the meal had not satisfied them, and only a childlike tantrum would do. And then they just swept a bunch of things from the freezer, the refrigerator, and various cabinets onto the floor, in a jumble of the perishable and the canned.

The corridor that was visible from garage to kitchen was a welter of these ransacked items, and to step into the corridor was to step into the chaos. The police led us in as though they were the tour guides, wordless docents, just sort of taking it in, waiting for us to say: *No, we don't live like this, this is different.*

And so it went on the basement floor, and on the second floor, where the bedrooms were. They spared exactly one room: my daughter's room. It was sprawling with brightly colored gewgaws of the sort that would appeal to any five-year-old, and it was arrayed as usual, therefore. Was it merciful that she had been spared? This was the sort of thing we brooded about later on. It's worth noting that there was nothing to pawn in my daughter's room. They did, however, take the baby car seat out of the garage. And they left the bikes.

In our bedroom, the thieves went straight for the dressers, and they upended the dressers like they were Cold War–era operatives attempting to locate and pry loose any miniature recording devices. Laurel's underwear was catastrophically strewn about the bedroom floor, for example. There's no shock quite like the shock of seeing that someone has been through your underwear drawer, and that it is now strewn around the bedroom for the local police to witness. And the bathroom came in for a lot of interest too. Both bathrooms, on the first and second floors, were upended and all the contents spread wide across the floor. Probably, the perpetrators were looking for prescription drugs.

Our tour was completed with a trip down to my office

in the basement. It occurred to me about the time we came to linger in the basement level to wonder what exactly was missing. To commence to wonder. This was easier to do in the basement because what was missing was large enough to be obviously absent—for example, all of my musical equipment. There was a lot of stuff strewn on the floor, in the basement as elsewhere, but the corners of the room where my guitars had formerly sat—some in cases, some on stands—were now free of clutter. I had an amp, too, and a wide variety of cheap electronic keyboards, and a violin, and a bunch of percussion instruments, and a melodica, and all of this was gone. I stood there like an idiot with the police, scratching my head, halfheartedly totaling up in my mind what was gone, but without doing anything like a rigorous examination of my remaining possessions. *A lot* was gone.

Back up in the living room, where the French door was wide open, a discussion ensued about how the perpetrators had gotten into the house. The French door had a finicky lock, this was true, but I was highly doubtful that I had left it unlocked. Because, at any rate, if it was unlocked they would have had to have tried all the other doors first, and to have done so repeatedly, in order to be well enough versed in the specifics of our coming and going to spend the afternoon in the house pawing through our things. The police sort of insisted that I had left the door open, though I didn't think so, and there we left off the discussion. The door swung wide, as they went through the house taking pictures, looking at items they might dust for fingerprints, and so on, and in my recollection this period went on for a long time, more than an hour, in the autumn chill of night that had now come to impress itself on the interior of our residence. The shell shock, the sense of trauma that was only beginning to be perceptible, caused me to feel terribly exhausted. I wanted to get the cops *out* of the house and go to sleep, which was utterly ridiculous and contraindicated. Who knew what further traces of the perps were spread wide, disseminated, upon our belongings, which no longer felt like our belongings.

After a while, the cops fell into small talk. One guy said he'd almost hit a buck with some spectacular antlers on the way to the house. I remember one guy saying to another, "I'd bet you anything it's our client down the hill. No doubt about it." They were obviously concealing the particulars, but they already had ideas about who might be responsible.

The mind, in these moments, falls into theorizing, filling in the gaps.

The police asked me to sign a brace of forms, and to sketch out some preliminary narratives about what I thought had taken place, and then, about 2:00 a.m., they readied themselves to do what seemed almost cruel: leave the rest of the story to us. If I had known then how long-standing would be the echoing outward of that night, for Laurel especially, I would have asked for grief counseling or some local specialist in posttraumatic stress disorder. It was Laurel who knew what was obvious—that we couldn't stay in the house that night. I had to teach the next day in New York City in any event. I suppose some college professors would have very reasonably missed class the next day, but I felt (and feel still) like showing up for class keeps me tethered to the world.

We got in the car, therefore, to drive back to Brooklyn, to which we arrived sometime after 4:00 a.m. With just what we had on our persons when we'd left for Pennsylvania, a couple of days before. What a weekend.

The project of itemizing our losses, and trying to figure out how to react, and what to do about our reactions to the burglary, which I had started thinking of as a "home invasion" because of the violence and intensity of the destruction, remained to be worked out. We had a few hours' sleep, to the extent that we could sleep, and I called the insurance company, and agreed to meet them back in Amenia on Tuesday, and then I went off to class. I have probably taught more effectively than I did that day.

The claims adjustor agreed to meet us around 11:00 a.m. on Tuesday. I remember it being a particularly crisp day, and clear, and Laurel and I made the drive back up sort of the way you go to visit the oncologist for the first time after the confirmation of your diagnosis, with a dread and a grief and a clarity about the circumstances. We were going to be there in the daylight, and then we were going to get the heck out of Amenia, and that was that for the time being.

If you thought that we had already seen the worst of the break-in, you would be thinking how we thought about it, that we had already seen the worst, in which the violation was of a scale we could now begin, in some fashion, to narrate, to control. But in thinking this way, the most logical way, we were wrong.

When the police left, two nights before, I had, with

their assistance, closed the French door on the deck and made sure that it was dead-bolted. They had done so because they were trying to figure out whether the door could be pried open from the outside. This was because they believed I had left the door open. But when, at Laurel's suggestion, we went around the perimeter of the house upon arriving again on Tuesday, we found, again, that the porch door was *open*. Which meant not only that it could be opened from the outside (with a crowbar or similar tool), but also that the perpetrators had returned. They had broken in a second time.

We called the police, and the police came again, this time in daylight, and we got busy with all the same rounds that we had made before, except that this time in addition to the chicken nuggets on the floor, and Laurel's underwear strewn wide, we went down to the basement and found that every piece of copper piping in the basement had since been removed, with a hacksaw, from the boiler room, with the result that the water tank had sprung a leak and flooded the basement with water, the basement that had all my papers and books (and formerly my musical instruments), etc. There was even a bootprint *on the wall* of the boiler room, where someone had leaped up to grab some pipes on the ceiling to haul them down. So, in addition to the losses from theft, there were now losses from vandalism.

The second visit from the police had its own theme, different from the first visit, and the theme of the second visit was: *Is there someone who has a vendetta against you?* The destruction was so immense now that it was hard to imagine, for the police, whether mere methamphetamine addicts or heroin addicts or opioid abusers, on the lookout for the quick buck, would possibly vandalize a house on this scale, just for the purpose of funding the next dose. The copper pipes were only worth a couple hundred bucks.

It is a real occasion for reflection in life when you are invited to look back and see if there is someone who might be willing to do you harm. When the police ask you this question it has a bright, menacing aspect that it doesn't have in your own depressive musings. I had to look back, as I had done at various points in my recovery from addiction, to attempt to see all that I had done wrong in my life, and who, of those done wrong, might still be hanging onto it. Or, to put it another way, once you begin this process, you can uncover a great many instances in which you have done things you wish you had not done. The stories spool out in front of you, on a loop.

Faced with the police, I even wondered if my ex-wife wished me harm in this way (unlikely!), and then there were the various affairs, and there were the various husbands and/or partners of other people with whom I had been involved. I could imagine any of them wanting to see me this morning, this Tuesday morning, looking at the sheen of water over the mangled and upended manuscripts in my office. And who could blame them? Then I had also written a long piece about a friend preoccupied justifiably with threats he had received (from a former pal, now estranged), and this piece had also attacked another writer at great length, and taken a firm stand on some literary injustices I had perceived. Such stories crawled up and out of the sewage of memory.

But once you go down into the spiral labeled "vendetta" it is hard to return, and as my experience of depression in my twenties was of just this kind of compulsive thinking, this self-hatred meted out relentlessly, I didn't really want to allow myself to go there, and, anyway, I didn't think it fit the facts. The facts were that someone was watching our house, and to do so they must have been nearby, and if they were nearby it was likely I didn't know them well.

Because how did they know when it was safe to go back for their second visit, having seen the house swarming with police, unless they were watching the house and had a firm grasp on our comings and goings? How did they know? The only explanation was that one or more participants in the burglary lived close enough to us to know that we weren't there all the time, and that, in particular, we hadn't been there since the police secured the premises early Monday morning. That implied that they lived just down the hill, and may have been there, at home, that very Tuesday morning, as the cops went about their business again, and the insurance company adjustor arrived, and began taking a look around. He wasn't allowed there until the police left, so he sat in his car for a while, went out for a sandwich and came back.

Laurel, that morning, began to try to go through her things, and what she found, as you might imagine, was that every single piece of jewelry in the household was gone. There were a number of pieces of jewelry among my things (all concealed in the sock drawer in my dresser, so let me use the bullhorn of publication right now for a public service announcement: don't put your jewelry in the sock drawer), including my grandfather's watch, the crucifix that my late sister wore at her baptism, and some other small items that were going to be given to my daughter, and perhaps a niece or nephew. But my collection of jewelry was nothing when compared to Laurel's.

As I've said, when we were engaged, before our marriage, Laurel went through a long period of trying to collect antique rings for an art project. As a result many weeks passed in which we went to jewelry stores both new and used, all around the Hudson Valley and in New York City, looking at rings. The ring I used to propose to her with in Oregon (now stolen, probably already pawned and melted down) was among these rings.

And all of these rings were gone. In place of the rings were a whole lot of empty jewelry boxes strewn across the floor of her office. Because no one *wants* used engagement rings (or this is the commonplace thinking) these rings would almost certainly be melted down after the seventy-two-hour waiting period at the pawn shop, if we didn't find them immediately. They did constitute a very large collection of engagement rings, which Laurel had wanted to preserve from being melted or lost, only to have them either melted or lost, or both.

For me, the loss of the ring I'd used to propose with was a deep wound, and, frankly, it hasn't entirely healed even now. It's the same with my sister's crucifix. There are moments like this, when the rage that comes with losing these things is powerful, and all you can think of is what aspect of vigilantism would appeal if you could have the guy who performed the robbery in the room with you.

Laurel, as a person who will always tell her side of the story in no uncertain terms, is better at it than I am, but what I'd like to tell the guy is these stories, these love stories, these stories of hardship. Perhaps these pages can be a beginning.

I had four guitars upstate in those days. A Taylor twelve-string, a Mexican-made Fender Telecaster, an acoustic six-string that Laurel's brother had picked out for me, and a Padron three-string cigar-box guitar. These were all gone. Because it is important to give the context to these things, I want to tell you about my Telecaster. The Telecaster had a real tuning issue, especially on the B string. I think the neck warped slightly when I lived on Fishers Island. The climate there was humid and salty, and it destroyed a lot of things—appliances, for example. I think the neck warped there from too much humidity. So the Telecaster, which was burgundy with a white pick guard, was nobody's idea of a good electric guitar. And yet it was *my* electric guitar. I bought it in the mid-nineties when I had my first substantial book advance, and I had to go to Manny's in Midtown to get it, with a friend of my brother's who was knowledgeable about these things (I think he liked the Fender Jaguar better). Manny's, as any aspiring musician will tell you, was in those days a daunting experience. There were always a bunch of guys standing around playing faultless imitations of Yngwie Malmsteen, while the sales staff ignored anyone without rock star credentials. It took me a long time to get anyone to pay attention to my desire to pay for the Mexican Telecaster, and they also tried to dissuade me from buying the distortion box and the wah pedal because, as a particularly bored salesperson told me, good guitar players don't need all those pedals.

I am not now, nor was I then, a good guitar player. Nor am I particularly good at playing anything else, any other instrument. But I never played in order to do much beyond make myself, and a few collaborators, happy, and the Telecaster, chosen in part for its comeliness, was an example of this. Other people buy cars with a first book advance, or they renovate a kitchen. I bought a guitar, for $450, and put the rest in a savings account.

That guitar traveled a long way with me after that. I played a few gigs with it. I remember playing it at a Bennington College event with my friend Syd Straw one time. I played it at a *Tin House* benefit one night, and sang "For the Turnstiles," by Neil Young. I had lived with it for twenty years, by the time it was stolen from the house. Ironically, the one guitar of mine that I passionately disliked, my Taylor six-string cutaway with onboard pickup for electrification, which was very difficult to play, because the action was too high, was not stolen, for the simple reason that it was in Brooklyn at the time. I sort of wished that one *had* been stolen.

By the time we had called the emergency contractors suggested to us by the insurance company, who had to come demo the basement and put in new drywall; by the time we had dragged all the wet carpets out onto the lawn, and set about packing up the three thousand books in the basement; by the time we had begun to itemize the lost jewelry, all of which we did on the occasional afternoon junket in which we drove upstate and turned around and drove back down before the sun went over the hills, by the time we had accomplished all of this, the horror had truly set in. The kind of permanent changes to a worldview that come with calamity. Laurel plans for the worst, but really believes that the best is liable to happen, and when the opposite is the outcome, when the planning for the worst turns out to be the right approach, she becomes deeply upset, in a way that seems to involve the very core of her. Laurel had no intention of sleeping in our house ever again, the house where we had been married.

I was experiencing feelings of rage. I was fine with being in the house. The police suggested to us that once a house was robbed, in our case twice, and depleted of all of its valuables, it was understood in the criminal demi-monde to be "used up." This is how they put it. I didn't think anyone was going to come again. But what I did think was that I really wanted to apprehend the guys who had done it, preferably in front of a jury, and tell them what it felt like. I wanted them to have that experience.

We were then assigned a detective, from Poughkeepsie. It was really hard to tell who was who and from what jurisdiction, but we collaborated on processing the break-ins with this guy from Poughkeepsie, and he was a little bit like that deputy marshall Sam McCloud of television infamy, offhandedly warm and unassuming. And he went over and over the story with us, and we told him what we knew over and over. He put a deer cam in the tree by the driveway, so that we could see anyone coming up the driveway, and he helped us affix a bike lock on the French door so that it would be inoperable from the outside. And he told us that they had a lead, in that there had been several other houses robbed in the area, and they had picked up a guy for one of these robberies. Apparently, in one of the other cases, a house only a few miles away, an ATV had been stolen. And then just a few days later, the police spotted a guy riding around town on an ATV. They gave chase.

That guy was locked up.

As the detective said, the goal was to prove somehow that this guy, the automotive enthusiast, had also committed the robbery on our house.

In the weeks that followed the robberies at our house, Laurel and I, when we weren't managing repairs and alarm installation from a distance, were using all of the internet tools at our disposal to attempt to figure out who was involved, where our stuff was, and what we could do about it.

It would not be inaccurate to say that my beloved spouse is an extremely good law enforcement volunteer. The kinds of skills that would make her good are integral to her work. Or, to put it another way, detail-oriented thinking is how Laurel does what she does, and during the period when she turned her detail-obsessed thinking on the two guys, barely into their twenties, who robbed our house, she turned up many, many more leads than we ever got or heard about from the detective assigned to our case. Conversations with the detective usually involved information going in one direction primarily: from Laurel *to* the detective, not vice versa.

For example, as I had been warned to expect by friends, my guitars very quickly turned up on eBay. They were being offered by a guy who had apparently bought them from a certain pawnshop in New Milford, Connecticut. Because he had bought them from the pawnshop, however, he had no obligation to return them to me. And because he had the Telecaster and the twelve-string, each of them with small problems, it was hard to conclude that I needed to *pay* to have them back, which is how this worked. Similarly, we concluded that the jewelry had been sold to the same pawn shop in New Milford, and that it was already melted down. Because they are only obliged to put a hold on jewelry for three days.

Assembling all of these threads of narrative—the arrest of the dirt bike enthusiast, the names of all the neighbors living down the hill from us, a few tidbits from the detective—in short order we knew the name of the guy who all but certainly had robbed our house and several other houses in the area. Of course, if the detective had just served a warrant to examine his collection of work boots, and matched them to the bootprint on the wall in the boiler room, he would have had his man, but the neighbor and his pal from New Milford (he had someone to help him out, to drive the stolen goods over the state line) wore rubber gloves, and even took an ink pad out of my desk, rubbed the ink on their rubber gloves and touched a lot of stuff *on purpose*, in a way that the detective described as taunting. As a result, the really straightforward proof was lacking and apparently still is.

Laurel also found out that the accomplice of the felon down the road had three kids. And she of course checked out the Facebook page of his wife, or partner, or, at least, the mother of his children, whose Facebook posts were morose and despondent, presumably because the ATV enthusiast (whose interests on Facebook often orbited around NASCAR) was going away to the penitentiary. We felt really sorry for him about his kids, but we also wished that he had found a way to pay for his kids and/or his drug habit that did not involve melting down our jewelry and cutting out the copper pipes from the utility room.

On it went, the police investigation, and the aftermath of the break-in, through our first wedding anniversary. By which I mean, that the break-in, or break-ins, occurred almost exactly on the anniversary of our wedding, namely the day on which we went to City Hall in New York City with Amy Hempel and Randy Polumbo. On our first anniversary, therefore, we were getting an emergency release of funds from our insurance company, after which the construction company arrived on the premises, taking all three thousand books out of the basement, boxing them up, and tearing out the floor and the drywall, removing the appliances in the basement including the destroyed water heater, and replacing most of these, all of this owing to the very legitimate fear, on the part of our insurance adjustor, of mold. The price for the initial repair was $19,000, but when we finished paying for everything that had to be repaired, the repainting, the stolen items, the insurance claim rose to $100,000. All of this so that a guy from right nearby, and his friend from New Milford, could pawn some rings, and sell a couple hundred dollars' worth of copper pipes to a disreputable metal dump in the area.

The construction took almost six months to finish, and

in addition to the repairs in the basement and the repaint-ing, we installed (as you could imagine) a very deluxe home alarm system, including cameras on the three doorways, which we could then watch remotely from New York City. When the avuncular detective from Poughkeepsie finally told us that he needed his deer cam back, we bought our own, and trained it on the driveway, and then collected, over the ensuing years, really powerful and moving sequences in stills of the seasons changing on the front yard, UPS trucks going by, the occasional deer (as adver-tised), the azaleas blooming, the leaves falling, the grass getting cut, winter sweeping in again, drifting snow, the melt, the blossoms.

We had our fingerprints taken, and various possessions were borrowed from us to be fully combed for fingerprints other than our own, but the perpetrators and their rubber gloves were more diabolical than that. We funneled infor-mation back to the detective, like the appearance of my guitars on eBay, and we figured out, in the course of our researches, which pawn shop was used for the jewelry. There were threads of information that seemed as though they might lead to the illusory *closure* that people want when they have been the victims of a crime, but we never particularly got *closure*, unless you mean seeing the wife of one of the perpetrators post on Facebook that she was "going through a hard time," after he was picked up for the theft of the ATV, or when the local police told us that they had asked a known associate of the perpetrator, who had been apprehended for driving under the influence, if he knew whether the perpetrator had committed the robbery on our house, with the understanding that if he told the truth they would go easier with respect to his DUI, to which he said that he did know, and had heard, *yes*, that the perpetrator had robbed our house.

I wrote a particularly savage short story about the experience.

But that was about it. We were left to try to re-create the feeling that it was acceptable to live on five acres in the barren middle of farm country *at night*, when we understood that someone very nearby knew how to open our porch door with a crowbar. When we put this matter to the contractors working on our house—can you please find a way to ensure that this door cannot be opened by force from the outside, using the tools of your expertise—one of them said, "You know, if someone really wants to get in, they're going to get in."

The first round of IVF, which followed not long after the break-in upstate, did not result in a pregnancy. We had a great many fertilized embryos coming out of the retrieval process, and then as the days passed, these great many embryos, twelve or so, started to fail, and by the time we went to transfer the one genetically normal embryo (a girl, because they tell you these things), she did not take, and we were out the many thousands, plus several more thousands for medication, and thus most of the money we had borrowed to attempt to bring about a pregnancy was spent, and we were in the meantime living part-time in a house completely haunted, a house whose new silent partner was the felon down the hill, whose ghoulish Facebook page we could regularly peruse, whose bootprint we had left on the wall in the utility room in the basement as a sort of reminder, and the rest of the time we were trying to have a baby, and failing to have a baby, while I tried to parent my daughter to the best of my ability, taking her out to the playground, going to the movies with her—in short, anything she wanted.

If you'll allow me to skip ahead here, there is a sort of an ending to the story of the break-in (excepting that it never ends, because you can still go to the Facebook pages of the two guys who did it, and they are still friends, and they are apparently out of jail now, and at least one of them is a very ardent booster for marijuana and its ancillary' products, and is also, well, a Juggalo, though it's unclear what kind of Juggalo), and it is as follows. On our way to see my brother, in Wilton, Connecticut, where he lives with his family, we sometimes drove through New Milford, Connecticut, which is only twenty minutes or so from Amenia, where we lived in Dutchess County then, and in this capacity, on one occasion, we stopped for gas, or for some other ephemeral need, in a shopping plaza in New Milford, and pulled the car up in a parking space, without meaning to, *right in front of the pawnshop* where some of our stuff had been pawned after the robbery. It was sort of terrifying, in a way, to happen on this close encounter, in part because, despite all the rioting emotions after the break-in, I still sort of felt like I had made it up, or exaggerated it, or misconstrued it. I sort of felt, after the bright red horror of arriving home to see all of our stuff trashed, strewn about, that it was some kind of evil fairy tale I had composed. I didn't really believe, as a practical matter, that the perpetrator lived nearby, though he did, or that he was capable of watching the house; I sort of felt like it was a story we told to make sense of the trauma of the break-in, something that Laurel and I could share to keep the panic of living at bay. But then we arrived at the pawnshop, and it upset the sedimentary activity of the whole thing, the silting over of it, stirring it up once again.

It took a little while for this knowledge of the pawnshop to fester sufficiently, but then one day as we were anew driving near New Milford, Laurel insisted she was going to march into the pawnshop in New Milford, and have a conversation with the owner. If you have read this far in the book you know that Laurel *definitely* meant that she was going to do just that, was not exaggerating at all. Sometimes, with Laurel, she has to get really mad about something else (as when, for example, I have done something unusually stupid), and then she busts through any remaining inhibition and clears the deck on any lingering discontent. She gets it all out. And it was a frequent conversation we had, in fact, that pawnshops were *immoral*, and not because they cater to a particular economic rung that is full of desperation, or because they charge obscene interest rates, not immoral according to these traditional arguments. No, we believed that pawnshops were immoral because they don't, and can't, fully prevent stolen merchandise from entering their product stream. They look the other way on this stolen property, and they are protected by the lax statutory framework that excuses the pawn business from having to do more than look the other way, and thus all the melted-down jewelry, and the guitars that are quickly sold for cheap to a reseller, etc. The people who do the work of the pawn business traffic with thieves, and they know they are doing so, if they are being honest, and that is how they make their living. This was a subject we had often discussed. And Laurel, eventually, was going to discuss it with the owner of the pawnshop in New Milford.

And so the day came to pass. Laurel said, "Pull over, pull over, I want to go in there."

"Where do you want to go in?"

"I'm going in to talk to the guy at the pawnshop."

I wasn't going in, and Hazel wasn't going in, but Laurel didn't need us, she only needed to be on the side of justice, and so she went into the store (this is her recounting it now, and my reconstructing), and she waited while a woman paid outlandish interest on some item that she wanted to get back but couldn't afford to, and then, when the woman was done, she said to the pawnshop manager, "You sold items stolen from our house."

The pawnshop manager, not surprisingly, took issue with the diminutive lady walking right up to him and getting into the fine print on the items he had for sale, but Laurel was not through, at all, and she sketched out the entire thing to him, not forbearing to mention that my dead sister's crucifix got melted down, and my grandfather's pocket watch got sold, and the ring I had proposed to her with got melted down, and she could even tell him exactly who had brought the stuff in, which caused the pawnshop manager to go through his database, believing that she couldn't possibly *know* who had brought the stolen merchandise in, whereupon he did in fact turn up the name of the perpetrator among his clients, after which he said that he would "freeze the account" of the perpetrator, so that he couldn't continue to do business with the pawnshop. But still Laurel wasn't done. She stood in front of the guy and said she would not leave until he apologized. A long standoff ensued. Laurel was not going to leave. The guy was definitely going to have another customer at some point, with the very forceful lady standing in front of him, waiting him out, so in due course he decided to yield: "I'm sorry, I didn't know that stuff was stolen."

It didn't change the outcome of the story, but it made us feel a bit better.

This is one of the many reasons I love Laurel Nakadate. You definitely want her on your side when justice needs to be done.

Then, after several months of licking our wounds, and incrementally coming to feel that we could sleep in our house in Dutchess County again, we got the final payout from the insurance company, who reminded us that we could use the money in any way we wanted. We didn't, for example, need to buy four guitars and a bunch of used engagement rings. It was ours to do with as we saw fit. They were very nice about it. We paid the contractors, we paid off the car, and we still had enough left for two more rounds of IVF.

Afterword:
Winter and Spring 2014–15

While we were living through these twelve months I have described, we thought of them as a stretch of mounting sorrows, each incident of loss or calamity adding onto the ones that had come before as an additional rude slap, and we felt that way despite the ultimate bounty that landed in our coffers through the good graces of our insurance company.

Mounting sorrows are bad enough, but are they not compounded by writing about them? Why is it that I needed to write about these sorrows, these wastes that stretched out in front of us?

In part, the compiling of these months has been automatic. Trouble this repetitious wants to be spoken about, wants to be shared, so one feels less alone. Trouble wants to be shared, contextualized, so it can be understood better, so that it might be avoided again. And because it's hard to understand trouble of this density until it's written down—the writing helps with the making sense—writing is a thing that in my case will inevitably happen. No useful accounts of life until they are committed to writing. Many were the points in this year I've described when I found myself telling Laurel that the stress was unbearable, not a thing to be borne, and yet in such moments I always knew I had to write about the period, too. Indeed, at one point, I was not sure I would be able to write anything else until I had attempted to render in words this, our *annus horribilis.*

It was also worth writing about these months because of how they celebrate marriage, the stabilizing force of marriage, which never occurred to me at all until this year I've described. There wasn't a need for marriage to be a stabilizing force, for me, until there were so many moments of instability, no need for marriage itself until the idea of marriage was in danger because of our difficulties.

These are some of the things that happened to us in 2013 and 2014, therefore, and though there were bad days, and though Laurel and I have been known to toss a few choice obscenities in each other's direction when really short-tempered, we have in fact been made stronger and more loving for all that we have gone through. We are humans in a marriage, not idealized figures out of a contemporary novel, and we have had a lot to get through. But in a great majority of cases we got through it by supporting each other, and our marriage has provided ample opportunities to learn more about how to support, when to support, and where to support.

However, the best argument for setting down in print

all of the *annus horribilis* is that it has, in fact, a happy ending. So let me try to get to the happy ending at last.

In the months after the break-in, while Laurel's mother
was getting decidedly more ill, it was finally decided that
Mary Ivie should move out to Portland, Oregon, to be
nearer to Laurel's brother Nick, and, by extension, her
children in general, as Portland was a place that was, for
most of her family, easier to get to than the middle of the
state of Iowa. This was a difficult relocation to mount
logistically, but once Mary was in Portland, where Nick
was the first responder (in a way that was no doubt very
difficult for him), Laurel, though concerned about being
so far away, was freed up a little bit, for a time, and as a
result there was a little extra room to concentrate on our
own medical challenges.

We did two more IVF cycles, therefore, paid for with
our homeowners' insurance payout, and while we made
more viable embryos with each cycle, we were again
unsuccessful with our second transfer. However, Dr. W.
seemed to be getting closer to a theory of why we could
not carry a baby to term, and the theory seemed to be that
Laurel's autoimmune challenges required serious medication at the beginning of each attempt at a cycle. He also
believed that the embryos really did not like being outside
of her body, did not like the storage medium they sat in
when outside, did not like being tested, did not like the
time in the lab.

Which caused us, as a group, to come up with what I
began to refer to, jokingly, as the Nakadate Protocol. (Of
course, Dr. W. really came up with it, had probably used

it before, and is probably using it still.) The Nakadate Protocol was simple, and, for us, a new approach: you should, if you're worried about testing embryos, or about the embryos surviving outside of the mother, just avoid these steps. Just transfer several of the embryos, a surfeit of them, and don't test. Surely, according to the Nakadate Protocol, one of those embryos will thrive.

Our approach, it bears pointing out, is sort of dangerous if you don't have a good idea about how many embryos are likely to survive the transfer. That's the only way you avoid high-order multiples, as they are called. I joked with Dr. W. that if we had quintuplets, he had to agree to be photographed with them (and us) when we sold our story to the *National Enquirer*, and it was the one time I ever saw our doctor look briefly uncomfortable. But over the course of our four cycles, and two failed in vitro fertilizations, we had come to understand some of how Laurel's body worked, and our much more potent worry, more potent than the threat of high-order multiples, was of being unsuccessful again.

In the meantime, despite the love for and celebrity of our doctor, there were forces militating against his continuing to practice in New York City. In the middle of our last attempt at a cycle (the last attempt we had the money for, despite our many attempts to find insurance coverage *somewhere* for infertility), he relocated to Trumbull, Connecticut, where his medical group was trying to set up a satellite office, on the appropriately named Technology Drive, an address we never failed to laugh about. We therefore had to do all of our office visits in Trumbull. The Connecticut office of the medical group with which he was affiliated, where Dr. W. had reestablished himself, was never crowded, was always easy to deal with, and the people in the Trumbull office, Dr. W.'s staff, were really rooting for Laurel.

So, in September 2015, with the Nakadate Protocol as our conceptual framework, and while Laurel's mother was getting moved into the skilled nursing wing of a nursing home in Portland, we transferred five embryos. Dr. W. showed us a photograph of all five. It seems really odd that one could get emotionally attached to *photos* of embryos, but Laurel, who is after all a photographer, felt emotionally attached to the photos. The reproductive endocrinologists tend to *rate* the photos of the embryos, you know, and Dr. W. suggested that one of the embryos in the group portrait looked really good, according to these official standards. The one in the lower right of the group portrait was sort of a standout, so we had at least one very well-formed embryo, and unlike in earlier cycles, we had no idea if it was a boy or a girl. We agreed to transfer the other four, along with that one shapely one.

The tech who prepares the embryos for transfer is called an embryologist, and at the Trumbull office, the embryologist was an Eastern European fellow, and he was also the embryologist of a western branch of the medical group where Dr. W. practiced. He was considered a superhero of embryology, and he jetted out to the East Coast to assist with transfers on particular days, and then flew back west. The regimented and closely monitored systems during the transfer procedure were fascinating. The stakes were high, of course. And this was especially the case when there were multiple embryos being transmitted. A kind of extreme and intensely serious hilarity hung in the air, especially when the embryologist tried to pronounce Laurel's surname, which catches off guard even the best informed. We watched and waited, and the transfers went multiply according to routine, and then Laurel was carrying enough human embryos to bankrupt us completely, and to make the college education of our offspring completely out of reach.

At first, as usual, we were sure it had not worked. Laurel, who *can* see a faint double line on a pregnancy test that no one on earth can see but her, who can see a *desire for a second line* as an actual thing, did multiple tests every day, but once inside the testing window, she still did not see a double line. Convinced we had failed, Laurel contacted Dr. W., who ordered a blood test to confirm the end of our last cycle. And that test failed to confirm the end. In fact, it was positive.

Of course it didn't mean anything *certain*, and getting a positive blood test at that point in our journey was like the homeowner with the underwater mortgage hitting the lottery ticket—you just don't believe the luck is going to turn, so used to the bad luck are you, and you save the winning ticket and put it in a drawer for a few hours. The next day Laurel did see a second line, and after a few days even I could see it.

From there we sailed through all of the traditional signs of a human pregnancy. There was a sack and it wasn't empty, there was a heartbeat and it sounded good, and then Laurel, because she had PTSD, wanted to go back to register the heartbeat a couple more times, and we recorded the heartbeat with our phones, and Dr. W. made time for us and for multiple ultrasounds, and then he helped us with finding an OB-GYN, and we got a really great OB from New York–Presbyterian, and somewhere in there we got a phone call telling us the baby was genetically normal, after which the nurse said "... and would you like to know the sex?" To which Laurel said *yes*, she did want to know, and then, because I was driving, I heard her say, "That's amazing," which I interpreted correctly. In this way she was telling me what I already knew. It was my turn to be a father to a son.

The rest of the pregnancy, including the very bad morning sickness, proceeded mostly the way these things are going to go, which is to say that the baby got bigger and appeared normal in every scan, and the mother appeared more pregnant as a result. Even the final trip to the hospital was routine. We were upstate, in Dutchess County, one morning, and Laurel was taking videos of herself with a heat-sensitive lens, and she was actually lying on the floor with the camera when suddenly there was liquid. This, according to Laurel, followed some similar liquid from the night before at a dinner party, some liquid that she had thought nothing about. The cumulative evidence seemed to suggest (though two weeks early) that something notable was taking place. No pain, no anxiety particularly, just fluid on the carpet, and we called the excellent OB-GYN, and she told us to drive to the hospital, which we did without any drama at all. It was a beautiful day in June, not too hot, and clear, and we arrived to check in, when Laurel flooded the chair in the insurance guy's office, and he waived the signing of forms, and we were admitted. Laurel's labor was extensive, but exactly long enough to do the job, and we actually watched some of *The Bachelor*, or was it *The Bachelorette*, in the hospital room, while a brace of intermittent thunderstorms caterwauled across the Hudson River from New Jersey. Laurel got her epidural, felt better, and then through some incredible technological innovation our room became the delivery room (full of, among others, a number of first-year med students, because we had signed a form welcoming them), and there was a momentous skidding out of our son, Theo.

Given the struggle to get to him, he happened without fuss, and we were able to concentrate on trying to get to know him. And as I write these lines, he has just turned two, and we do know him, and he's a big happy cherub of a boy with an easy smile, very dark brown eyes, and an obsession with trucks that I in no way caused.

I tell you these things not because a child is the solution to infertility in all cases, nor because all bad luck gets reversed in the course of life, because neither is true. I love all my friends who want a child and have been so far unable to have one and I feel their ache. The more than four years it took for us to carry a pregnancy to term looked destitute and hopeless at many points, and that hopelessness was keen enough to still feel fresh. This story is not about the miracles of science and how they conquer all. There are no such miracles. And if science could be perfectly miraculous or at least entirely reliable we would have another daughter and/or a pair of twin boys, for whom we still grieve. But this story instead orbits around questions of grace, and by that I mean grace as an unearned outcome, an undeserved bit of good fortune that arrives for no other reason than that it just does. Not because we had suffered enough, but because sometimes grace is what happens. Sometimes life does take a turn for the better.

Laurel's mother was gravely ill at the time Theo was born, and she was just well enough to understand Laurel's pregnancy, and when he was born, Laurel took to contacting Mary by FaceTime to show her Theo and images of Theo, to which on one occasion Mary said, while bearing another grandchild in her lap in Portland (and it was the last thing she said to Laurel): "The kingdom!"

Which *kingdom* was this exactly? Should we think of Mary as having had one foot on the other side by that point, such that she knew she would not be long among us, such that she was feeling the expanses beyond? Is "the kingdom" an allusion to her interplanetary transit away from us? Should we think of the *kingdom* as meaning that children are a catalyst through which it is realized that the kingdom of heaven is *at hand*? Mary Margaret Ivie Nakadate was mother to five children, and she obviously believed in being a mother completely, and no doubt she was happy that Laurel was at last going to be a mother, and so maybe motherhood was the kingdom for Mary. Or maybe the instant of joy that she felt in beholding the picture of Theo was what she was referring to with the phrase. Maybe "the kingdom" is another way of expressing joy at becoming a grandmother again. Whatever the exact meaning of the image, which we will not ever know, for the speaker was someone whose language was failing entirely, it is an exceedingly powerful thing to say, and not a forgettable one. Laurel and I have often returned to wonder at "the kingdom" ever since.

We waited for Theo to have his first vaccinations before we took him on the plane to see Mary in Portland, and that delay was at the suggestion of Theo's pediatrician. We got the vaccinations a week early, and then we hastened to the airport, and landed at Mary's bedside for her last days. Not long after we arrived, Mary's further suffering was at last commuted.

There are limits to grace, there's an inexplicability to it, then, because Mary Ivie was the grandparent most equipped by circumstances, and the most outwardly enthusiastic about playing an active role in Theo's life, and she never got to embrace him, hold him, sing to him, delight in him completely. And there are limits to grace in that Laurel should not have had to go through her mother's death when her child was newly born. And yet that is how it went.

I felt honored to be at Mary's bedside, as I have so often felt honored to be among Laurel's family. And the night after her death, Laurel and I drove out to Cannon Beach, where I had proposed to her, and spent the night in a hotel, one of those nights when all of the stark and unvarnished truths of life are obvious to you, but where love is mostly possible too. We'd been there with Mary less than a year before, just ten days after the embryonic Theo had been transferred in Trumbull, Connecticut, and the stairs on the back side of our hotel led directly down to Haystack Rock, that primordial place, with its funnel cloud of seabirds, and its skeins of fog, with its ancient geological riddles and immensities, and in the half-light of that evening it was hard not to feel Mary with us, both of us lucky to be there with our son.

Acknowledgments

I am most grateful to everyone at Henry Holt and Company for their generous and warm welcome of myself and my memoir. The entire Holt team has treated me with warmth and kindness, even as I was waiting around for the ending of my book, which took a while. I won't forget their kindness. I would like especially to single out my editor, Barbara Jones, to whom I am much indebted here, as I have often been, for her wise counsel and her writerly instincts; likewise her excellent associate Ruby Rose Lee. Barbara and Ruby each helped me over many hurdles on the way to this book.

Melanie Jackson and Matt Dissen at the Melanie Jackson Agency have also been instrumental in this work coming to fruition. Working with Melanie has been among the greatest honors of my writing life.

Laurel, my wife, was a collaborator and a source of inspiration throughout this project. Laurel is shrewd, uncompromising, wise, and effortlessly original. I could not have written these pages without her. The same is true of Hazel Moody and Theo Moody, who have made me a better person and a better writer.

Thanks, as well, to Jeffrey Wang for all that he has given Laurel and me, and to my cousin the Reverend Jack Moody, who has never failed to support my family, even when we were at our lowest ebb. Thanks also to my comrade of many decades Randy Polumbo, whose generosity is self-evident in these pages, as in my life, and special thanks, too, to my many writer friends who have made my up and down creative life possible: Amy Hempel, Susan Minot, Darcey Steinke, Adam Braver, Melora Wolff, Marc Woodworth, and of course thank you to Helen Schulman, writer, empath, ethicist, sister. Thank you to the Moodys and the Davises. And a special thanks to the Nakadate family—to my brothers-in-law, Nick and Nate, and to Neil Nakadate—all of whom could not have wanted another writer in the family. Mary Margaret Ivie Nakadate, we miss you every day.

About the Author

Rick Moody was born in New York City. He attended Brown and Columbia Universities. He is the author of the award-winning memoir *The Black Veil* and of the novels *Hotels of North America*, *The Four Fingers of Death*, *The Diviners*, *Purple America*, *The Ice Storm*, *Garden State*, and multiple collections of short fiction. Moody is the recipient of numerous awards, including a Guggenheim Fellowship, and his work has been anthologized in *Best American Stories*, *Best American Essays*, and the Pushcart Prize anthology. He lives in Rhode Island.